Advanced Custom Motorcycle Wiring
REVISED

Jeff Zielinski

Published by:
Wolfgang Publications Inc.
PO Box 223
Stillwater, MN 55082
www.wolfpub.com

Legals

First published in 2013 by Wolfgang Publications Inc.,
PO Box 223, Stillwater MN 55082

ISBN - 13: 978-1-941064-07-8
Printed and bound in U.S.A.

Advanced Custom Motorcycle Wiring

Introduction/Acknowledgements

INTRODUCTION:

I feel that this book will provide beginners with the basic knowledge and understanding of 12-volt electrical systems found on most Harley-Davidson models. There are many-detailed wiring schematics found throughout the book that can help even the most experienced technician or builder through a difficult repair or installation. My goal was to provide as much technical expertise and experience about the methods and original equipment used by Harley Davidson since the middle '80s. The book discusses how to repair, re-install or create new wiring harnesses from scratch. You learn the basics, find answers to common electrical problems and see the what, when, where, how and why to install, repair and replace all electrical components, terminals and connectors. In closing, all motorcycle enthusiasts can use this book for years to come as a technical point of reference.

ACKNOWLEDGEMENTS:

When you partake in an effort of this scale it's very difficult to do it alone. Trying to come up with all of the content and photographs is tough but making sure it is accurate is even more of a challenge. With that being said, I would like to take the time to thank some really important people. Many of you I talk to on a regular basis and some of you have been friends for many years but ALL of you were a big help and for that, I thank you.

I would like to thank Rick and Dan at Badlands Motorcycle Products, Mike Merrit at Dakota Digital and Dave Withrow at Maverick Publishing. An extra special thank you to Jeff & Huey at Cleveland Motorcycle Company, Mike Allerton and the legendary Don Hotop from Hotop Designs. Lastly, I would like to dedicate this book in the memory of Chuck Shearer, you will always inspire me. I couldn't have done it without your help!

FROM THE PUBLISHER

Just a quick list of thank-yous, first to Jeff Zielinski for agreeing to do the work necessary to produce this revised edition, which like everything else was more work than either of us thought it would be. For last minute photos I'm grateful to the following: Lance Kugler and the crew at St. Paul H-D. Don Hannon from Kustom Werks. Brian Klock and crew at Klock Werks. George Munger and staff at Kuryakyn. Dave Withrow from American Bagger.

Timothy Remus

About the Author

Growing up, it was my two older brothers who made sure I stayed out of trouble. In Mom's eyes, I could do no wrong but I think my Dad knew better. I spent my early teenage years applying body filler to my 1949 Ford, and hiding dirt bikes at a friend's house so my parents wouldn't find out. My father's rule, "no motorcycles," made me hesitant, but didn't stop my two-wheeled dreams.

Needless to say, I purchased my first street bike in 1990 and my first Harley later that same year. My wife Pam didn't like the idea, but in 1996 I purchased a brand new 1997 Sportster 1200 Custom. After thousands of dollars of custom parts, I traded the Sporty six months later for a 1997 Softail Custom. It didn't take long for me to start changing and customizing everything possible.

All the new chrome looked great, but what about that ugly wiring? What if I covered the electrical wiring with stainless steel braiding? The bike received a lot of attention at local shows and after taking first place at a show a fellow enthusiast said, "you should start a business selling braided wiring harnesses."

In 1999 I created NAMZ Custom Cycle Products, Inc. Nine years later we are a well-known distributor and a manufacturer of electrical components. Before I jumped into NAMZ full-time I was in the wireless telecom industry from 1988 through 2006. I was also co-founder of a custom bike shop in 2001 and co-owner of another in 2005. Over the years I have had motorcycles featured in magazines, written many technical articles and been featured in other non-industry publications. I created technical drawings and developed wiring schematics for several published motorcycle books. NAMZ products have been distributed since 2001 starting with Arlen Ness and now we are in most after-market catalogs worldwide. We are a contract manufacturer of wiring harnesses, pigtails and other electrical components for many companies within the motorcycle industry.

Sorry Dad, I just can't seem to quit messing with motorcycles.

Chapter One

Basics of DC Electricity

Volts, Amps and Ohms

There is much to know about electricity. Whether it is high voltage AC or low voltage DC, it is a science that should never be taken lightly. In this chapter we will discuss the "basics" of DC electricity then apply what we have learned to motorcycle wiring as we move through the book. A very, very long time ago a man was flying a kite with a key attached to it during a thunderstorm, then... just kidding, we are not going that far back. Sit back, relax and put your thinking cap on.

When it comes time to pick the wiring and the components, basic knowledge of DC electronics and ohms law helps enormously.

12v Basics

Direct Current or DC electricity is the continuous movement of electrons from an area of negative (-) charge to an area of positive (+) charge through a conducting material such as metal wire. A DC circuit is necessary to allow the current or steam of electrons to flow. Such a circuit consists of a source of electrical energy, such as a battery, and a conducting wire running from the positive end of the source to the negative terminal. Electrical devices are included in the circuit. DC electricity in a circuit is measured in terms of voltage, current and resistance. To understand the basics of DC electricity in this section we will imagine it as the flow of water through a hose.

Electrical Current (I)

The number of electrons produced in DC voltage is called current. Its unit of measurement is the Ampere or Amp. Electrical current is like the rate that water that flows through a hose.

Voltage (V)

A potential or pressure builds up at one end of the wire, due to an excess of negatively charged electrons. This is like the water pressure in the hose. The pressure causes the electrons to move through the wire to the area of positive charge. This potential energy is called Voltage. Its unit of measurement is the Volt.

Resistance (R)

Resistance is the restriction to the flow of electrons and is measured in Ohms. Think of this as a kink in the hose which reduces the amount of water flowing through.

The way these three forces interact is explained by a simple formula known as Ohm's law:

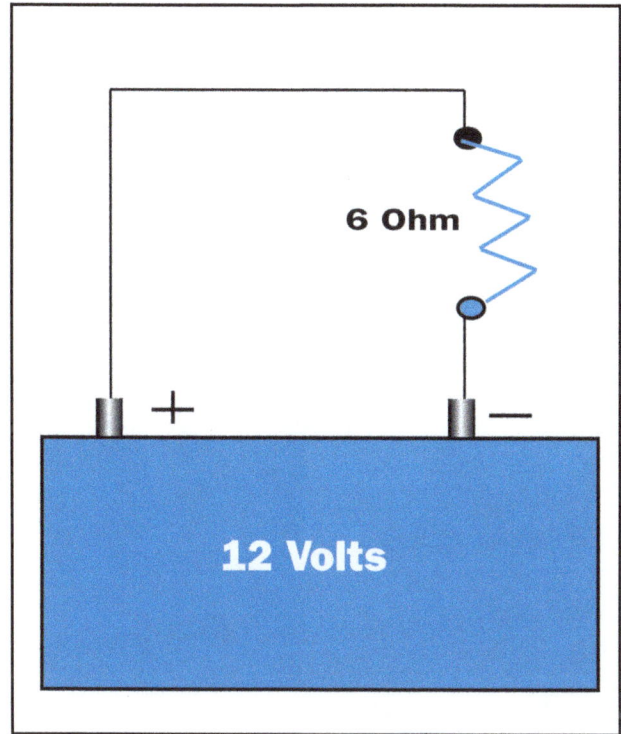

Using Ohm's law (I=V/R) we determine that the current in this impractical circuit is 2 amps.

Length Current	0-4ft.	4-7ft.	7-10ft.	10-13ft.	13-16ft.	16-19ft.
0-20A	14ga.	12ga.	12ga.	10ga.	10ga.	8ga.
20-35A	12ga.	10ga.	8ga.	8ga.	6ga.	6ga.
35-50A	10ga.	8ga.	8ga.	6ga.	6ga.	4ga.
50-65A	8ga.	8ga.	6ga.	4ga.	4ga.	4ga.
65-85A	6ga.	6ga.	4ga.	4ga.	2ga.	2ga.
85-105A	6ga.	6ga.	4ga.	2ga.	2ga.	2ga.
105-125A	4ga.	4ga.	4ga.	2ga.	2ga.	0ga.
125-150A	2ga.	2ga.	2ga.	2ga.	0ga.	0ga.

Wire size chart from the IASCA handbook. The size of wire used in any circuit is determined by the current load and the length of the wire. This chart is for copper wire (don't use aluminum wire).

If you're going to build a harness from scratch, it helps to have all the common H-D colors available in the most common gauges.

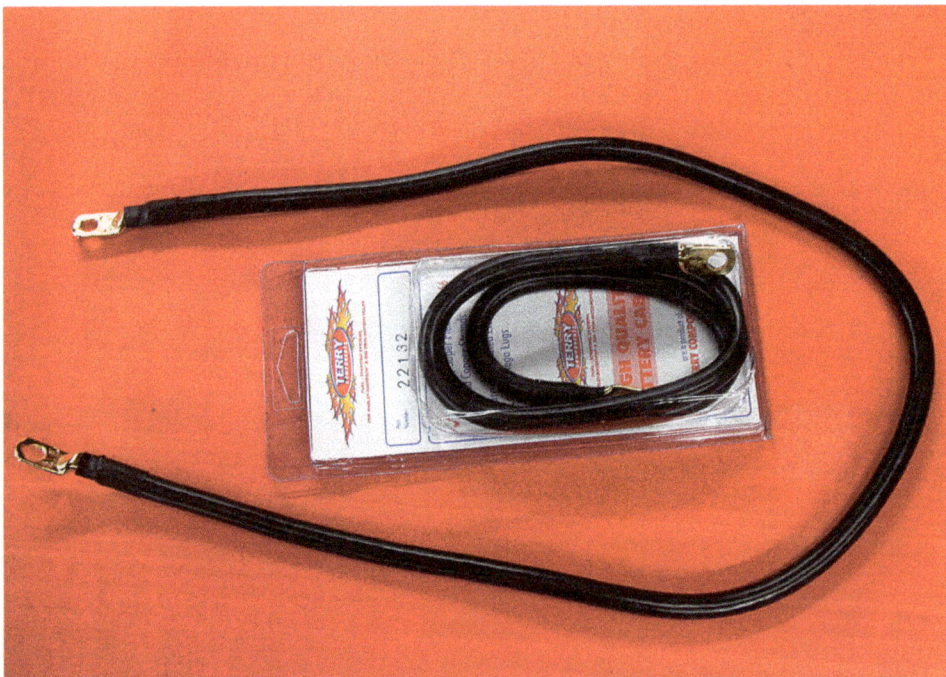

Heavy cables are designed to carry heavy current, like a starter motor. Remember, not all cables are the same, the very good ones are made up of hundreds of very small gauge wires.

V=IXR, or stated another way, I=V/R and R=V/I.

GROUND

A motor vehicle uses the frame as the "ground" or return path back to the battery. You will generally find that the battery is grounded to the chassis or frame of the vehicle. Nearly any electrical device can be grounded to the frame or a metal bracket that bolts to the frame. Note, all grounds must have metal-on-metal contact in order to complete a circuit, paint or corrosion between the terminal and the frame or bracket will make for a poor ground.

CIRCUITS

The simplest example of a DC circuit would be a flashlight. In order to make the flashlight operate you will need the following items to complete the circuit: a battery, a light and a switch. A wire from the positive (+) side of the battery attaches to one side of the switch. The other side of the switch attaches to one side of the light. The other side of the light attaches to the ground (-) side of the battery. Since DC voltage does not have polarity it does not make a difference on what side you attach the wires to on either the light or the switch.

TESTING

There are many different ways to test the existence of DC voltage. Here in Chapter 1 we will go over basic DC testing procedures that can be performed on a motorcycle. Throughout the rest of this book we will talk about detailed testing methods used on actual components found on a motorcycle. As with any procedures performed on a motorcycle, you need to have the right tools in order to test for DC voltage. Some of the basic tools needed for testing are a 12-volt test light. This is one of the least expensive tools you can buy. I have seen them sell for as little as $1.99. It looks like a screwdriver that has a sharp point on one end and a see-through handle with a light on the other. Coming out of the handle you will find a long wire with an alligator-clip on the end. Attach the alligator-clip to a ground or the negative (-) side of the battery and the pointed end to the positive (+) side of the battery and the light should illuminate if there is voltage found in the battery. Note, before you get pissed off thinking that your battery may be dead, be sure that the bulb in your test light is working. The test light can also be used to test power wires throughout the motorcycles wiring harness.

Another way to use the test light is to test grounds. If you were to attach the alligator-clip to a known ground wire in your wiring harnesses and the pointed end onto the positive (+) side of the battery and the light does not illuminate then you can be sure that you have a faulty ground somewhere. The other most common testing tool would be a multi-meter. Multi-meters are available in all shapes, sizes and price ranges. For this particular tool, I would recommend spending at least $75.00 in order to be sure that you are getting a quality, accurate unit that will last. The multi-meter can show you the actual voltage output of a battery or how much voltage is getting to a particular component. It can also show you if there is a direct short in any electrical device or wiring harness. Keep in mind, the better multi-meters allow you to do more detailed testing procedures.

THE IMPORTANCE OF WIRE SIZE

The size of wire is very important in the flow of electrons. The larger the wire, with more strands in the wire, the more current it can carry. Different wire sizes and types are manufactured with different amounts of strands. Most household wire is made of a single heavy strand, good for carrying high voltages and low current. In automotive and motorcycle applications the wire is sized from light to heavy and is always made up of many strands, which is good for carrying higher current flows at relatively low voltage. Multiple strands also makes the wire flexible and less prone to breakage from vibration.

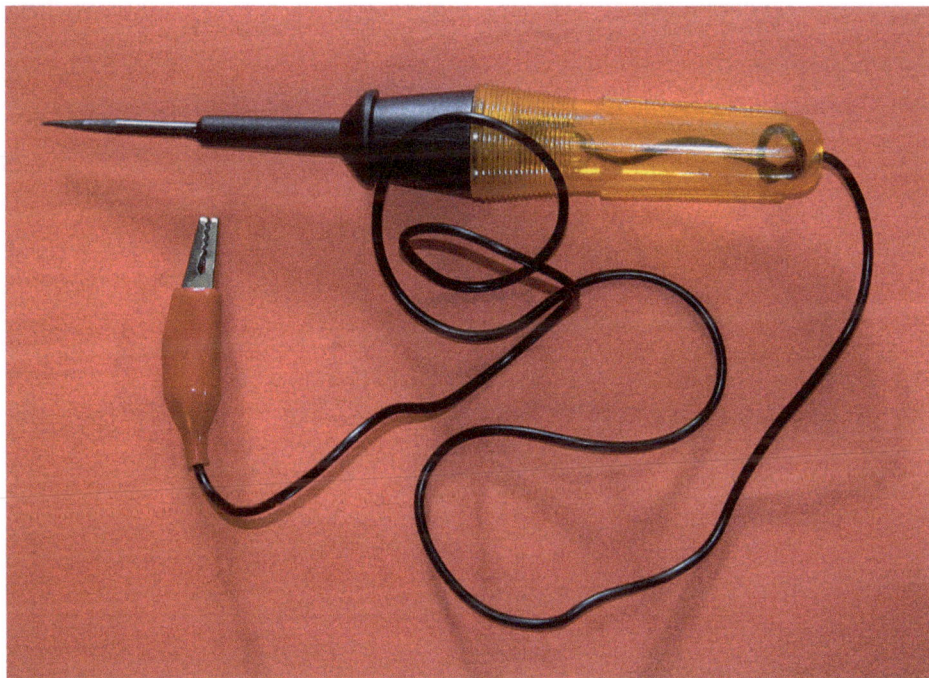

When it comes to trying to diagnose an electrical malady, the simple 12 volt test light is perhaps the best and certainly the cheapest, tool ever invented.

This TXL wire from Painless uses a very high quality, high temperature insulation that is actually thinner than the insulation on the hardware-store wire most of us are familiar with. The high temperature insulation means a short in one wire is likely to damage only that one circuit and not take the whole harness with it.

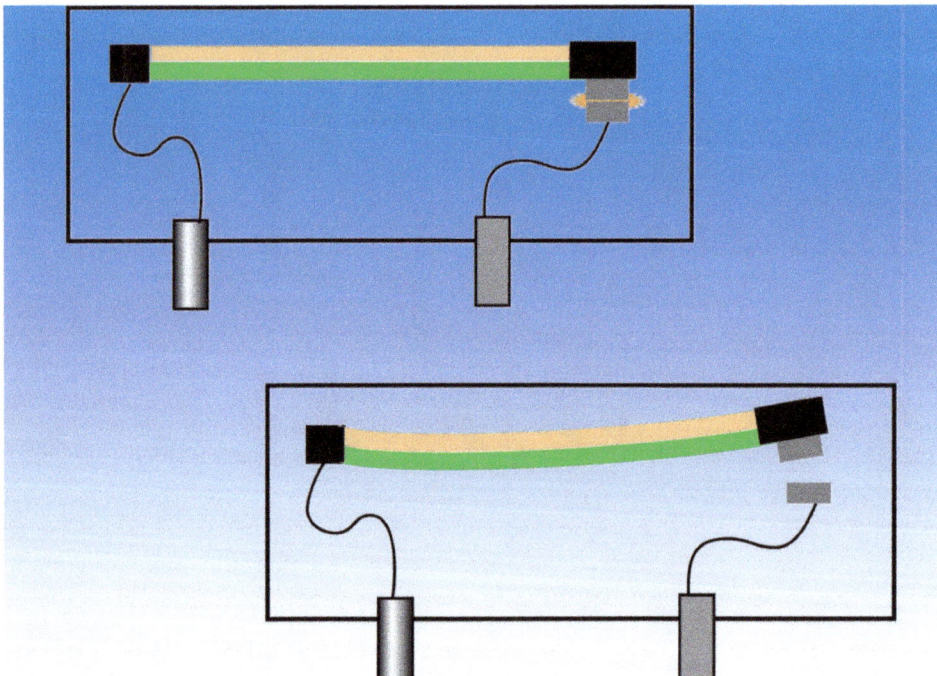

Too much current moving through the bi-metallic strip in this auto-reset circuit breaker causes the dissimilar metals to expand at different rates - and open the circuit.

The size of a wire is known as its gauge. Bigger numbers indicate a smaller wire able to carry less current. A 22 gauge wire might be used for a gauge or very small bulb while a 4 or 6 gauge wire would make a good motorcycle battery cable.

Even within a given gauge, different types of wires will have different numbers of strands. Higher quality wire generally contains a larger number of smaller diameter strands. As a general rule of thumb, always use the highest number of strands per wire size as possible.

WIRE SIZE IN A CIRCUIT

The two things that determine the gauge needed for a circuit are the current load the wire will need to carry, and the length of the wire that carries that load (see the wire size chart). More current requires a larger diameter wire (smaller gauge number). The same current, but in a longer piece of wire, will require a larger diameter wire. When in doubt about the diameter of the wire you need for particular application always go larger, not smaller.

The other thing to consider when buying wire is the quality of the insulation. The best automotive grade wire is TXL, with insulation that is thinner, yet more heat (125 degrees C) and abrasion resistant than anything else on the market. A more common rating might be GPT, this is common "auto store" wire with insulation rated at 85 degrees C.

Remember that the new high temperature insulation like that used with TXL is thinner than the insulation used with lesser grades of wire making it hard to determine the gauge of the wire. What looks at first like a 16 gauge wire might actually be 14 gauge wire with the new, thinner insulation.

CIRCUIT PROTECTION DEVICES
Fuses

A fuse is one of the most important parts of the electrical circuit. The fuse is the weak link in the passage of current and is designed to allow only a preset amount of current to flow through the circuit. By using a fuse regulation of current flow is possible and damage to sensitive electronic parts and powered circuits can be avoided. A fuse works by having a small conductive strip between the two contacts that is designed to melt at a certain temperature. When current flow reaches a certain maximum level the natural resistance of the strip creates enough heat to melt the strip, thus stopping current flow. If a wire rubs through the insulation and contacts the frame the fuse will blow well before the wire melts. Without a fuse (or circuit breaker) you run the risk of melting the wires in one or more circuits and possibly starting a fire.

Circuit Breakers

Circuit breakers, like fuses, are designed to protect circuits from overloading. The major difference between fuses and circuit breakers is that fuses are not reusable and circuit breakers are. Circuit breakers have a bimetallic strip that heats up under overload conditions causing a break in the current flow.

Circuit breakers come in various sizes, though the capacities are generally either 15 or 30 amps. Most are auto-reset, meaning that as soon as the breaker cools off it will reset and power will be restored to that circuit.

Most of the circuit breakers used with V-twins are what you might call automatic reset. This type of circuit breaker will automatically reset itself when the bimetallic strip cools. This is the most commonly used type and will continue to turn current off and on as long as the circuit is overloaded.

Physically smaller circuit breakers are now available in the standard 15 and 30 amp ratings. The smaller size makes it easier to neatly locate these breakers.

CIRCUIT CONTROL DEVICES
Relays

A relay can be thought of as a remote switch controlled by another switch. Most relays have two "sides," a control side and a load side. In most cases when you hit the switch you put current through the control side of the relay which then closes the contacts on the load side (check the illustration).

A relay is designed to pass relatively large amounts of current to specific devices, rather than have that current pass through switches and major harnesses. Relays are often used to prevent overloading of circuits or switches. A relay is usually mounted close to the device that requires the high current. Power is transferred directly from the battery source to the device through the relay.

A good example of how a relay is used would be the starter circuit on most V-twins. When you hit the starter button on the bars you're actually sending current from the button to the control side of the starter relay. Current passes through the coil in the control side of the relay to ground creating a magnetic field as it does so. The magnetic field causes the contacts on the load side of the relay to close. With these contacts closed, current moves from the battery to the starter solenoid (check the diagram). Without the relay the heavy wires needed to power the solenoid would have to run up to the switch in the handle bars. Note: some of the new relays are solid state which eliminates the moving armature and the contacts described above though they do exactly the same job.

Relays are also a good way to control any circuit with heavy current draw, including accessory lights used on dressers and quartz fog or driving lights, often added for improved vision at night. By using a relay to power the lights you need only run the small wires needed for the control side of the relay up to the switch. The current to run the lights moves from the battery or main circuit breaker, through a fuse, through the load side of the relay, and on to the lights.

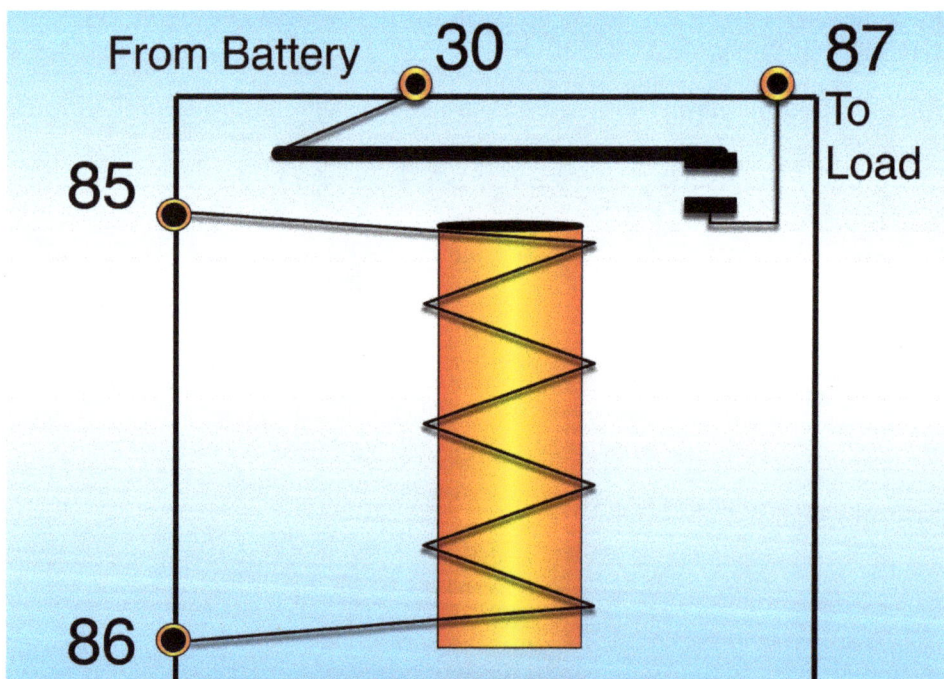

This schematic shows the internal workings of a basic 4-prong electric relay. A small current moving between 85 and 86 (the control side of the relay) creates a magnetic field which pulls down the small horizontal steel strap, and closes the load carrying part of the relay.

Solenoids

A solenoid used in a starter circuit is really nothing more than a specialized relay. In the case of a V-twin starter circuit, the solenoid is activated by the relay. Inside the solenoid are two coils of wire (a hold-in and a pull-in winding) with a movable plunger in the center. A copper disc is attached to one end of the solenoid. When the coils are energized, a magnetic field is created which causes the plunger to overcome spring pressure and be drawn into the coils. As this happens the copper disc is brought into contact with two terminals inside the solenoid. One of these terminals is connected to the battery, the other connects to the starter motor. Once the copper disc makes the connection between the battery and the starter, current no longer flows to the pull-in winding and only the hold-in winding is used to hold the disc in place.

In addition to moving the copper disc up against the two larger terminals and thus acting as a switch between the battery and starter, the plunger also moves the starter pinion gear into mesh with the gear on the outside of the clutch basket.

The most common use of a relay in the V-Twin world is the starter relay, which takes the load off the starter button and also ensures a good power to the starter trigger terminal.

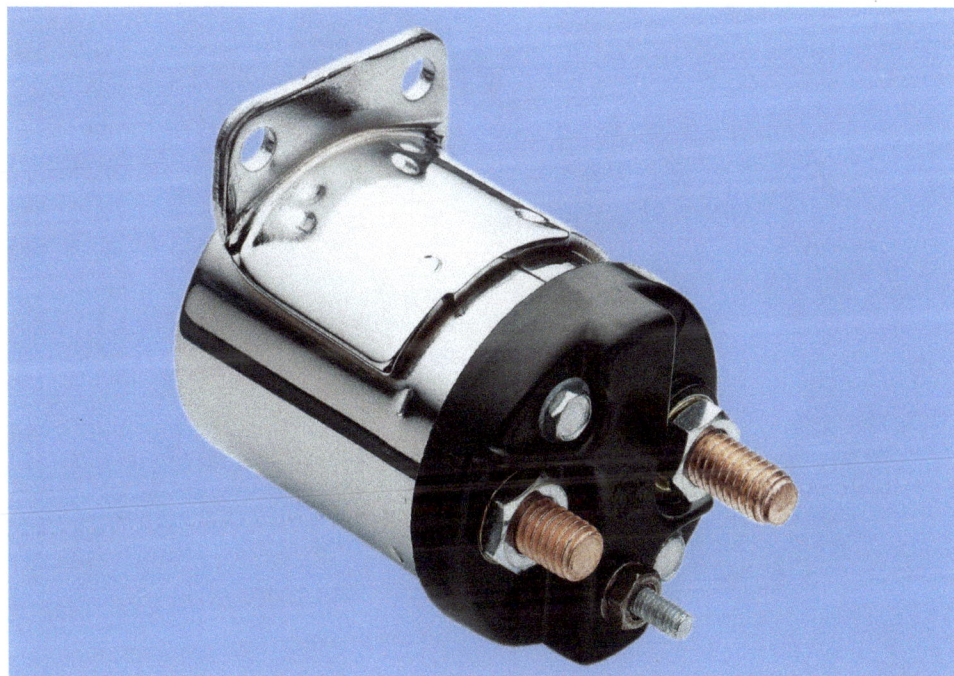

A starter solenoid, whether it's meant for a Harley or a Ford, is just a specialized relay or switch. When energized, the solenoid closes the circuit between the battery positive terminal and the starter.

Chapter Two

Batteries, Starters, Alternators

The Foundation of Your Electrical System

See, that wasn't so bad. Now you understand the basics of DC electricity, if it was only that simple. In chapter two, we will begin to apply our knowledge to charging circuits, starters and alternators. Taken in that order, let's examine the charging circuit first. It is important to understand how each part of the charging system relies on the others. When one component is not functioning properly it can make all of them seem faulty. We will discuss testing methods for

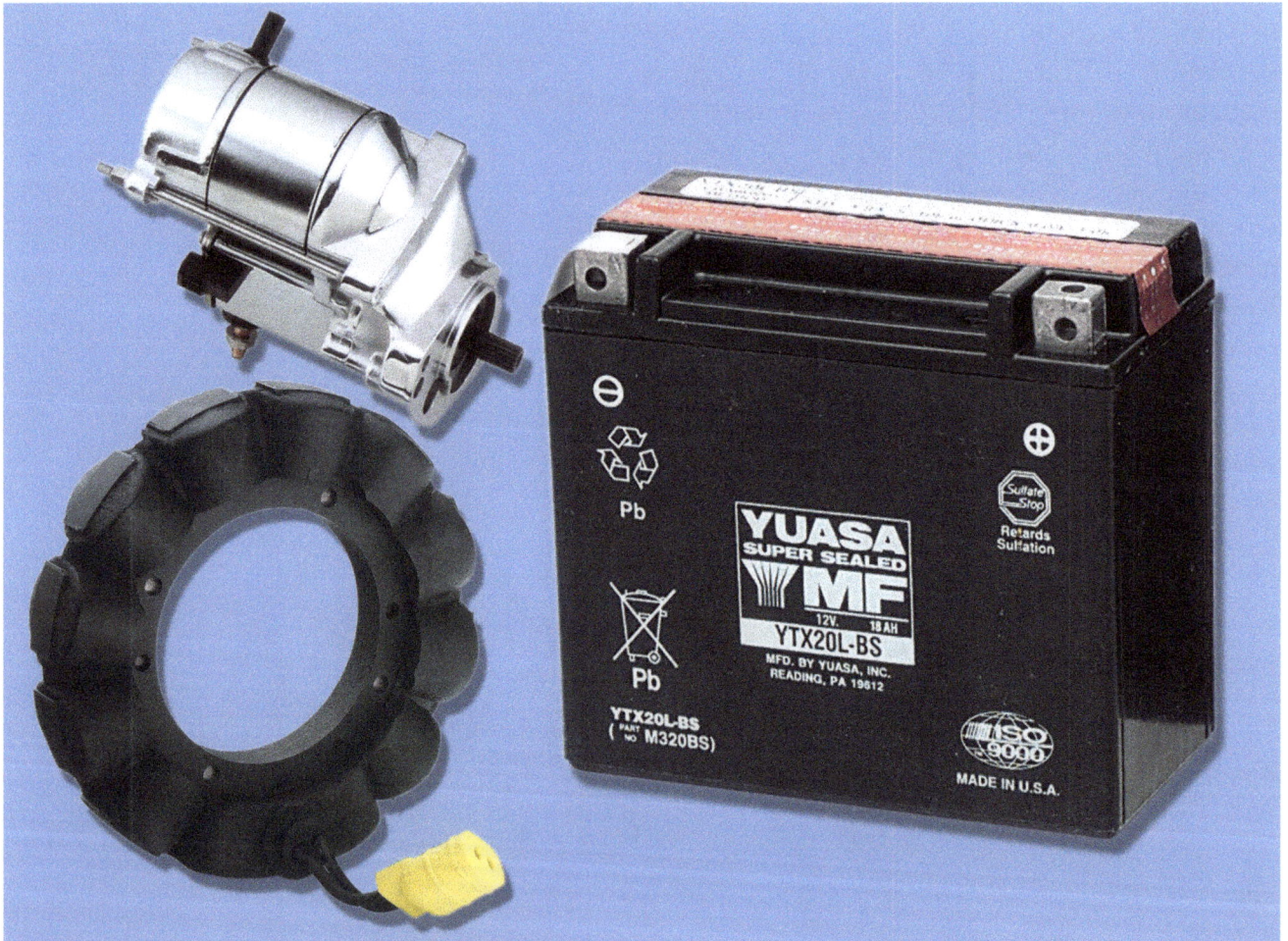

Starting your bike requires a good battery to turn the starter, and a good charging circuit to replace the energy used in starting, and to keep the bike running.

each of the components, basic preventative maintenance and show you how and when to replace these parts. Before we dive into the details, lets go over the basics.

HOW IT WORKS

Almost all production motorcycles use the following components for their charging systems: a stator, rotor, regulator, battery and starter. These parts play an intricate and crucial role in the day-to-day operation of the motorcycle. Let's start from the beginning. In order to understand a charging system, you have to know how it works. A basic motorcycle charging system works on the simple method of supply and demand. When the engine is running the charging system supplies energy to run the bike and any excess to charge the battery.

HISTORY

The components of a motorcycles charging system are very similar to those in an automobile. Before the late 1940's and early 1950's, most automobiles and motorcycles used a 6-volt generator-style charging system. Generators make DC current that batteries needed in order to be charged. One of the downsides to a generator is the inability to spin at higher RPM's while producing a reliable and

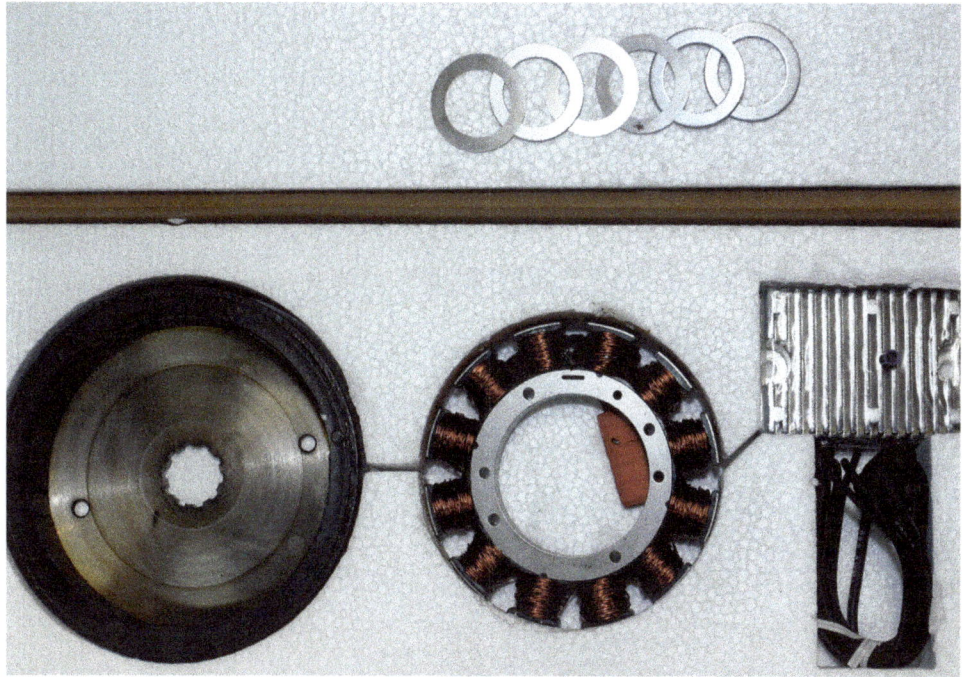

Above is a picture of a complete Big Twin charging system. Top: rotor shims, from left to right; rotor, stator and chrome regulator.

Two different styles of stators: The one on the left uses heavier gauge copper wire. Though it's not always true, most companies use a heavy gauge wire in order to produce a higher-amperage charging system. The heavy gauge style rotor will hold up better to extreme heat and vibration.

A picture of an early style generator used on 1969 and earlier Harley Davidson models. Generators were replaced with the stator, rotor and regulator, in 1970, the components still used today.

consistent charge. With problems like this you can see why a change was needed. Generators were used in automobiles until around the mid 1960's. The alternator's biggest advantage was its ability to spin at a much higher RPM thus providing more efficient charging. An alternator is also capable of supplying more power at a low RPM than a typical generator. Coupled with a regulator, the alternator became the charging method of the future. Harley-Davidson made their change from the generator to the new alternator style by 1970. Now, with a 12-volt battery and a more efficient alternator-style charging system, motorcycles became more electrically reliable.

CHARGING CIRCUIT

A motorcycle charging system can be a rather complex bunch of electrical components. When all of the parts are working in unison life is good. When one of those parts fails, it can damage others components and create a situation that's hard to diagnose. The worst part about a charging system failure is it usually results in a dead battery.

The charging system is made up of a stator and rotor, which creates AC energy/voltage when

A complete charging system, rotor, stator and regulator with rotor shims. This is a typical system used on 1984 to 1999 Evolution Engines.

the motor is running. The regulator takes the AC voltage from the stator, converts it to DC and regulates it before sending it to the battery. The regulator monitors the voltage preventing spikes of higher and lower voltage from making their way back to the battery. These voltage spikes can damage battery cells, overheat the battery or even destroy it all together. Keep in mind, in some cases low voltage can be just as damaging has high voltage. It is a known fact that most Harley Davidson motorcycles will not begin to charge a battery until the engine is running at least 2000-RPM's or revolutions per minute. A simple test to ensure your charging system is properly charging your battery is to start your motorcycle, get the engine to about 2000-RPM's and the voltage should read about 13.4-volts when using a multi-meter connected across the battery.

Now back to the supply and demand scenario. A 12-volt battery is supplying power at the push of a button or turn of a key. This power is used to energize the starter's solenoid and supply power to the starter to turn over the engine. Once running, the charging systems begins to supply a steady flow of voltage to the battery in order to keep it charged. The demand is for the bike to start once the key is turned on. In order for this to happen, the battery must be able to supply the power and the battery can only supply power if it is charged. A classic example of supply and demand. Now lets look at the flow of a charging system and discuss the role of each component.

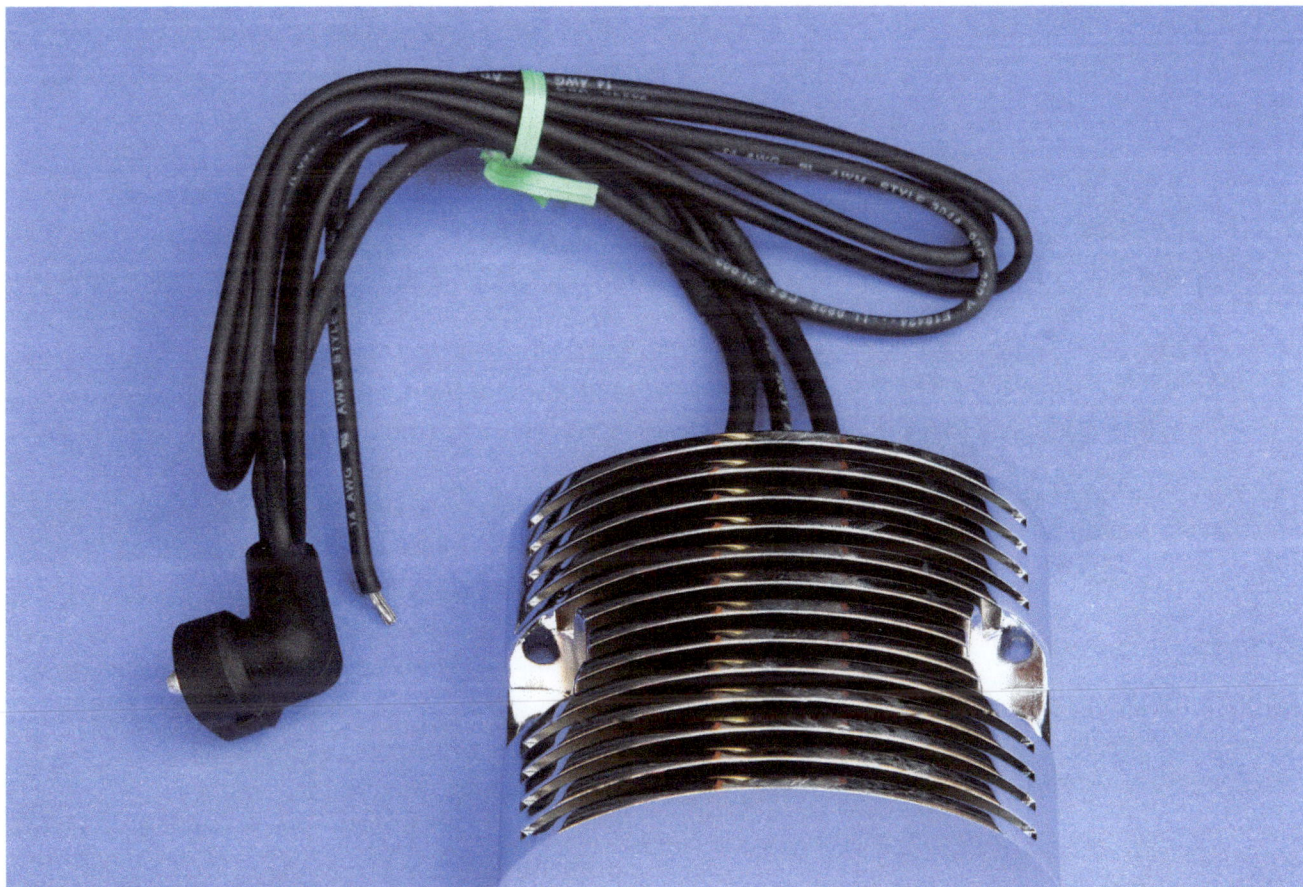

Though the shape is different, this Arlen Ness regulator is a standard 32 amp unit. Always make sure the plug on the regulator matches the plug on the stator.

STATOR AND ROTOR

Be sure to use caution when installing the rotor. The magnetic field will pull the rotor right out of your hands before you know it and can damage the stator or rotor as a result.

Though it looks like an old generator-Shovel, the new Shovels from S&S use an alternator left side case, and a modern sprocket shaft so this motor provides a 32 amp charging circuit and bolts up to a modern primary. S&S

To explain the stator and rotor we need to first revisit high school physics. You will recall that when you cut through a magnetic field with a wire you induce a small current in the wire. Whether you move the wire through the magnetic field or the field over the wire doesn't matter. To increase the output of this simple generator you can either increase the strength of the magnetic field, or you can increase the number of "wires."

As we've said, alternators are made up of three components: The stationary stator (the wires), the spinning rotor (the magnetic field), and the regulator.

Most automotive alternators regulate the voltage of the alternator by regulating the current to the rotor. By increasing or decreasing the current to the rotor they control the strength of the magnetic field. V-twin alternators on the other hand use permanent magnets in the rotor, so the strength of the magnetic field is fixed. The voltage is controlled by "shunting" some of the alternator output to ground. What this means is that the typical V-twin alternator is putting out full power (for that particular RPM) all the time. This power is sent to the battery through the 30-amp circuit breaker.

Where is the Stator? The stator is not the easiest part to get to on your motorcycle. They are located behind the rotor, which is behind the compensating sprocket, nut and shaft, that's in your inner primary, which is behind your outer primary. Another words, it's a pretty big job. It will take you a good part of four-hours, start to finish to replace a stator. You will need to purchase at least one quart of inner primary fluid, an inner and outer primary gasket and be sure to have the proper torque specifications for the inner, outer primary and primary chain tensioner bolts. Be sure to consult with your user manual for specific manufacturer instructions.

When should it be replaced? If you purchase a new motorcycle with a warranty, you really don't need to worry about a stator failure for many years. Although, just like any electrical part, there really is no rhyme or reason why or when parts stop working. The best time to replace a stator is when you know it has stopped working. Sounds simple right? It can be a bit more difficult than that. The life of a stator on a motorcycle is predicated around one major factor, mileage. The more miles you put on your ride, the more the charging system is in use and greater the likelihood the part will fail.

Another factor that can cause stator failure is the regulator. Since the stator and regulator work in tandem, it is possible that if one goes bad, it may damages the other. This holds true if you have taken your motorcycle in for service due to a dead battery. The mechanic can quickly inform you if you have a bad battery, but there is a chance it could be dead

due to a defective stator, rotor or regulator. In a worse case scenarios, one of those components can cause the entire charging system to go bad. However, if your motorcycle is kept in good condition and all routine maintenance is followed according to the manufacturer's specifica-

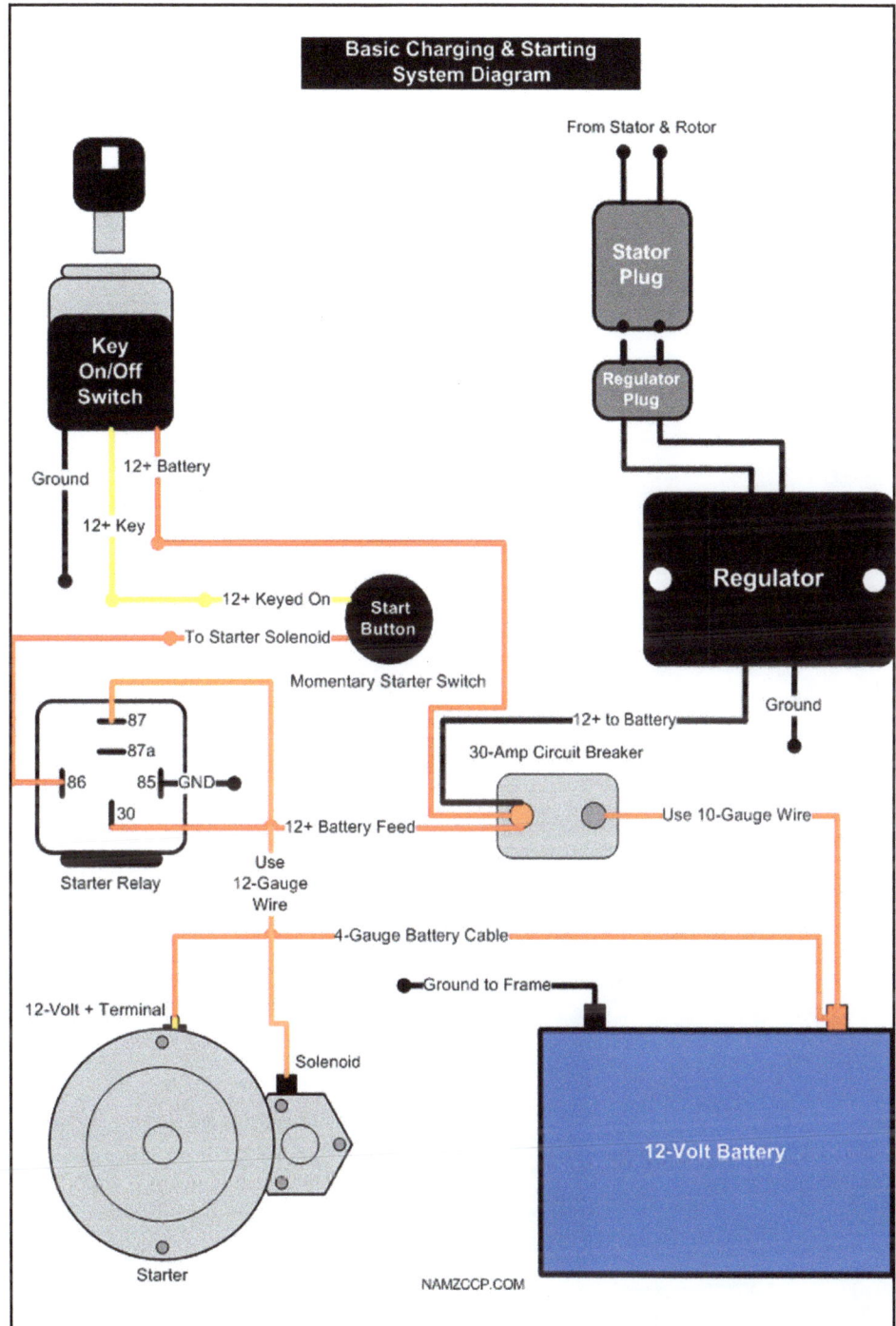

Above is a sample of a basic wiring harness that can be used on all Evolution engine based motorcycles.

tions, it is safe to say these components will long outlive your motorcycle's warranty. This is why it is very important to purchase a good stator, rotor and regulator when these parts do go bad. Install quality parts from the get go and you can generally forget about it for several years to come.

Are they all the same? There are many different brands and varieties of stators. They can differ by brand, amperage and by year, make and model. There are so many brands available today, it's hard to keep track of them. If you have a factory Harley-Davidson motorcycle, you may choose to use a factory brand stator. Your local Harley Shop will know what fits your bike best. If you are more the "forget the factory" or aftermarket person, one of the big names in quality motorcycle electrics is Accel Motorcycle Products. Either way, you have to make sure that you purchase the right one. Since 1970 when stators were first used on a Harley Davidson, there have been several different versions for Big Twins and Sportster models ranging from 15 to 45 amps. Charging systems work in tandem with each individual component. Having a matching combination of a stator, rotor and regulator is crucial. Mix and matching any one of these components could cause serious damage to your charging system, battery or any other electrical device on your motorcycle. Be sure you only purchase what is specified by your user manual.

Here is a sample of a stator installed on a TP Engineering Evolution style engine. Notice how the stator plug slides through the engine case in order to connect to the regulator. Be sure the screws that hold the stator in place are treated with loctite and tightened to factory specs.

HOW TO REMOVE AND REPLACE

Servicing a stator and rotor, as I said before, can be a pretty big job unless you have done it before. If you're a beginner, it's recommended that you follow your service manual to a tee. Disconnect the battery first! The second thing you will need to do is to locate the drain plug under the outer primary cover. The drain plug is a torx-head, tapered thread plug that was tightened up by the factory using liquid thread sealer. Be careful when removing to be sure that it is not cross-threaded! If you bind these threads or over-tighten the plug, you risk damage to the outer primary cover. When that happens you will have a lifetime of leaks or even crack the cover all together. Reference the service manual for torque settings.

Once the primary fluid has been drained, (should be about a quart's worth) you can then begin to remove the outer-primary bolts using a 3/16 inch Allen wrench. Some models used long bolts on the inspection cover, which thread directly into the inner primary for additional support. Make sure you remove these bolts if applicable. Once all of the bolts have been removed, you will see that there are several different lengths of bolts. This is done for a reason and each bolt must go back into the same hole it came out of. If you put a longer bolt into a short bolt whole, you risk cracking the outer primary. In order to prevent any mistakes, position the bolts in a way that you can put them back the same way as they were removed. One trick you can use is to number the bolts and the primary using a back sharpie. This will make easier for you to reinstall without damaging the chrome.

Now that the outer primary is off, you will be looking at your inner primary chain, compensating sprocket, nut and shaft and the clutch basket. In order to remove the compensating nut you will need to have access to air tools or a high torque electric impact gun. The threads on the nut are standard right hand threads but the threads on the clutch basket are left-handed.

This is the start of a typical primary assembly sequence done at the Shadley Bros. Shop - what you will have to go through to install a new stator and rotor. Mark is torquing the bolts for the inner primary.

You can now re-install the compensating nut, clutch basket and inner primary chain, they go on as an assembly.

Install the clutch basket nut using a touch of red Loctite. Remember that the nut has left hand threads and should never be over tightened. Be sure to use OEM torque specs.

Once the hub-nut is tightened, install the clutch pushrod adjusting screw and plate as shown.

Now you can install the adjuster plate retainer clip.

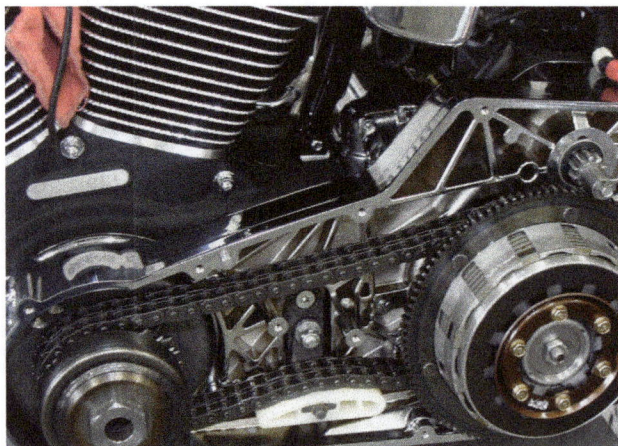

Before you go any further, be sure to tighten and adjust the primary chain.

This means in order to loosen the clutch basket your impact gun will be spinning to the left. Be sure to reference your service manual for proper foot-pound settings. You will now need to loosen the primary chain tensioner and remove accordingly. Both the compensating sprocket and clutch basket should slide off at the same time.

Once all of the primary components have been removed, the rotor will be in plain view. Make sure to remove the spacer that is on the crankshaft and sitting against the rotor. This "spacer" is installed to keep the compensating sprocket aligned with clutch basket and primary chain. Now you will be able to remove the rotor using a rotor removal tool or you can use a pair of dental picks. Depending on the model you are working on, the rotor can be very difficult to remove due to the magnets pulling in the opposite direction. Once you have removed the rotor you will see the stator and the four torx bolts holding it in place. These are hardened bolts and are installed using blue Loctite. Harley Davidson recommends that these bolts be replaced with a new set once removed. You may need to heat up the head of the bolt in order to break it free. Be careful not to use too much muscle when trying to remove these bolts. It is possible to snap off the head of the bolt, which will require a lot more work to remove. When the four bolts have been removed you can unplug the regulator from the stator and push the plug through the engine case. Now the stator can be removed from the motorcycle and replaced with the new unit. All the parts you removed can now be reinstalled in the same manner you removed them. Be sure to reference the service manual when reassembling.

TESTING

The easiest way to test the operation of the stator and rotor is with an ohmmeter. Unplug the stator plug located on the primary side of the engine block and insert the meter probes. If you see .2 to .4 ohm's then you know there is not a direct short. If your meter has audio output and you hear a tone when testing, that would mean there is a direct short. Usually when the stator has a direct short it smells horrible. You'll know right away when you finally remove the outer primary cover. Another test, a bit more daring, is performed with the engine running. Place an AC multi-meter into the stator socket and rev up the engine. If the voltage climbs as the RPM's increase, then at least you know it is working. Considering the time needed to replace parts of a charging system, it is usually recommended when replacing a stator that you also replace the rotor and regulator at the same time. It's better to be safe than sorry.

Once chain tension has been set, you can begin to install the outer primary cover. Again, be sure not to over tighten, and follow the OEM torque specs as noted in the service manual.

REGULATOR

Because the stator produces AC voltage, the regulator has two jobs. Not only does it perform the duty of a voltage regulator, but it also operates as a rectifier. A rectifier transforms AC voltage into usable DC voltage. This process is relatively simple but can generate some serious heat. I'm not sure if you have ever had the unfortunate experience of mistakenly touching the regulator after an hour ride in the middle of the summer. Not a good idea

A picture of an installed complete inner and outer primary system.

A picture of a Twin Cam regulator, mounted where it gets plenty of cooling air.

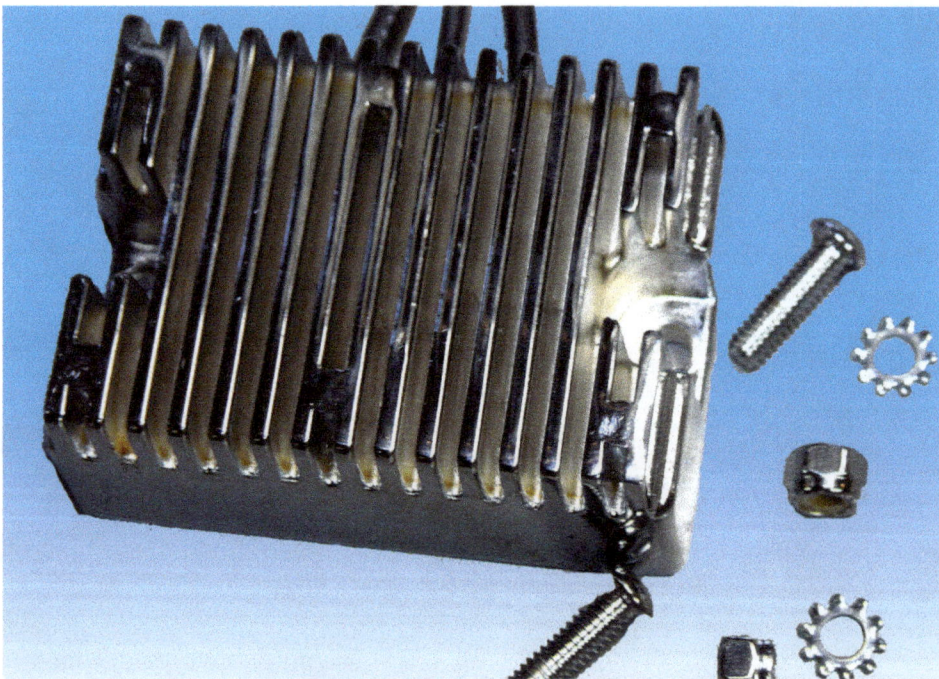

Here is a sample of a chrome Evolution style regulator with mounting hardware. Note the star washers, used between the regulator base and the frame-mount to ensure a good ground connection.

to say the least. For those of you that have, I'll bet you won't do it again. The regulator function supplies the required load to keep the voltage within specified limits. It does so by consuming the excess electrical power as heat. For example, a resistor removes heat from an electrical circuit in order to allow continuous operation without component failure. The regulator function is very similar. It "regulates" the DC voltage that is being sent back to the battery. It does so in a way that keeps excess voltage from being sent back too quickly which would damage the battery.

The best way to explain this process is to think of a battery charger. It converts AC voltage and turns it into DC voltage. It then sends lower voltage at a low amperage rate to the battery, which will in turn charge slowly. If the amperage or rate of charge was increased in order to charge the battery faster, you may risk damaging the battery. It's a pretty simple process.

This simple yet complex part of the charging system is able to handle both functions without much maintenance or special care. The worst enemy of a regulator is overheating, though this tends to happen mostly in hotter climates. If you were ever to ride a long distance, say across the country in the summertime, you may have a pit stop due to a burned out regulator or dead battery. Once a regulator begins to fail there is a good chance that it will damage the battery as well. You can see why we talked about how each part of the charging systems works in tandem with all the others. All four components really do depend on each other in order to operate properly.

Where are they located? On most stock motorcycles, regulators are bolted onto a bracket located on the frames down tubes. You can usually find it right in front of the engine or below the front motor mount. The reason for this location is because of the good airflow. Increased airflow means a cooler regulator.

When should it be replaced? Like all other electrical components, the only time you would want to replace the regulator is when it fails. As we discussed above, many people choose to replace it when they replace the stator and rotor just to be safe. It is a really good feeling to know that you replaced your entire charging system at once.

Are they all the same? Like the rest of the charging system, each component is specific based upon year, make and model. You need to be sure to purchase the correct regulator for your bike. Today, there are several manufacturers that produce quality regulators available in chrome or even billet styles. Some riders that have been around a while say the chrome regulators get hotter since they are dipped in chrome. I would agree with this statement but at the same time, I have used chrome regulators over the past 10-years and have never had any problems. The best way to look at it is if you find a chrome regulator that you like, buy it. On the other hand, chrome won't get you home. It is a matter personal preference only.

REMOVE AND REPLACE

Since we now know how difficult the other charging system compo-

nents are to replace, we saved the easiest for last. The regulator can be very simple job but yet will take some time to do it right. Before you do anything, disconnect the battery FIRST! Remember, the regulator connects directly to the battery through a 30-amp circuit breaker. Now that you have disconnected the battery, start the removal by unplugging the regulator from the stator located on the primary side of the engine. Keep in mind that Twin Cam and Evolution engines have slightly different configurations. We are using a Harley-Davidson Softail model with an Evolution engine for our example.

If you look on the inside of your rear splashguard you will see the circuit breaker that the regulator is attached to. If you are working on your motorcycle for other reasons and you have your rear wheel off, you can gain simple access to the splashguard thus making it much easier to remove the circuit breaker. The studs on a circuit breaker are usually color-coded. For example, the copper looking color is the battery side and the silver color goes to the component, in this case the regulator. This is key for proper protection.

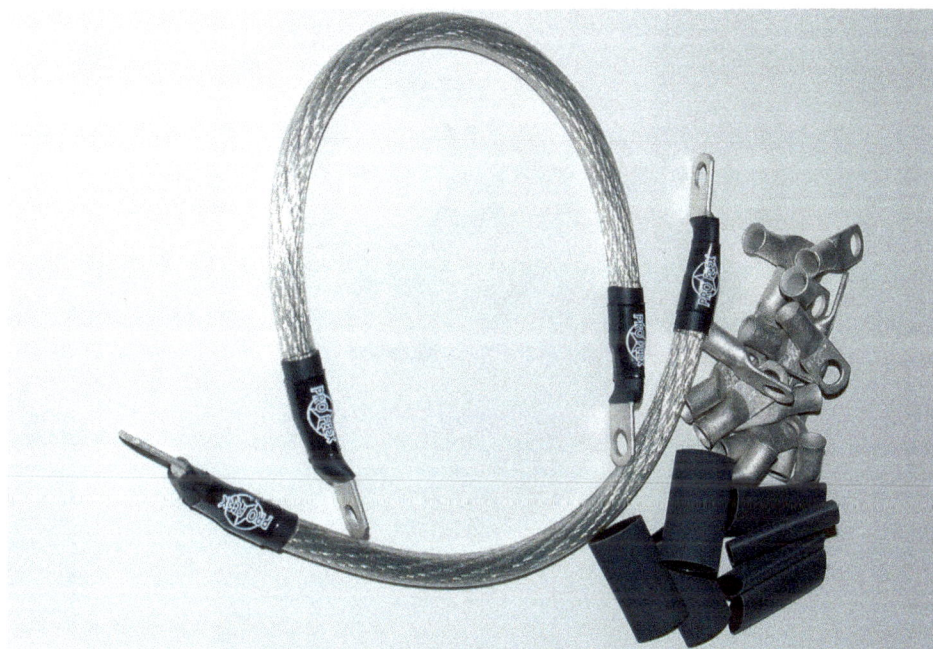

Big motors put big loads on the starter, which means you need large-gauge, high-quality cables like these from NAMZ. Most companies make terminals available in case you have to shorten a cable as shown in Chapter 10. Be sure to protect the positive cable so a sharp edge can't possibly rub through the insulation.

Now that you have located the circuit breaker, loosen the nut on the sliver-side in order to remove the ring terminal on the regulator wire. Note there will be many cable ties along the underside of the right frame rail keeping the wire snug to the frame. These will need to be removed and replaced during re-installation. The new regulator should also come with a new ring terminal. This should be crimped on once the regulator has been installed and the wire has been run back to the circuit breaker. Once the new unit is in place and attached to the circuit breaker, replace the cable ties that were cut during the removal process. Be sure not to over tighten. This could possibly damage the wire's insulation and cause a direct short. Lastly, plug the regulator into the stator before reconnecting the battery. Expect to spend about 2 hours, start to finish, if you've never done it before.

TESTING THE REGULATOR

Testing a regulator is very simple. Unfortunately, the test may start when you are riding down the road and your bike begins to kick, spit and sputter until is finally shuts off. Besides running out of fuel, a battery or regulator issue is usually the only other time your bike will act like this. Now that you are on the side of the road, the first thing you should do is the check your battery connections making sure they are tight. Then you want to make sure that your regulator is plugged into the stator. This has been a common problem over the years where the plug would vibrate out of the stator. With the regulator unplugged, the battery stops charging and once the battery finally dies, the bike shuts off. If this is the case, plug the regulator

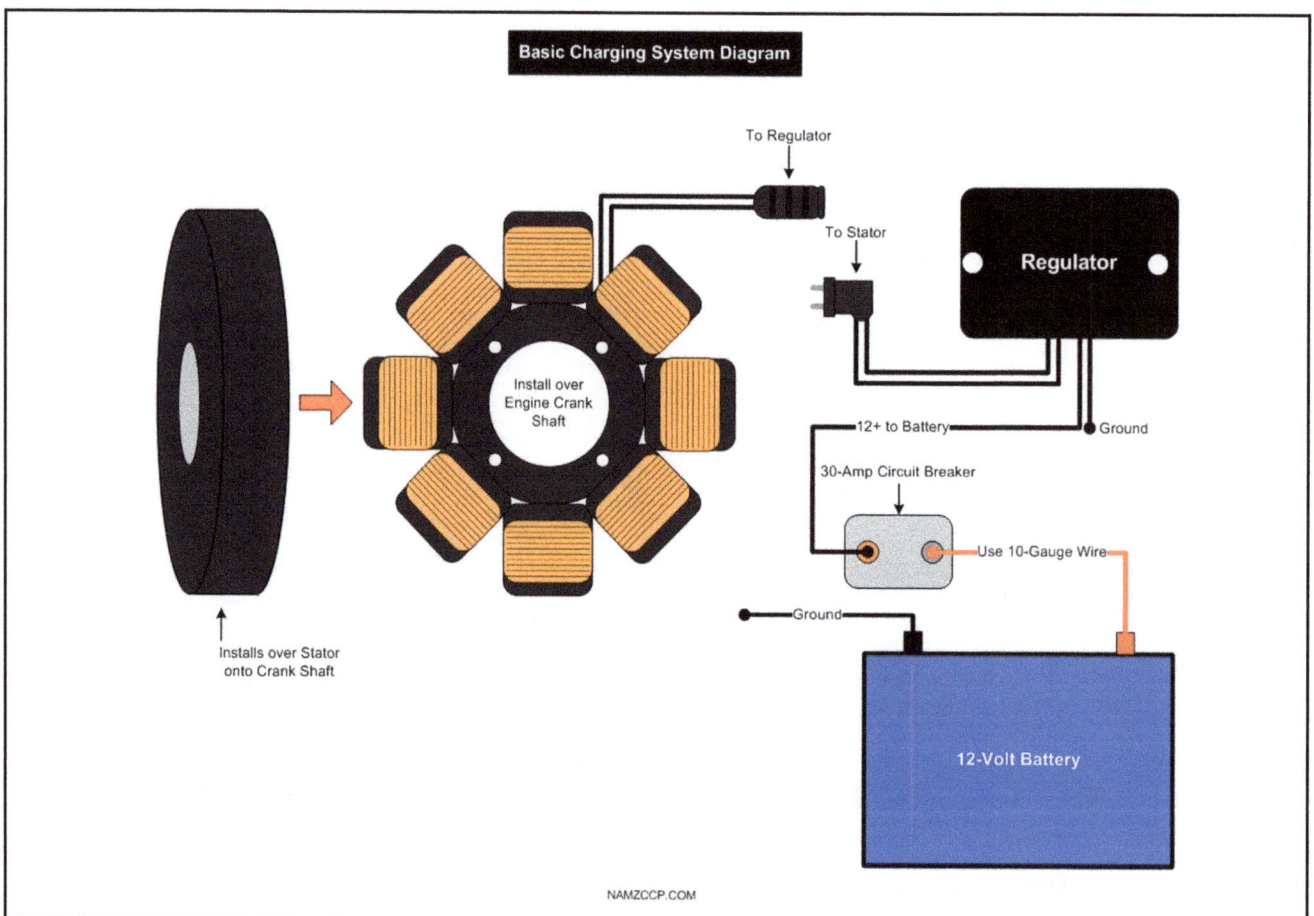

Basic Charging System Diagram

To Regulator
To Stator
Regulator
Install over Engine Crank Shaft
Installs over Stator onto Crank Shaft
12+ to Battery
Ground
30-Amp Circuit Breaker
Use 10-Gauge Wire
Ground
12-Volt Battery

NAMZCCP.COM

A typical V-Twin charging circuit is pretty straight forward. The spinning rotor induces an AC current in the stator, which is then converted to DC and controlled to about 14 volts by the regulator, and sent on to the battery via the main circuit breaker.

back in and try to bump start your bike. There is a fix to prevent this problem. Most aftermarket catalogs sell a retainer that bolts to the motor while pushing tightly against the back of the regulator plug. This makes it impossible to unplug the regulator unless the retainer bolt was loosened first. If the regulator was not unplugged and the battery is dead then chances are you have a bad regulator.

BATTERIES

The most common source of DC electricity is used by most of us every day. When you wake up in the morning and turn on the television, you are probably using a remote. You turn on your cell phone, look at your watch and see that you're running late for work. So you put on your coat, grab your keys and use your car's remote to unlock the door. Once you're in, you put the key in the ignition and start the car. Now you're off. You may ask why I wasted your time talking about this simple every-day scenario. It's because a battery powers every item we talked about with DC electricity.

SEALED OR WET

If you have ever had to go and buy a new battery for your bike I'm sure you have been asked the question, "sealed or wet?" Sealed batteries are also known as maintenance free batteries which means that it is not necessary to add water or battery acid in order to keep a sufficient charge. Sealed batteries generally require no maintenance except for keeping the terminals tight and clean. Wet batteries on the other hand usually require much more supervision. A wet battery needs an initial supply of battery acid mixed with water. These batteries have to be

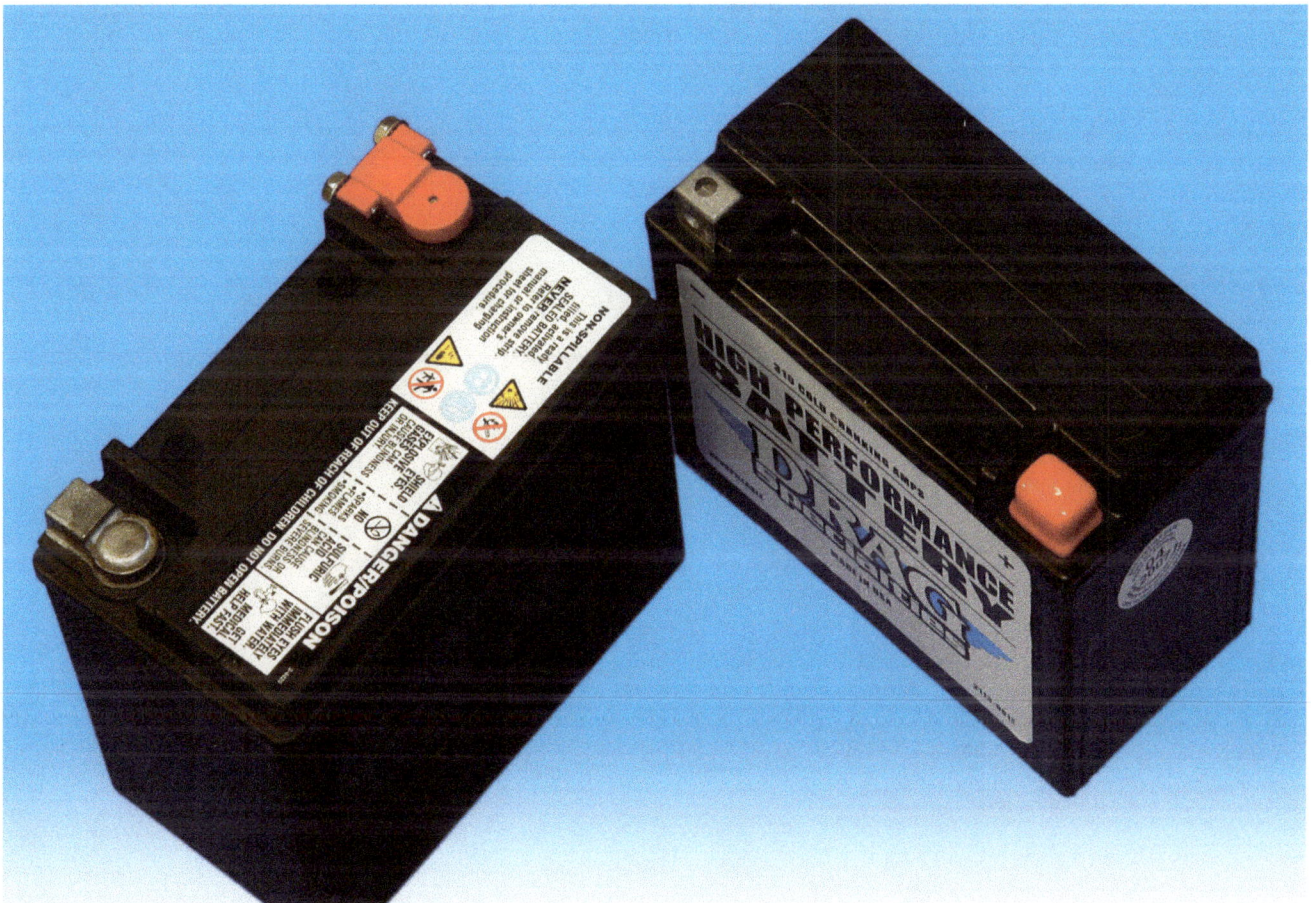

Here is a picture of two different style maintenance free batteries. Notice the difference between the positive and negative location on the two styles shown. Be sure to order a battery that fits your battery box and has the terminal in the right location for your application.

monitored more frequently to be sure that they are topped off with water in order for the battery to perform properly. If it's a matter of value, buy the sealed battery, it's worth it every time.

RATINGS - CCA OR COLD CRANKING AMPS

Did you ever wonder how a little 12-volt battery could turn over some of these new high-performance, huge cubic inch motors? There are two major factors that will make the difference. First, CCA or Cold Cranking Amps is the amount of amperage stored in a battery once the starter is engaged. The higher the CCA, the easier it is for the battery to turn over those big cubic-inch engines. Second, the bigger the battery the better. Smaller batteries may turn over a big motor once or twice but repeated attempts will drain the smaller battery much faster. If you are building a big motor, be sure to purchase a name brand, high CCA battery that will fit in your motorcycle.

MAINTENANCE

It's a good idea to perform general maintenance on your battery in order to prolong the battery life and prevent other possible electrical issues. With so many of the new motorcycles having sensitive electronics it's important to understand that low voltage can be just as damaging as a spike of higher voltage.

The most common practice for maintaining your battery is to be sure that both terminals are clean and tight. Check each of the battery cables to make sure they are tight on the starter and where they bolt to the frame. A loose ground wire either on the battery or on the frame can cause many issues. For instance, a loose ground wire can burn out a starter, wiring harness or your battery very quickly. A loose positive battery cable will do the same but could also cause a fire due to arcing near other metal objects. Tighten those terminals but not too tight, you don't want to strip out the threads.

Make sure the contacts are clean and free of debris. If you live in a cold weather climate be sure to purchase a battery-conditioning charger or battery tender. Battery conditioners/tenders provide a small but constant flow of low-amperage voltage to the battery as it sits unused. This will prevent the battery from dying when it gets below freezing thus prolonging the battery's life expectancy. It's safe to say that if a battery conditioner is used your battery should remain in great shape for many years. Harley Davidson uses sealed batteries that will last a very long time if properly taken care of. It's not too uncommon to see a factory battery last for five to eight years.

The smart chargers and battery tenders are self-regulating and will not allow over charging which will ruin a battery.

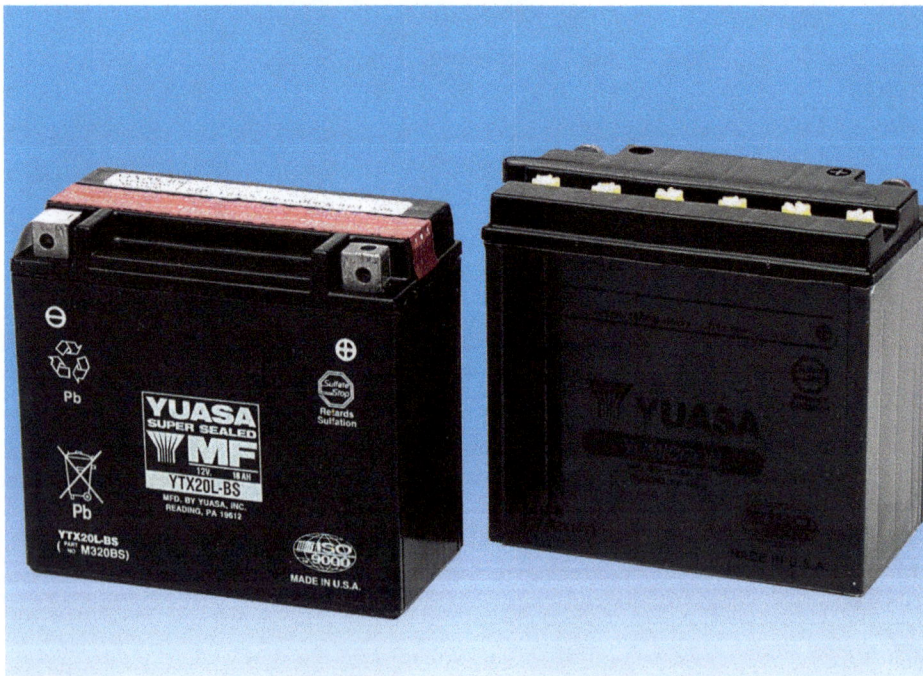

The battery on the left is a maintenance free (AGM or Activated Glass Mat) battery and the one on the right is a standard lead acid battery that requires filling when needed.

Overcharging a battery occurs when too much voltage is supplied to the battery's individual cells and the over load causes these cells to become damaged or burn out. For example, if two cells are damaged due to overcharging, they may never hold the correct voltage again. They may not accept a charge at all. Even worse, the damaged cells may begin to operate intermittently. You could hop on your bike, start it up fine and off you go. Then, two hours later, your battery could be dead as a doornail. Intermittent batteries are no fun to diagnose. If the damaged cell in the battery is the third cell in-line, (Battery's cells are wired in series) and it decides to stop working, the rest of the circuit will become interrupted. A net result will be a battery registering about 3-volts of DC output. Once the cell decides to start working again, the battery will be back to normal. There is no fix for an intermittent battery except to replace it with a new one.

All new motorcycle batteries are 12-volts and contain a positive (+) and negative (-) terminal. When you attach a pair of battery cables to the battery you are enabling the flow of 12-volt DC electricity to a specific source. If you connect the positive cable to the starter and the negative cable to a ground on the frame, the starter is ready to be energized. When you press the start button the starter relay energizes the starter solenoid, which engages the starter motor. Now that you have confirmed proper installation, whatever else you connect to the battery will automatically become energized as long as it is grounded.

STARTERS

Back in the day, before 1966, all Harley Davidson models were available as kick-start only. Can you imagine not having an electric start on these new, big inch, high horsepower engines of today? It's pretty funny to talk with some of the old time bikers hearing them refer to 21st century riders as "yuppies." One of the funniest answers I ever heard explaining a "yuppie biker" was, "Did you ever see a suit, (business man) try to kick-start an old Panhead"? If you think about it, the addition of the electric start has made all of us take those old kick-starters for granted.

How does it work? Electric starters have evolved a great deal over the years. The starter motors of years ago were generally unreliable and rather bulky. When they worked, they often times did not have the power that was needed to turn the engine over. Not to say that all starters didn't work, they just needed improvement. The starters you will find today are very reliable, have much more kilowatt power, use less amperage and are much more compact. The common

Here is today's standard "battery tender" available from any aftermarket shop or dealership for around thirty dollars. Unlike the old trickle chargers, these can be left connected to the bike all winter long.

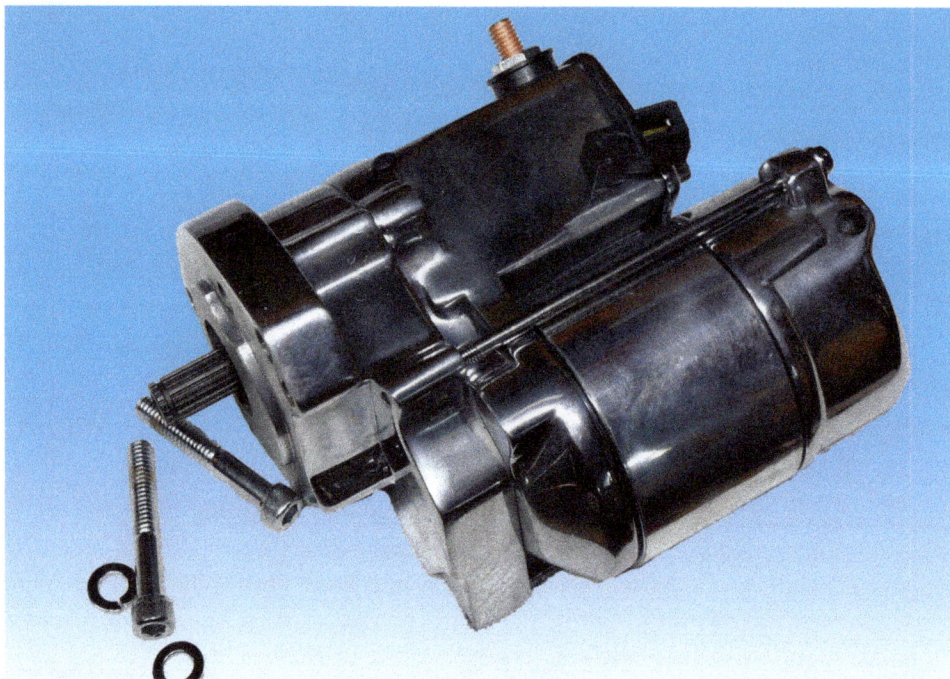

Above is a sample of a small kilowatt polished aluminum starter motor.

starter found in a Harley is a 1.4-kilowatt motor utilizing a starter solenoid and clutch assembly.

Starting a motorcycle is generally a six-step process that begins with the push of a button. On the right side handlebar controls found on a factory Harley Davidson you can find the starter button. This switch is momentary which will only provide power while the button is pressed. The power from the switch flows down to a starter relay. A starter relay is used as a high-current switch in most motorcycle starting circuits. The purpose of a starter relay is to provide high-current power to the starter while only needing a small amount of current to activate the relay.

Relays contain a set of windings and a pair of contacts that move when energized. A starter relay is usually mounted near the battery on the motorcycle's fuse panel. Once the relay is activated, electrical current is sent to the starter solenoid located on the starter motor. Although similar to the starter relay, the solenoid converts electrical energy into linear motion. The solenoid contains a set of windings that, when energized, cause movement of the solenoid's

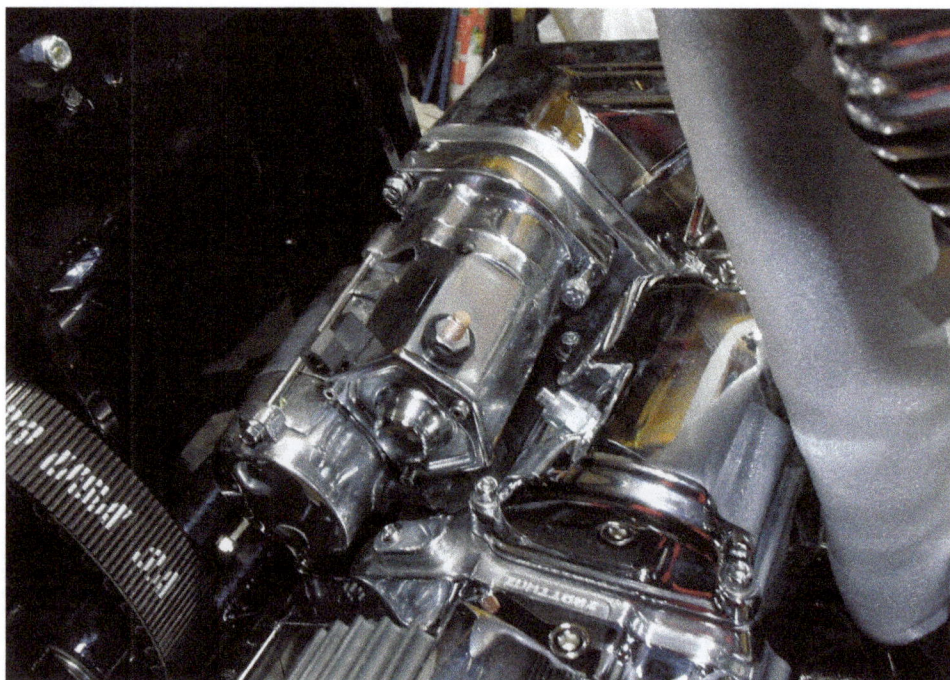

This is the start of a starter installation sequence. Note the starter body is bolted in from the right side. Be sure there's enough clearance that the starter stud can't touch the bottom of the battery box.

30

plunger, which then engages the starter. Once the starter is engaged, the jackshaft will engage with the ring gear that is mounted on the clutch hub found in the inner primary. When the ring gear begins to rotate, the primary chain connecting the crankshaft to the clutch hub will turn over the engine. Though it seems like a lot of things need to happen at the right time in order for this process to work correctly, it all happens in a split second. As long as there is power to the ignition system and the fuel is turned on, your ride should fire right up.

Where is it located?

The starter on a factory motorcycle can be found on top of the transmission. Most transmissions made after 1965 have a machined area, which is designed to mount the starter. Today, there are transmissions that actually reposition the starter behind instead of on top of the transmission. When using this system, a completely new, redesigned inner and outer primary must also be used. The starter mounting area on a transmission helps to properly align the starter with the jackshaft and ring gear. The inner and outer primaries also play a major role in this align-

Next, the bare jackshaft is installed as shown with a connector that is not shown.

Here you see the jackshaft coupler being installed.

Now the starter bolt, lock tab and pinion gear are installed.

Once the starter bolt is tightened, use a pair of vice grips to pull the jackshaft assembly in and out of the primary to ensure proper movement.

ment as well. Most new style starters are bolted in through the transmission and into the inner primary using two 5/16 inch thick bolts with lock washers. Before ever working on your starter, be sure to disconnect the battery FIRST!

How do you know if it is bad? There have been many instances where a misaligned primary caused people to think their starter was bad. The sound a starter makes when your battery is dead is the same sound it makes when you have a misaligned inner and outer primary. This "clicking" noise caused by a dead battery is due to the starter solenoid not getting the power it needs to engage the starter motor. The "clicking" noise is the solenoid partially engaging the starter. If your battery is fully charged and your starter is still making that clicking sound, it could also mean that you have a battery cable issue. A loose battery cable, either positive or negative, or a loose ground wire to the frame can also cause this problem. Check the battery and cables for damage due to excessive heat that is caused by a loose wire. If your battery and cables have been checked and you still have the clicking noise, there is a chance that the starter clutch is bad or that there is a misaligned primary.

STARTER CLUTCHES, SOLENOIDS & JACKSHAFTS

The function of the starter clutch is to connect to both the starter and the clutch gear while its one-way operation prevents engagement when the engine is running. The sound of a defective starter clutch is like a bunch of loose nuts and bolts placed in a blender. For some reason, whenever I hear a motorcycle with a bad starter clutch, I think of the dentist. Maybe it reminds me of the drills they use. Anyway, it's not a pretty sound. Starter clutches can be replaced for much less than the cost of a new starter, usually under a hundred bucks. Not a very easy job for the beginner. From start to finish, an experienced mechanic could spend about 4 to 5 hours replacing a defective starter clutch. That's about the same time required to replace the starter itself with the additional cost of a new starter.

Starter solenoids can also go bad. They too are much less expensive to replace and do not require much more than an hour or two of labor. The average price of a replacement starter solenoid depends on the year, make and model but most solenoids or

Here is a picture of the installed jackshaft assembly.

You have to be sure the chain runs true by checking that it runs parallel to the inner primary at both the front...

33

...and the back, just ahead of the clutch hub. Shims, as seen in the photo on the top of page 15, can be used to move the compensator sprocket out away from the inner primary and thus align the chain.

A picture of a heavy duty starter clutch.

replacement solenoid re-build kits sell for between $20 and $50 bucks. This is an easy fix and is much cheaper to do than to replace the starter. Most late model starter solenoids have 3-metric hex head bolts holding on the cover located next to the starter motor. Be ready!

When you remove the solenoid cover the solenoid will want to slide out of the housing. You do not want to jam it back in place without making sure it is properly aligned. To do so would risk possible damage to the solenoid plunger or other internal components.

The starter jackshaft is located in the primary housing and connects the splined shaft from the starter motor to a two-sided splined coupler. This coupler is designed to attach the starter motor shaft to the splined jackshaft. If this connection binds for any reason, a damaged coupler, loose starter, worn out jackshaft bushing or a loose/mis-aligned outer primary cover, usually causes it. No matter what the reason, trying to find the problem can really drive you nuts and take up a whole bunch of time. The best advice for preventing this prob-lem is to only use original OEM replacement parts. If you decide to go with an open primary, use a popu-lar brand. Many open belt drive systems have a small cover over the jackshaft that may not have the strict machining tolerances needed to prevent mis-aligning the jackshaft with the ring gear. Your best bet when deciding on which belt drive is the best for you, is to try to look for a system with a three-bolt jackshaft cover instead of the more common 2-bolt. Using a 3-bolt cover will be stronger and allow for precise alignment of the jackshaft.

Are they all the same?

Since the inception of the electric starter, there have been many different manufacturers who have come and gone. There are still a few companies in the United States that make many of their own components for starter assemblies but the majority use starter motors from over seas. Even most late model Harley Davidson's use a starter that is made over seas. For a long while, it was the same starter that was used to start Toyota's. There are many riders who love Harley Davidson's since they are made in America but they do out-source some of their components. It's like the saying goes, why reinvent the wheel? If these starters are good enough for one of the world's best automobile manufacturers, then they've got to be good. Good they are, but they are not the best.

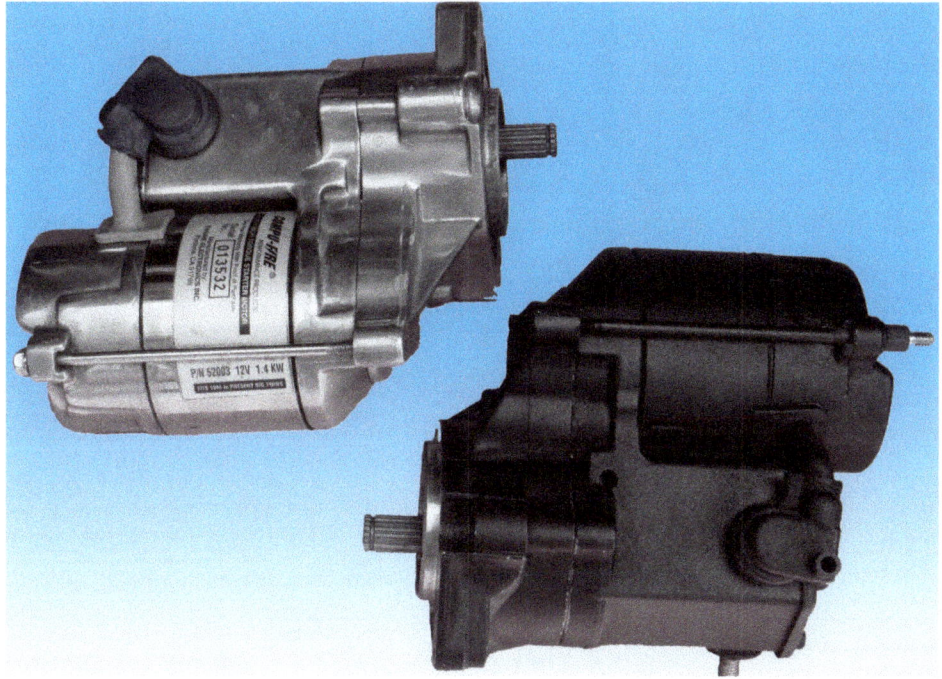

The starter on the right resembles a stock, wrinkle finish starter and the one on the left is a polished starter from Compu-fire. Most of these V-Twin starters were designed originally to start small Japanese automobiles, which means the fasteners, including the main stud, use metric threads.

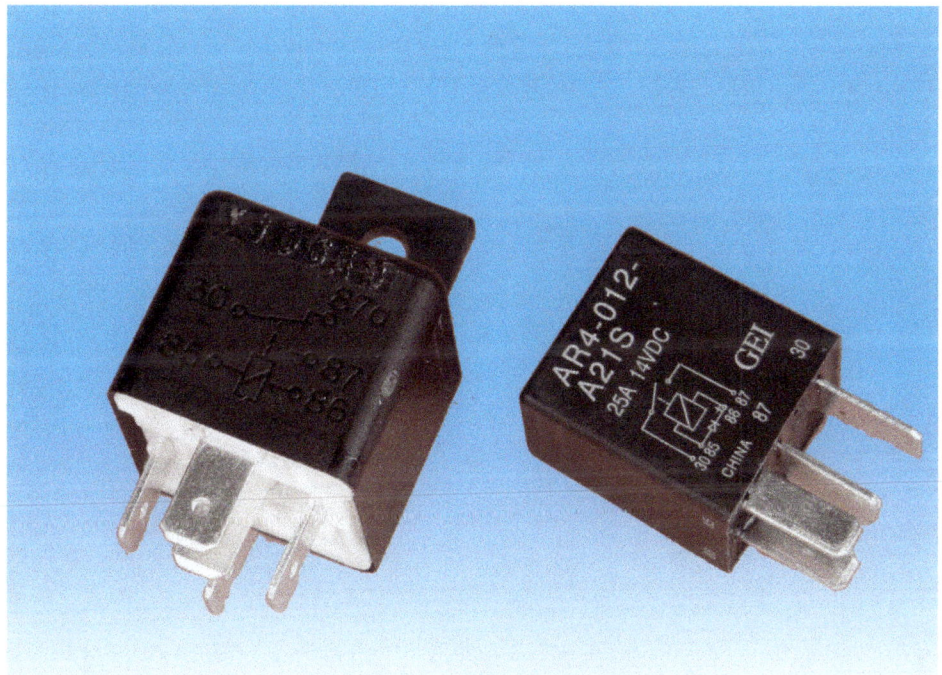

This picture shows two different styles of starter relays.

There are starters out there that are designed for use on high-horsepower motors. These starters have a higher kilowatt output than stock so they can turn over high compression engines. Starters come in different sizes depending on how much room you have on your bike. Some use quality billet aluminum gearboxes with hardened gears. You can find starters that come polished, chrome or colored anodized finishes. Some starters are very basic and some use only the very best electrical components money can buy. I'm not going to tell you what is the best starter brand to buy because that's not what this book is about. I will, however tell you to be careful what you do buy. Some starters out there are remanufactured. The only way to tell is to read over the fine print found in the packaging. Every company must state if any of the parts in the contents of their packaging have been made using remanufactured goods. So if you're trying to avoid buying junk, spend more money and get the good stuff. The saying, "you get what you pay for" is so very true with starters. The more they cost, the better they are. Just to make you feel better, two of the better starters out there are made in the US!

REMOVE AND REPLACE

When it's finally time to replace a damaged starter, plan on spending a couple bucks and a full day's worth of work. Replacing a starter is not fun so do yourself a favor a buy a good one the first time. No matter what type of American V-Twin motorcycle you may have, it is still a pretty big job. Besides needing to purchase a new starter, plan on getting an outer primary gasket, inspection and derby cover gaskets and a quart of primary fluid. If you're really unlucky, you may even need to drain your oil so the oil tank can be moved out of the way. Many factory Softail models must have the oil tank bolts removed so the tank can be pulled away from the starter in order to remove it.

Let's say for our scenario that a Softail does not have to have the oil drained or the oil tank removed in order to replace the starter. The first thing you will need to do is disconnect the battery! Now, this time I know you will not forget since the battery will need to be removed in order to access the starter's battery cable. Batteries do not need to be removed on most other models. Now the battery is out, you should remove the primary drain plug. Remember that the inner primary holds about a quart of primary fluid. Once drained, you can now go ahead and begin to remove the outer primary, inspection and derby covers.

When you finish removing the outer primary, locate the jackshaft towards the backside of the clutch hub. The small

Here is a sample of a stock starter installed in a motorcycle.

hex-head bolt should have a lock tab folded over the side of the bolt. This is done to prevent the bolt from breaking loose. Fold over the tab and begin to remove the long bolt. This bolt secures the jackshaft assembly to the starter shaft. As we discussed above, the jackshaft is attached to the starter using a splined coupler and the long bolt tightens the two together. You can now remove the jackshaft. From the bottom of the battery tray, you should be able to see the battery cable that is fastened to the starter. Loosen the nut and remove the positive battery cable. Now from the right side of the bike, access the back of the starter and remove the two 5/16" allen-head bolts. At this point the starter should be very loose and can be removed from the motorcycle. Repeat all of the same steps when reinstalling the new starter.

Some of the other things you want to think about when you're replacing a starter are whether or not you have any leaks? For example, if the inner primary is leaking at the jackshaft, at the transmission seal, or at the inner primary O-ring you should address these issues since the bike is already apart. Another area to address is the condition of the battery cables. Be sure that the wire is not cracked and the terminals are tight. Lastly, you may want to look at you primary chain and tensioner to be sure they are in good shape. If any of these items are worn according to your service manual, you're much better off replacing them now to avoid possible issues down the road.

Testing: Say you go out to the garage and your bike doesn't turn over. Besides being aggravated, you now have to find out what's wrong. The first thing you should do is check to see if your battery has a charge. Use a multi-meter and be sure that it reads over 12-volts DC. If your battery is OK then you may want to test the starter. The quickest and easiest way to test your starter is to run a heavy-gauge jumper wire from the top of your starter or from the positive side of your battery down to the starter solenoid. Make sure that the bike is in neutral first! Remove the single, 16-gauge wire from the solenoid. If the starter turns over when you connect the jumper wire then you know it's not a starter issue. If it does not turn over then you definitely have a starter problem. Now keep in mind, a starter is made up of a motor, solenoid and a gearbox. Anyone of these individual components could go bad but can be replaced or repaired. Once you have removed your defective starter from the bike, test the individual components until you find the problem. Refer to the manufacturer's service manual for further instructions.

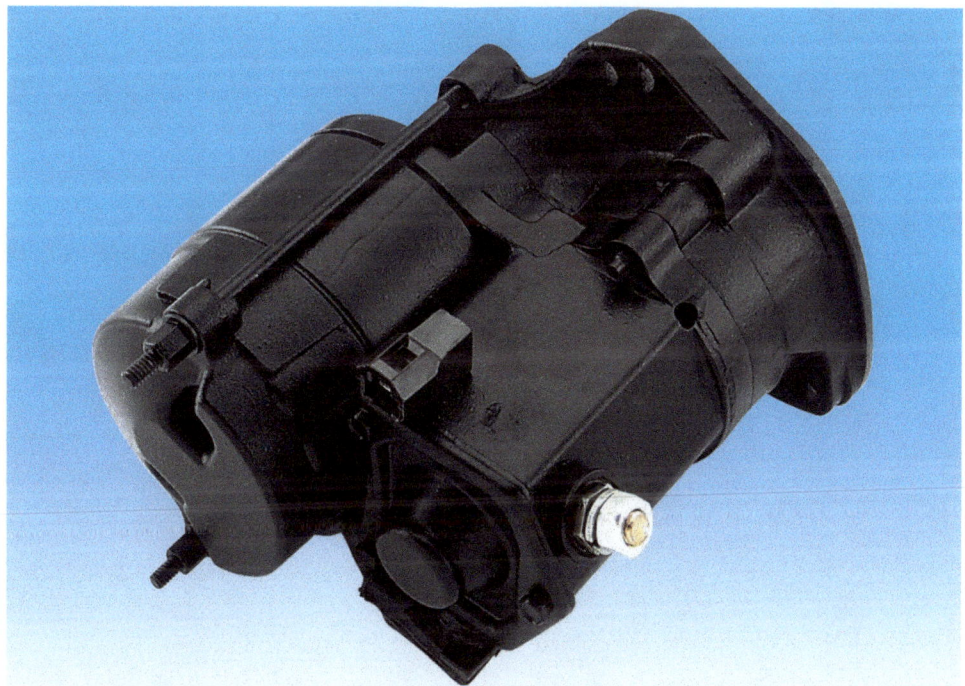

Here is another sample of a stock-style starter assembly.

Chapter Three

The Factory Harness

From AMP to Deutsch

Now that all of the heavy-duty learning is out of the way, we can begin to focus on the fun stuff. Well, maybe not that much fun, but it will be much easier to follow along. In this chapter we will discuss the differences Harley Davidson made during major model year changes. Once Harley bought the company back from AMF, two major areas the factory needed to focus on were making the motorcycle's engine reliable and leak free, and developing a wiring harness that actually worked. Hop on and let's go for a ride down memory lane.

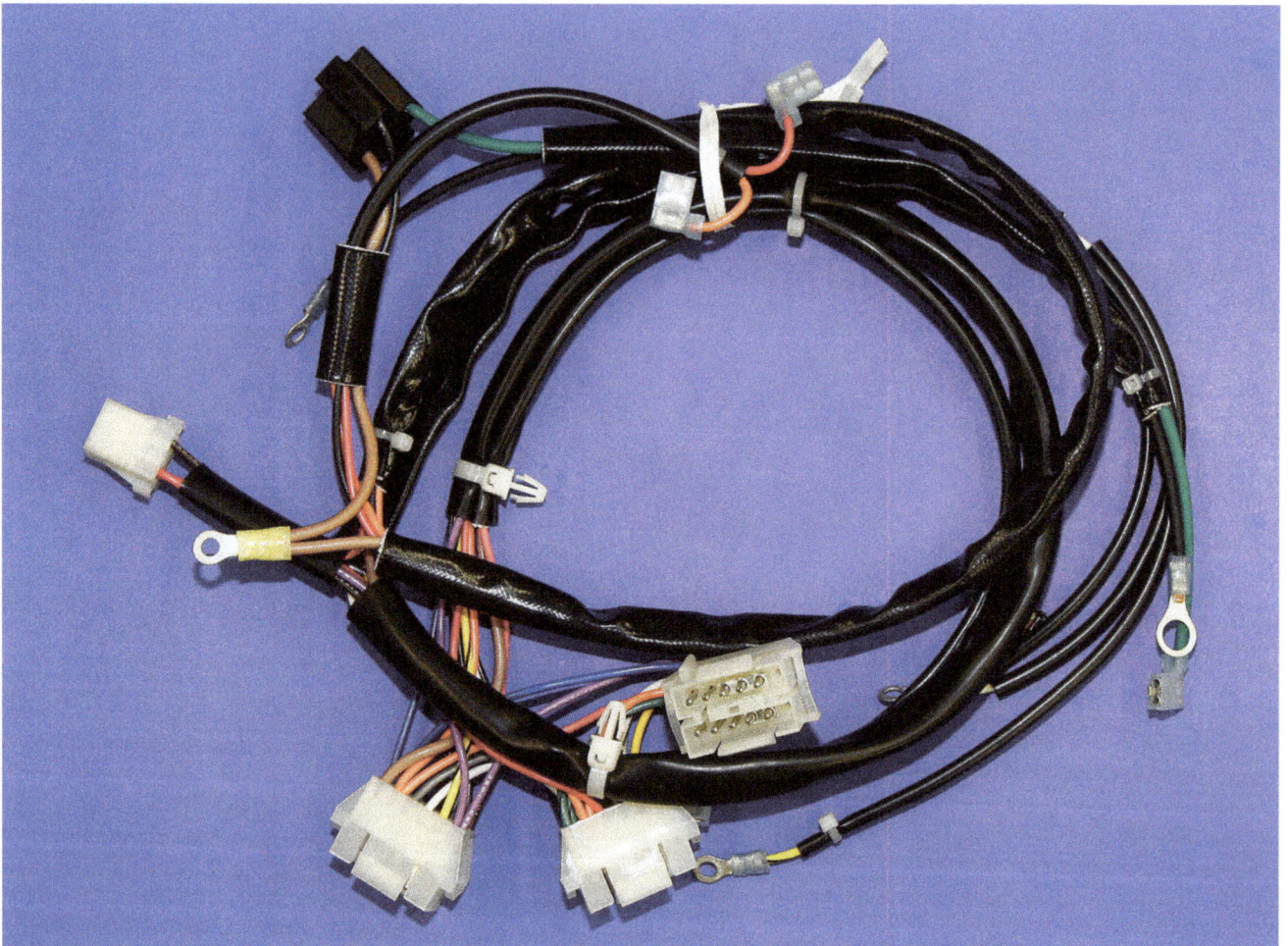

Here's a pre-1996 factory harness, complete with AMP connectors, very similar to the harness on the old white Softail seen a few pages farther along.

1982 TO 1995

Since the inception of Harley Davidson back in 1903, there have been so many changes that it would take hundreds of books to cover all of them. In this book, we will focus on the wiring harnesses that debuted in 1982 and up through 2007. The harnesses used between 1982 and 1995 were very similar between all models. The switches and housings on the handlebars during these years were similar to today's style. A square master cylinder reservoir was used with a 2-piece switch housing and blade style levers were some of the upgrades from previous years. It's safe to say that every after-market V-Twin catalog now offers these '82 to '95 OEM style switches, with or without housings, available in black or chrome.

With the earlier harness, the headlight and front turn signals connect directly into the same connector making it a bit more cumbersome to remove individual components. These connectors, manufactured by AMP, are not water tight by any means. Any of you who have worked with these connectors in the past understand how difficult they are to service. The handlebar switches, headlight and front turn signals all terminated under the fuel tank on most models. This was a real "rats nest" of wires. Older AMP connectors stayed together, you really didn't have to worry about them falling apart. In some cases, they used small metal tabs that

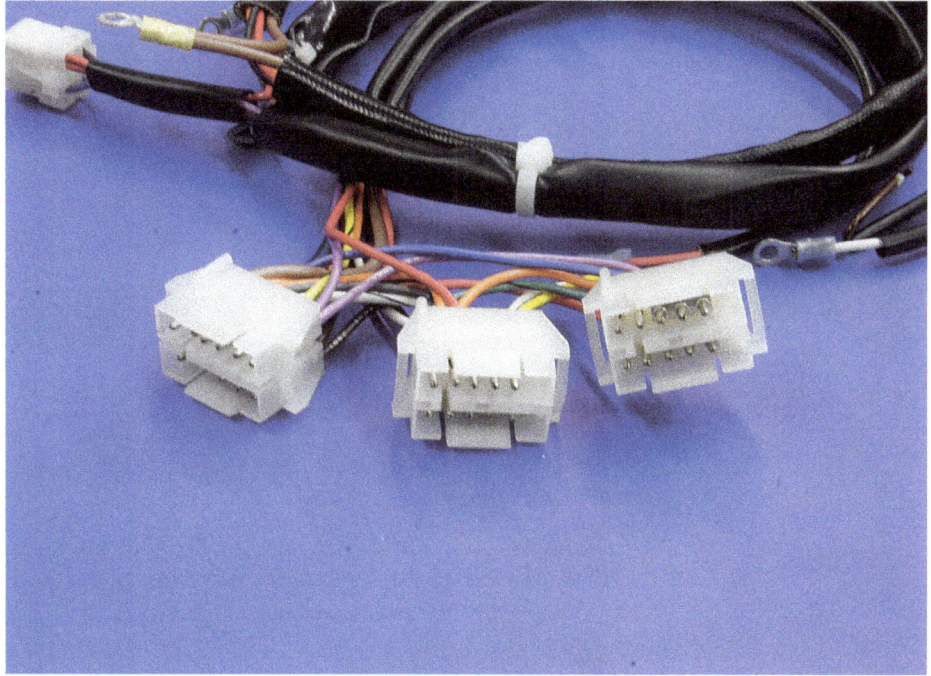

This close up shows the AMP connectors. If you look closely you can see the "bridge" in the upper right of the right side connector.

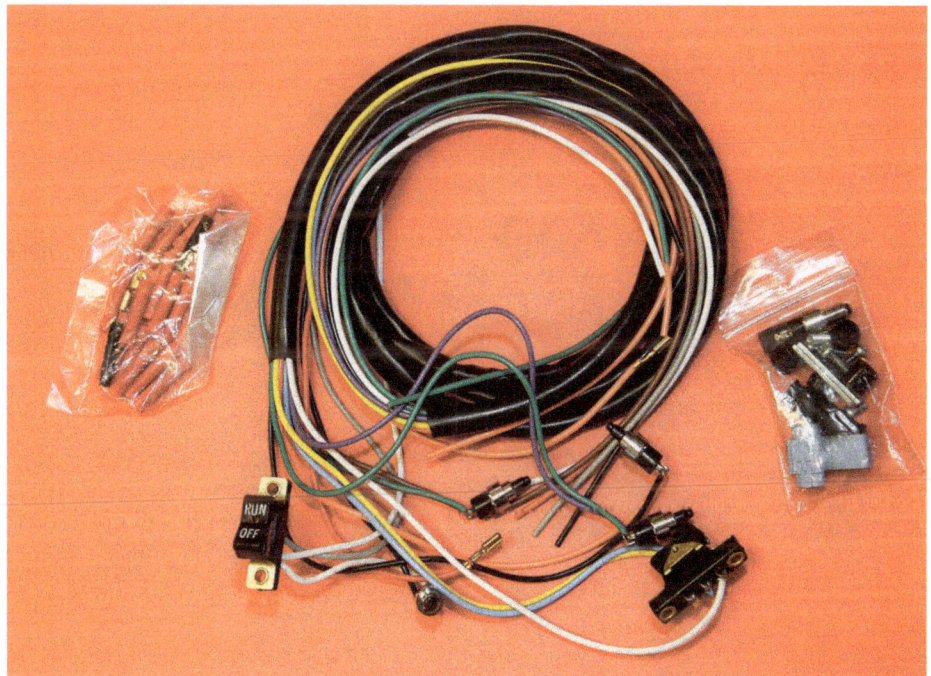

Another early harness - this one meant for the handle bar switches circa '73 to '81, which are very different from the later switches.

were wedged between two crimp terminals as jumpers. This would take 12-volt power (in most cases) from one wire and supply it to another wire. It was a great concept but it didn't last past 1995.

The key switch for FX and FL model Harley Davidson's was another rat's nest. These mechanical switches left much to be desired. They were open to the elements and not watertight. If you pushed down on them too hard in order to turn the bike on, you could easily short out a circuit or two. This was due to the numerous wires connected to the switch itself.

Factory ignition switches generally had a minimum of six wires connected to them not including any wiring used for custom add ons. This was also the area where you would find the circuit breakers and the turn signal flasher relay. There was a very good chance that any wiring problem you encountered would be found here. For the most part, the wiring harnesses used during these years were not waterproof in any way. The assorted AMP connectors are serviceable for the application, but the lack of wire seals definitely caused some issues with the wiring, one of worst enemies for the harnesses from this period is corrosion due to moisture. Corrosion can cause a connection of any sort to loose continuity and either short circuit, damage the device requiring the power - or even melt the wiring harness all together. Bad connections have high resistance, which

Though the dash and switch on this early 90s Softail looks a lot like the newer Softails, the electrical details are very archaic compared to the later bikes...

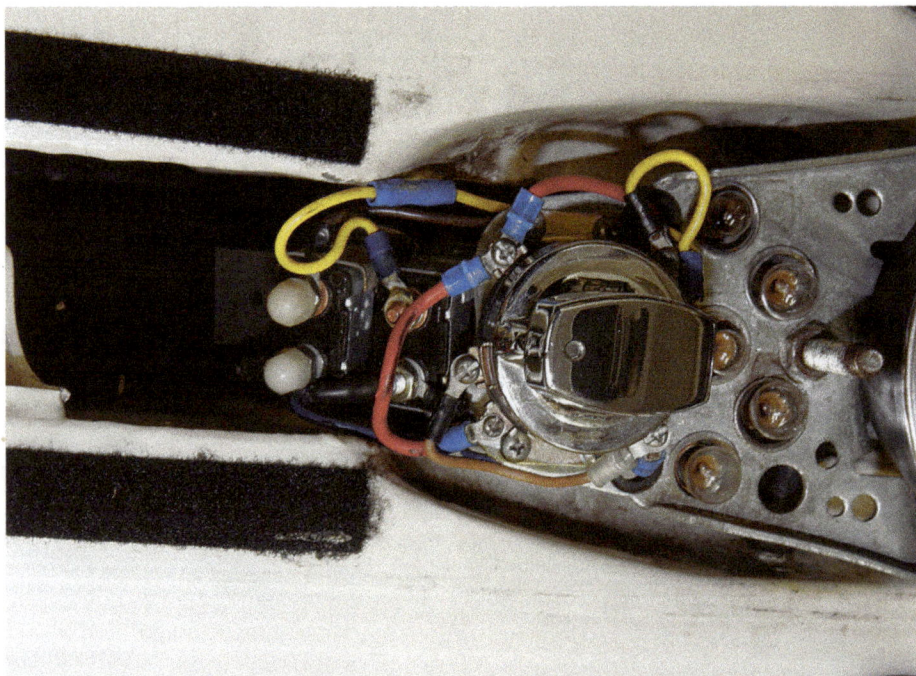

...here you can see the non-water-resistant ignition switch with the external, exposed connectors.

creates excess heat. Generally the voltage drop is not severe enough to cause damage to components but the heat can definitely cause issues with the wiring or normal operation of the motorcycle.

Compared to today's mainly "electronic" computer driven harnesses, the harnesses used between1982 and 1995 were mostly "mechanical". You may not understand what I mean by that. Here are some examples. Before 1989 self-canceling turn signal modules were non-existent. It wasn't until 1991 that all Harley Davidson models used a self-canceling turn signal module. Before 1989, the component used to make turn signals flash was a Wagner 552 mechanical flasher relay. These relays did the job but needed to be replaced often. It sounds like a joke but in order to stop a turn signal from flashing, you had to press on the turn signal button. As mentioned above, the ignition switch on most big twin models were also 100% mechanical with mainly internal moving parts, too many wires and not waterproof. Rather clunky if you ever used one and like the flasher relay, these switches do not have a long service life.

The main wiring harness from this period uses stiff 16-gauge wires throughout the entire motorcycle. Even the wire loom was a heavier gauge compared to today. If you think about it, mechanical components require higher amperage in order to operate properly.

1996 TO 2006
Say goodbye to the 20th and a big hello to the 21st Century! Not only was the custom market going through puberty back in

Those early harnesses plugged into recesses in the frame webbing between the tanks.

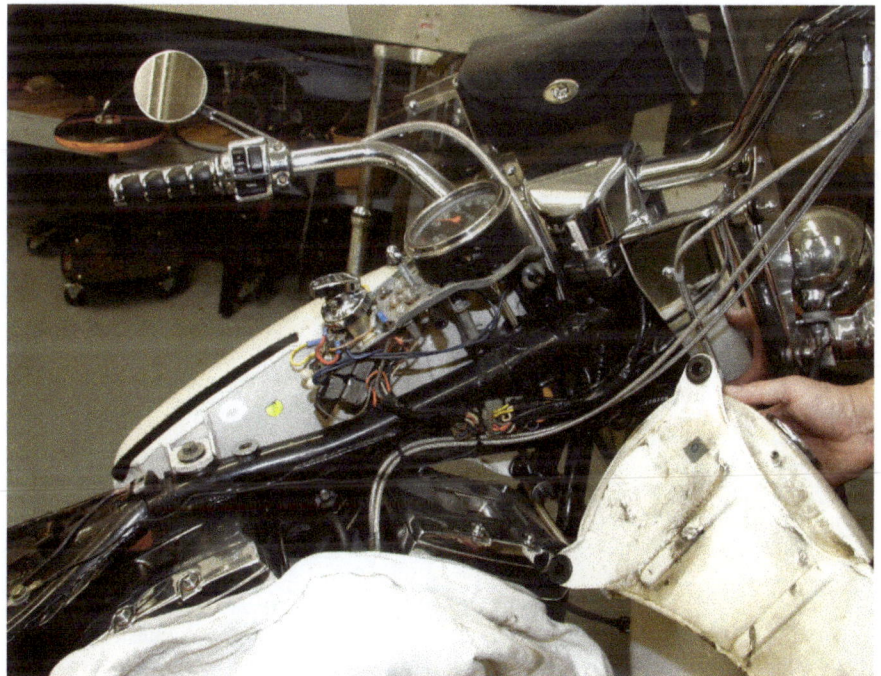

If you peel back one of the fat bob tanks, you can see the big ugly harness along with the circuit breakers.

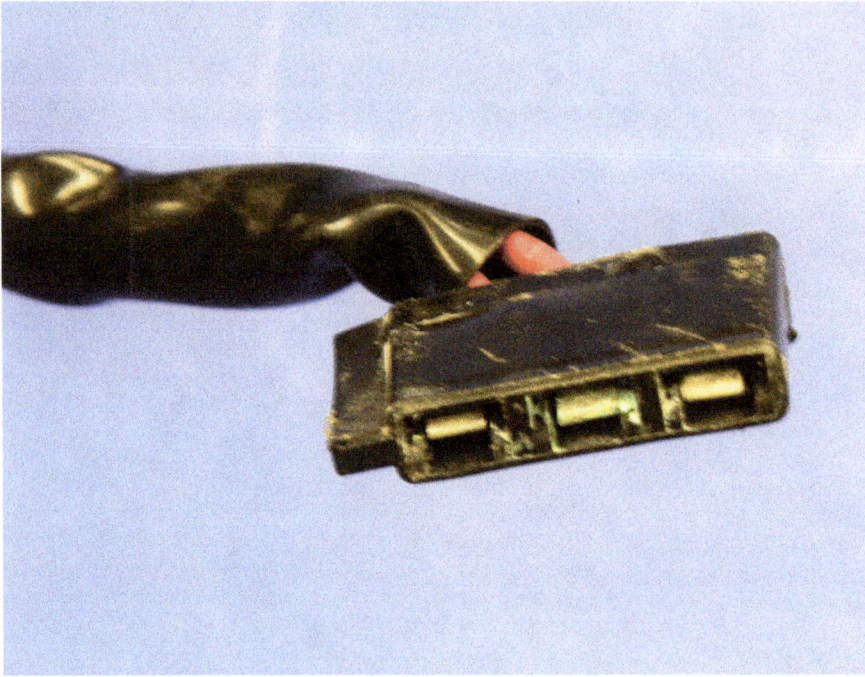

This close up shows the ignition switch plug from the '03 fuel injected harness, note the corrosion. Sealed connectors are a very good thing.

Circuit breakers are mounted in a bundle just under the ignition switch, not the easiest spot to get at.

1995 but the factory was also going through some serious changes. For starters, the entire wiring harness from front to back received an upgrade. As of 1996, some of the AMP connectors are gone, replaced with water-tight Deutsch connectors. These new connectors are much easier to install and service. Other improvements include handlebar switches and housings that are more ergonomic and feature a rounded-corner design. The housing themselves are a bit larger than previous years but they are definitely more attractive. Headlights and turn signals are the same. The turn signal module changed slightly but the basic operation is the same.

The new turn signal modules now work in conjunction with a reed switch, located in the bike's speedometer. What's a reed switch? A reed switch is an electrical switch operated by an applied magnetic field. It was invented at Bell Telephone Laboratories in 1936 by W. B. Elwood. It consists of a pair of contacts on ferrous metal reeds in a hermetically sealed glass envelope. On a motorcycle the contacts are normally open, closing when a magnetic field is present. The closing of these contacts is what shuts off the flashing turn signals and occurs when the motorcycle reaches a particular speed measured by distance traveled.

Along with the new harness, Harley replaced the ignition switch. This new switch is more of a sealed style, fed by only three, 12-gauge wires. The switch itself is much smoother to operate and can be locked with the new style barrel key that replaced the traditional key used in the past.

The keyhole door hinged on the right of the switch, unlike earlier years hinging from the top of switch. Once a rat's nest of wire, the area between the gas tanks on most models is now a clean open area. The circuit breakers are located near the battery box area, and no longer create a tangle of wires near the ignition switch.

Another major change that occurred in 1996 is the change from mechanical speedometers to electronic speedometers. Prior to 1996, the speedometer was cable driven, usually off of the front wheel. Except for some bagger models, the speedometer drive comes off the front axle on the same side as the brake rotor. A notch cut into the brake rotors accept the little tang from the speedometer drive. As the wheel turns, so does the speedometer drive. A speedometer cable is nothing more than a tightly wound spring, flexible enough to run up to a speedometer, but strong enough that it won't break easily. The drive turns the cable, which in turn drives the speedometer itself. Not a bunch of rocket science, but an older technology that gets the job done.

The new transmissions designed for electronic speedometers have a machined port so a hall-effect sensor can be mounted in the case, and measure the rotation of forth gear and send that data to the speedometer. This system generally works flawlessly.

In 1996 the ignition modules and trigger plates began using the new style of Deutsch connectors as well. For the

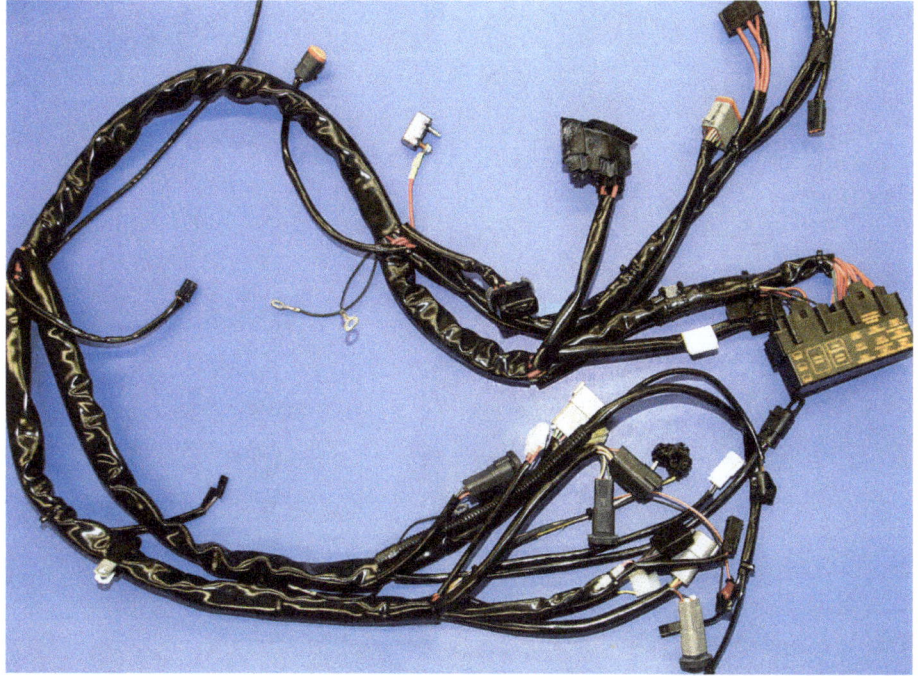

This late-model Road King harness is slightly different than a Bagger harness as the components are positioned in different locations. The late model bikes have the relays, fuses and breakers in easy-to-access locations.

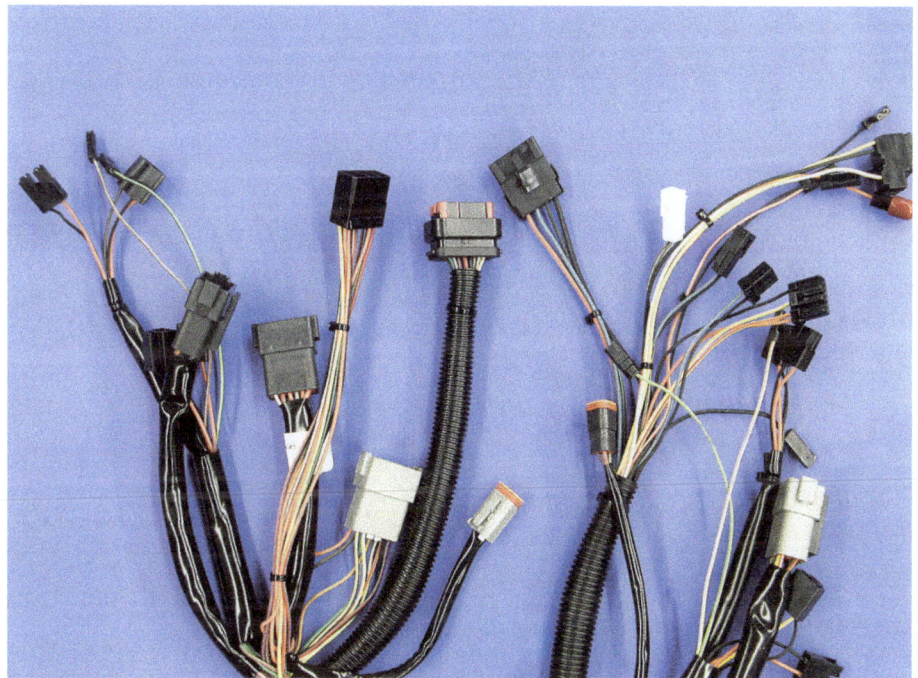

Close up of the variety of connectors (mostly Deutsch style) used on a late model harness.

The underside of the dash on a Twin Cam model: Note the switch is sealed, the idiot lights are enclosed and the speedo is electronic.

Notice how much neater and more compact the wiring is between the tanks than on the old Softail seen a few pages back.

most part, the wiring harness is tighter, yet more flexible and better constructed than in previous years. Harley apparently knew that wiring was their achilles heel for many years and used this redesign of the harness to eliminate all those old gremlins. With the introduction of the '96 models the wiring nightmares of the past seemed to disappear.

DIFFERENCES

Because of the changes introduced in '96, most of the electrical components produced for 1995 and earlier models are not compatible with 1996 and up models. For example, the headlight on a 1995 Softail is wired into a 12-position connector located under the gas tank, along with the wiring for the front turn signals (note the photos on page 43 and 44). If you ever had the chance to work on an early to mid 1990's Harley Davidson, you know how difficult it is to remove the terminals from Mate-n-Lock connectors. There are a variety of terminal removal tools available but most of them don't work that well. If you were unable to remove the terminals or you didn't feel like taking off the fuel tank to get to the connector, the only way to remove the headlight was to remove the bulb. Once the bulb has been removed, you would have to remove the terminals from the 3-pin socket then hope that the flag-style spade connectors would fit through the hole in the headlight bucket. No matter which way you go about it, this is not an easy job.

On a 1996 model, the headlight harness runs under the gas tank and terminates into a 4-

position AMP Multilock connector. There are no other wires in this connector. Having a connection dedicated for each electrical component is the way to go. In this case, it's very easy to remove the headlight. Simply unplug the connector and off you go. In some cases, and with a little luck, you can reach the headlight connector without removing the fuel tank. This also holds true with the turn signal connector. The front turn signals are wired into a dedicated 6-position AMP Multilock connection under the fuel tank. The 6-position connector has all the terminals in a single row, the 3-wires from the left and right turn signal making up the circuit. The difference from left to right is a small band of brown tape indicating the right side. The AMP connectors use a numbering system above or beside each position on the connector. This makes it easier to remove a couple of wires, record the number and the color of the wire, and know where to reinstall them.

You didn't have the same ease with the pre-1996 models. For example, in order to service the handlebar switches you have to remove the terminals (or pins) from the connector so you can fit the wires through the hole in the top triple tree. There was no other way around it. This is also true of the turn signals. On 1996 to 2006 models, you still have to remove the fuel tank(s) in order to get to the handlebar switch connectors but you don't have to remove the individual pins from the Deutsch connectors. These new connectors fit through the hole in the top triple tree intact, which makes service and repair

Here's the gray 6-position Deutsch plug from the handlebar switches. Gray is used for the left side and black for the right side.

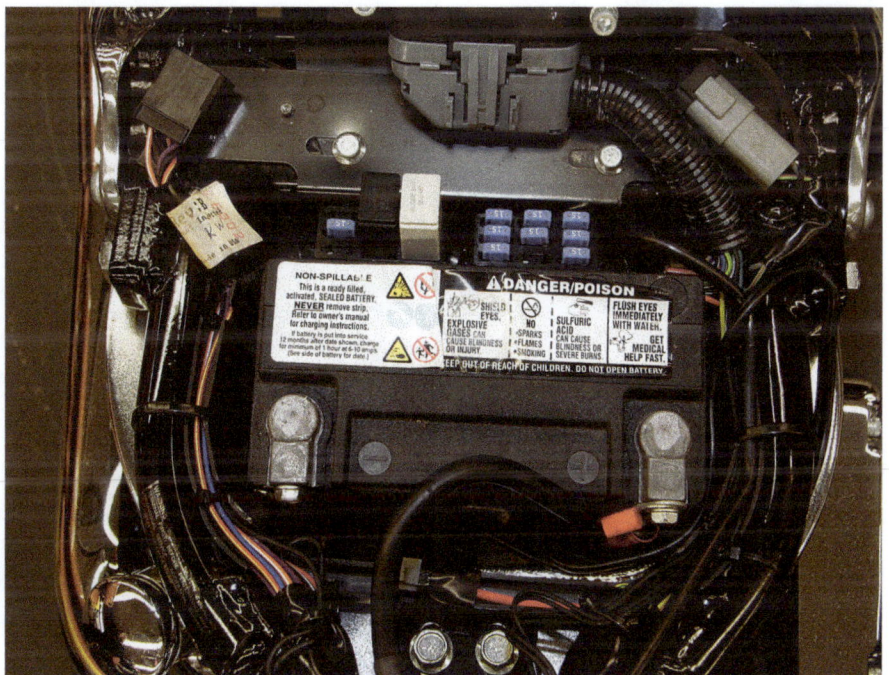

You can tell from this photo that this model is fuel injected, the large gray connector is a Delphi and it attaches the main harness to the computer. You can also see Micro relays and the small fuse panel.

much easier. The Deutsch connectors are also simple to take apart, you don't need special tools. In fact, a small straight-blade style screwdriver does the job perfectly, allowing the small connectors to disengage with very little effort. It is nearly impossible to damage the connector while removing the terminals.

There were other small differences in the wiring, connections and styles of terminals used. Neutral safety switches began to use a slide-on barrel-style terminal. The rear main harness located in the rear fender uses an 8-position AMP Multilock connector replacing the older "automotive style" 6-position Mate-n-Lock connector. The trigger plate in the cam cover also changed to a 3-position Deutsch connector located on the right side of the bottom frame rail. This makes it very simple to replace the ignition. Many of the mechanical components had a makeover as well. For example, wheel hubs, switch housings, switches, keys, clutch and brake levers, dash and speedometers just to name a few. The charging system, however, is essentially the same between the early and late bikes.

CONNECTOR TYPES AND JUNCTION POINTS

Throughout the book we have discussed some of the connectors used by the factory over the past 25 years. In this section we will focus on the names, number of circuits, locations and years in which the variety of connectors were used on Harley-Davidson models. Since there were so many changes in the middle of a production year some of our examples may vary. Let's focus on the Mate-n-Lock connectors that Harley started using back in 1984. You will find them at the turn signal module (10-position) and feeding the rear fender harness (6-position) and under the fuel tanks (12-position) connecting the headlight, front turn signals and both handlebar switches

Ignition modules use a Cannon connector starting in 1991, through 1995. The modules themselves are the same after 1995 but the connector did change. AMP Mate-n-Lock connectors were very popular in the automotive industry so they have a track record. Whatever the case may have been for using the AMP Mate-n-Lock, most people are glad that they are long gone. In fact, they are so gone that AMP has discontinued manufacturing them.

Beginning in 1996, the factory had a new outlook. As we discussed earlier in this chapter, the electronics are not the only components that they upgraded. Harley switched the configuration of their wiring harnesses in general. If you were to compare the '95 FXST harness to the '96 FXST harness, you would be amazed how much better they really are. Unlike previous years, the factory set out to make things simple.

Let's start with servicing. If you needed to remove the headlight, you simply unplugged the new AMP 4-position MultiLock

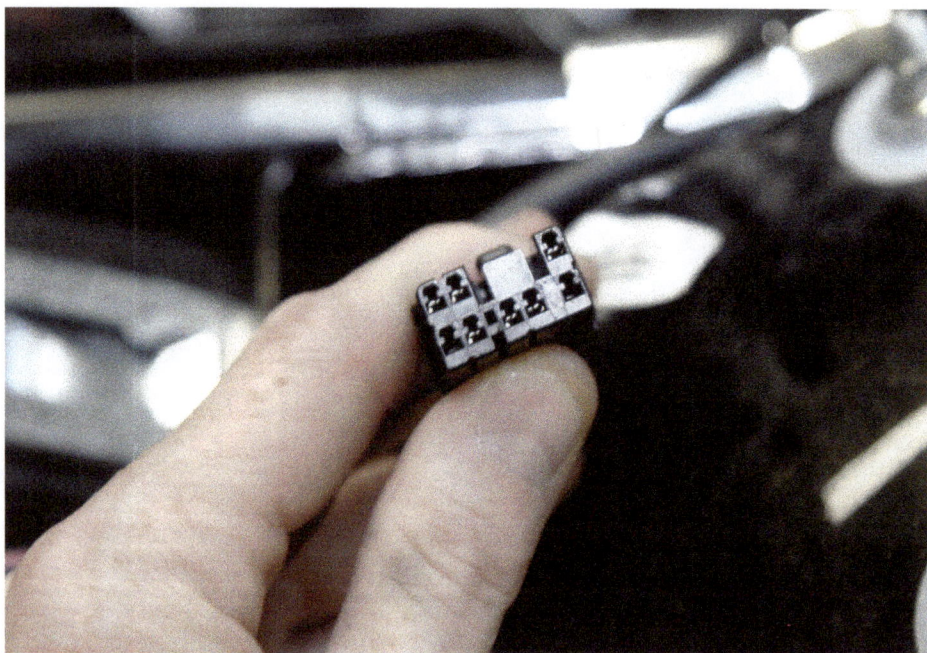

Under the Bagger's seat is the MultiLock junction for the taillights and blinkers, the male terminal block is numbered: #1 Brown = Rt turn. #2, Orange w white = 12V switched. #3, Violet = L turn. #4 & #8 are vacant. #5, Black = ground. #6, Red w Yellow = brake light. #7, Blue = running light.

connector located between the fuel tanks on the left side of the bike. These slim black connectors took up much less space than the Mate-n-Lock connectors. They were very versatile and when mated together made a much better connection. Like the Mate-n-Lock connectors, the MultiLock line was not watertight either. It is safe to say that making each component unplug on it's own from the main harness was utilizing the "keep it simple stupid" or KISS method. It just flat out made sense. Not only was the headlight easy to remove but the turn signals and handlebar switches were as well. The front turn signals us a 6-position MultiLock connector that was also located in between the fuel tanks on the left side on the motorcycle. This was the only connector on the bike that was "shared." This meant that on both front turn signals, 3-wires from each one used the same connector instead of being wired separately.

Since removing the terminals from MultiLock connectors is so much easier then the Mate-n-Lock, it's really no big deal to separate the turn signal connector. Handlebar switches went into a different direction. They began using 6-position Deutsch connectors that are top notch and watertight. This was a huge improvement and it was sure to cut down on wiring and component failures. Harley also used grey for left and black for right to separate the each sides switch harness.

The speedometer, which is now electronic, uses a Deutsch 8-position mini connector. You will also find that the VOES switch (Evos, 1996 and up) located above the manifold uses a 2-position Deutsch connector. Most of the Evolution's ignition system, starting with the trigger plate located in the cam cover, use a 3-position Deutsch connector located under the trans-

mission and mounted on the right side of the frame. Ignition modules changed from the 7-position Cannon connectors and went to an 8-position Deutsch. The console gauge cluster wiring harness is connected using a 12-position AMP MultiLock, and finally, the rear main wiring harness that went from under the seat and fed the rear fender lighting uses an 8-position Multilock connector as well. Describing all of these connectors and their locations seems so easy and to be honest, it really is compared to earlier models.

How to Repair and Modify

Making repairs on factory harnesses can be relatively easy if you have the right tools to diagnose the problem and the right parts to do the repair. Yea, sure, that sounds way too good to be true but it is. On pre '96 models you need to stock up on the AMP "automotive style" male and female crimp terminals. In order to remove any wiring from their respective connector, you will also need to have a removal tool. As we discussed earlier, these are not the greatest, and there are several varieties out there. Most automotive supply warehouses or aftermarket American V-twin catalogs

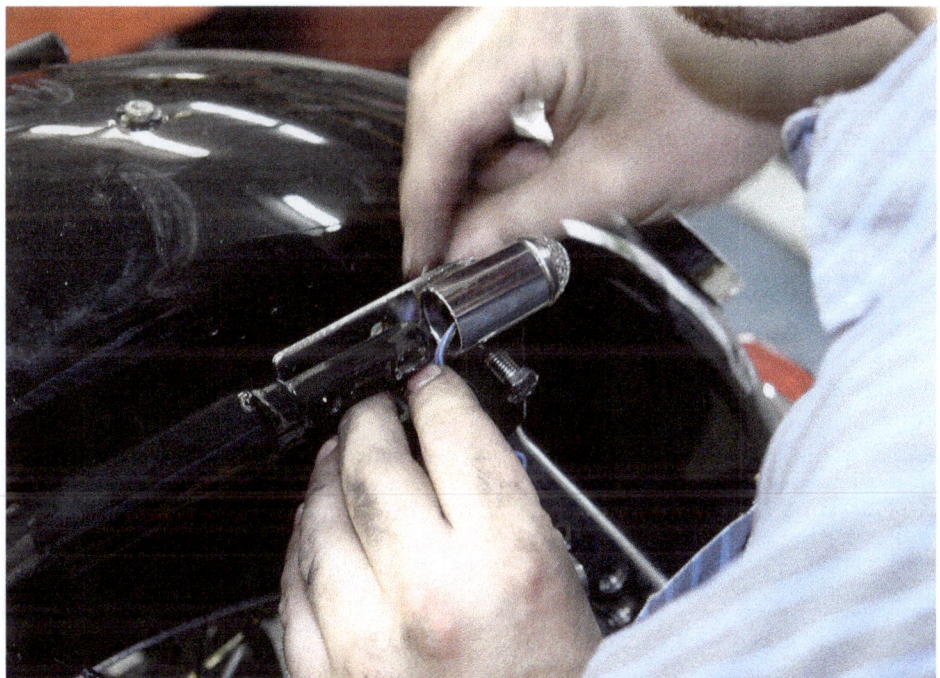

To clean up the back of an '04 Bagger we took off the rail and stock light bar, then added these little shotgun LEDs as the blinkers.

have these tools. They are not that expensive and can generally be found for under $30.

The way to remove crimp terminals from AMP Mate-n-Lock connectors is to insert the removal tool, which looks like a 1/8" ID aluminum tube that compresses the locking tabs found on both male and female terminals. The tabs are what hold the terminal in the terminal block, once the tabs are compressed, the wire and terminal can slide out of the connector. This is not as easy as it sounds. This process can drive you crazy because the terminals generally need much more coaxing to come out and before you know it, you're asking yourself, "How bad would it be if I just cut it off"?

Now that you have the right tools and materials all you need to do is understand what the problem is. A simple repair could be a short in the rear fender. Depending on the model, this could take you some time. A general rule of thumb is to look for the obvious things first. In this case, remove the seat and inspect the 6-position Mate-n-Lock connector. Be sure it's intact, plugged in to its matting side and that the terminals are making contact. Look for possible corrosion due to water. If the connector looks fine, test either side of the connector with a continuity tester or multi-meter. Select the Ohm setting on your multi-meter and place the test probes on either end of circuit. If you hear a tone this means that you have a complete circuit or continuity. If the tone does not sound, you have a short or open circuit.

A continuity test will tell you if there is good contact between the connections. If this tests out OK then it's time to look at the turn signals and rear tail/brake light assembly. Remove the lenses and inspect the bulbs, remove them and look at the socket for corrosion. Light sockets on older models are a common problem since the poor seal between the lens and housing often allows water into the housing. The socket gets wet and begins to oxidize, making for a poor connection and possibly causing a short. If the socket looks OK you can perform a continuity test from the 6-position Mate-n-Lock connector under the seat. This will tell you which or how many of the wires in the harness are shorted. Once you have narrowed down which wire(s) to look for, add some dielectric grease to the bulbs before reinstalling them to prevent corrosion.

Now the real fun begins. In order to get to the fender wiring harness, you will need to remove the rear wheel assembly. Once the wheel has been removed, you have complete access to the wiring harness. If the bike has been lowered there is a good chance that the harness was ripped out of its clamps and shorted as it rubbed against the tire. This also can happen when installing an oversized tire. Wheel travel in the fender is changed when the bike is lowered. The tire will travel further into the

Everybody wants to get the big ugly factory lights off the bike while retaining some vestige of turn signals. These fender rail lights from Kuryakyn are a great way to do exactly that.

fender causing possible fender, wiring harness or tire damage. Some Softails are so low the swing arm slams into the back of the oil tank, which can rip the tank off its mounting bracket. The proper way to repair this harness would be to replace any broken inner fender well clamps and replace each shorted wire with a new wire of the same gauge and color. Install new AMP terminals on the wire and re-insert into the Mate-n-Lock connector. The rear fender wiring harness repair scenario would be the same for '96 and later models except that the connectors are 8-position MultiLock.

Let's say you want to customize your ride, the first thing you decide to do is remove your turn signals. Before you go and rip them off, remember it may be illegal to do so in your state. Maybe instead of removing them, you change them. Turn signals are available in several different varieties. You can purchase single or dual filament signals, meaning just a flashing signal or a running lamp and a flashing signal. Most stock motorcycles have dual filament bulbs on the front and single filament turn signals on the rear. LED turn signals, big and small, have become very popular over the last 5 years. These signals tend to offer more lumens power or a brighter light making them more visible. It is important to know that not all turn signals are D.O.T. approved. Most states will tell you what the minimum exposed reflector size can be. This is the limit on how small the actual colored lens can be per D.O.T. requirements. This will help you purchase not only what is legal but also what are the brightest and safest signals available.

Say you decided to keep those turn signals, but change the look of your bike by mounting them in a different area. Positioning of turn signals can be a real

pain in the ass. Not only are the turn signals themselves obtrusive and un-appealing but trying to find a good spot for them can be a real chore. Since there are so many different styles to choose from it can make this daunting task a bit easier. You still have to pick out a pair that fits, physically and visually. The OEM signals found in flush or bracket-mounted styles are a safe bet but some of the custom models include mirror mounted, built-in-signal grips, or even handlebar levers with signals in them. Again, be sure that they fit your theme and that they're legal.

If you're more the adventurous type and you want those signals off no matter what, it will be a pretty easy job to do so. If you have a pre '96 factory model, you will need to use your AMP Mate-n-Lock terminal removal tool to take the turn signal pins out of the connectors located under the fuel tanks. You will need to repeat the same steps on the 6-position connector located under the seat. Front turn signals on later models are even easier. You only need to unplug the 6-position MultiLock connector under the tank, and remove the rear turn signal wires from the 8-position terminal block under the seat. The color code will be

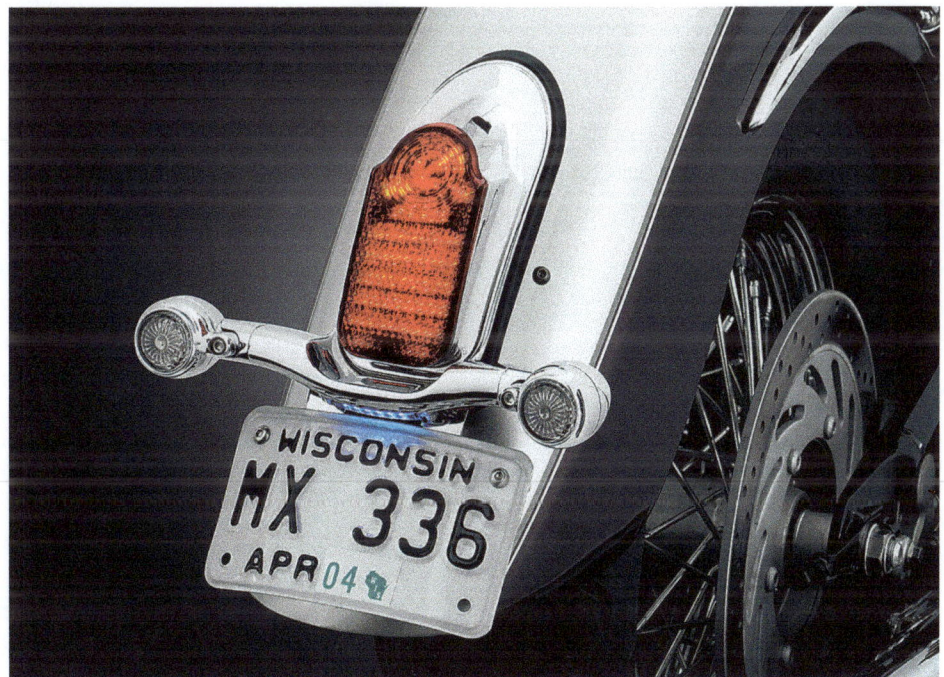

Take a timeless design, the tombstone taillight, and give it a modern twist, complete with light bar for turn signals. Kuryakyn

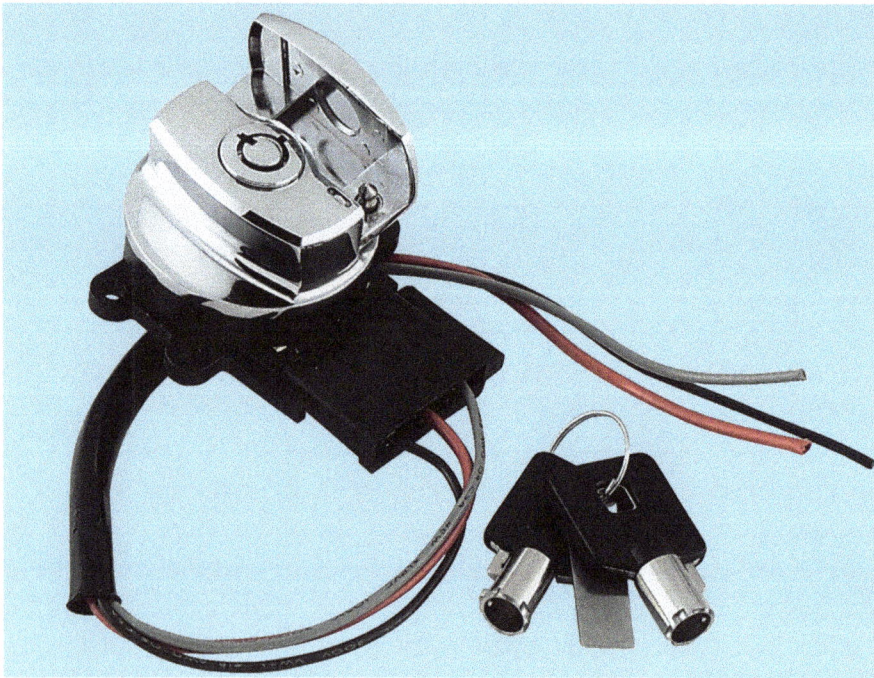

Here's a factory-style '96 and up ignition switch.

This ignition module from Crane is programmable and fits '96 and up. Note the 8-pin Deutsch connector.

violet for left, brown for right, blue for running light and black for ground. Be sure to test the connections once you have removed the turn signal wires to insure that all other components are functioning properly.

HEADLIGHT REPLACEMENT

Many motorcycle owners like the look of the chrome billet, stretched-style headlights. This is another easy job. The first thing you want to do is to remove the fuel tank to gain access to the headlight connection. On 1996 and later models, the 4-position MultiLock headlight connector will be located on the left side of the motorcycle and will contain a yellow, white and black wire. Simply unplug this connection, loosen the headlight bracket and remove the headlight. Most new headlights come with a bulb and pigtail-wiring socket. One method for installing your new light is to remove the "flag style" female spade connectors from the OEM headlamp socket and pull the harness our of the old bucket. Reinstall the OEM harness into the new light and connect accordingly. If you are unable to remove the wiring from the OEM light due to the molded grommet, you can generally cut off the lamp socket and pull the harness through the grommet. At that point, you can feed the harness back into the new bucket and solder on the new pigtail-socket. In most cases, your first choice should always be to crimp on new versions of the same terminal and reinstall as OEM. Your last resort would be to cut and splice properly using solder and heat shrink tubing. You may decide to purchase a new headlight wiring harness. There are after-market companies that make replacement harnesses for most components on a motorcycle. You can even purchase a braided, stainless steel and clear-coated wiring harness that would serve two purposes, aesthetics and function.

REPLACE AN IGNITION SWITCH

Let's take a look at another simple problem on '95 and earlier models. One issue that sticks out the most is the ignition switch. This poorly designed switch always seemed to have a problem shorting out something. This switch, compared to later models, was very mechanical with moving parts that were very clumsy and prone to falling apart. The contacts were out in the open and the six different ring terminals attached to it often came loose. Over time, the moving contacts began to break down and cause short circuits due to resistance. Back then, the option for upgrading was out of the question. There were not many options in the aftermarket world so going back to the dealership for a new "replacement" switch was about the only option. Today, you can buy a replacement, early-style switch either from the dealer or any good aftermarket shop.

In order to perform this repair successfully the first thing you should do is disconnect the battery. Now with the battery disconnected, you can begin to remove the dash. Once removed you will need to mark each wire that is attached to the existing switch. Some contacts on the switch may contain more than one wire so be sure to label accordingly. In most cases you will be able to loosen one contact at a time from the old switch and reinstall the same wire(s) on the new one. When you have all wires transferred over to the new switch you can now remove the old switch from

the motorcycle. You will find that the switch is held in place with 4 small screws, two on the front and two on the back of the switch. Simply reinstall the new switch in its place and tighten accordingly. Reconnect the battery and check your connections for any possible shorts.

This scenario on a later model would be much easier. You should still disconnect the battery first. Now you could remove the nut on the dash and pull upward. You will see a rather large and flat 3-position connector attached to the ignition switch. Slide the connector off to reveal the four torx-head screws that hold the switch in place. Simply remove the screws and replace the defective switch. In closing, there are so many different things you can do to modify or repair a stock harness. The best method is to be sure you do it right the first time to prevent any issues down the road.

IT'S JUST NOT THAT HARD

One of the biggest misconceptions surrounding wiring in general is how difficult it is. To be honest, it is not really that hard. Remove one wire at a time, trace that wire to its termination point, how could you make a mistake? The key is in the tools, materials and your patience. Don't make the job harder than it really is.

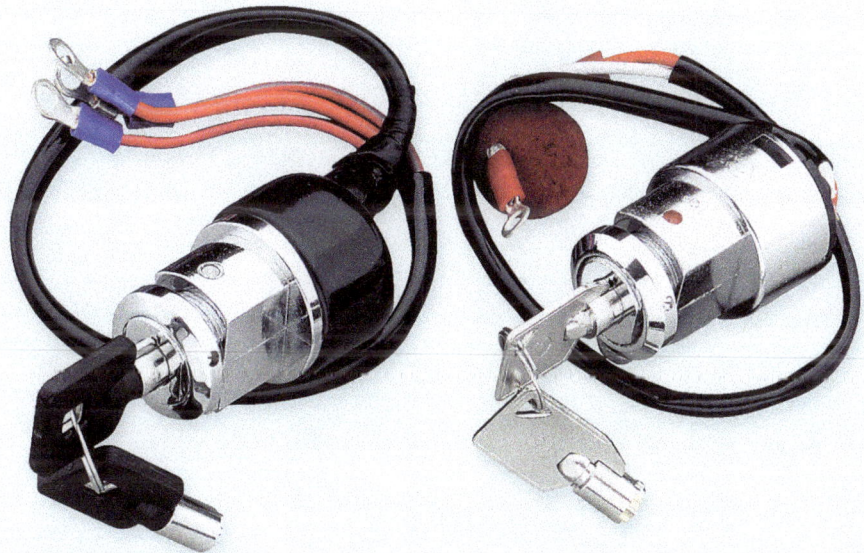

These barrel-style aftermarket switches would be great for a Sportster or a custom bike.

Chapter Four

Ignition Systems

Source of the Spark

We spent time talking about wiring harnesses. How they differ between model years, how to perform simple repairs, or modifications, and what connectors are used. In this chapter we will discuss all facets of factory and aftermarket ignition systems. From installation, repair, testing and performance we will spend some time understanding what makes an ignition system operate.

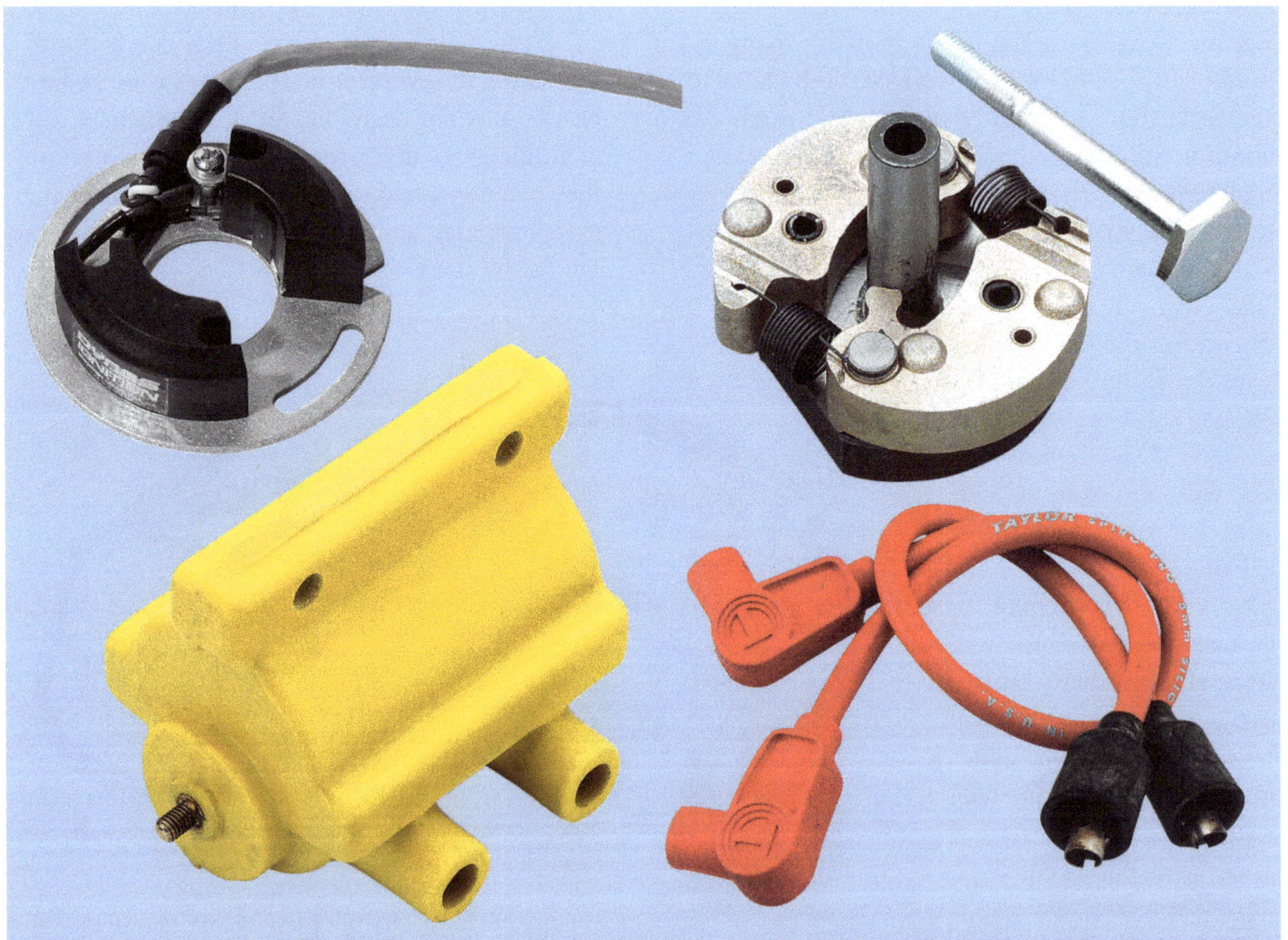

Like the other parts of your electrical system, good ignition requires that all the components in the circuit be compatible with the others, and that all of them be in good condition.

EARLY IGNITIONS

Starting in 1978 Harley Davidson began using electronic ignition systems. They wanted to leave behind an older technology, a system that included points, condenser and a mechanical advance unit. Late model points-ignition systems didn't last long since they started in late 1969 and were abandoned 9-years later. Earlier models, beginning in 1936, also used points, but these early bikes housed the points in a distributor. During this period the factory also used a generator instead of an alternator as the heart of the charging system. The last "generator Shovel" rolled off the line in 1969. In 1970 Harley introduced the "cone-style" engine, designed to accept an alternator in place of the generator, and a set of points housed under the cam cover on the engine's right side. In 1978 the points were replaced with Harley's first electronic ignition. When the factory replaced the Shovelhead with the Evo the cone-style cases with an alternator on the left side, and points on the right, remained.

Why switch to electronic ignition, you ask? The difference between mechanical and electronic is simple. Electronic systems are more reliable and efficient. A major disadvantage of the mechanical system is the use of breaker points. These points interrupt the low voltage current through the primary winding of the coil. When this happens the magnetic field created by that primary current collapses and generates a spike of high voltage in the secondary windings. It's this voltage that fires the spark plug. The trouble is, points are subject to mechanical wear where the rubbing block rides on the cam, as well as oxidation and burning at the contact

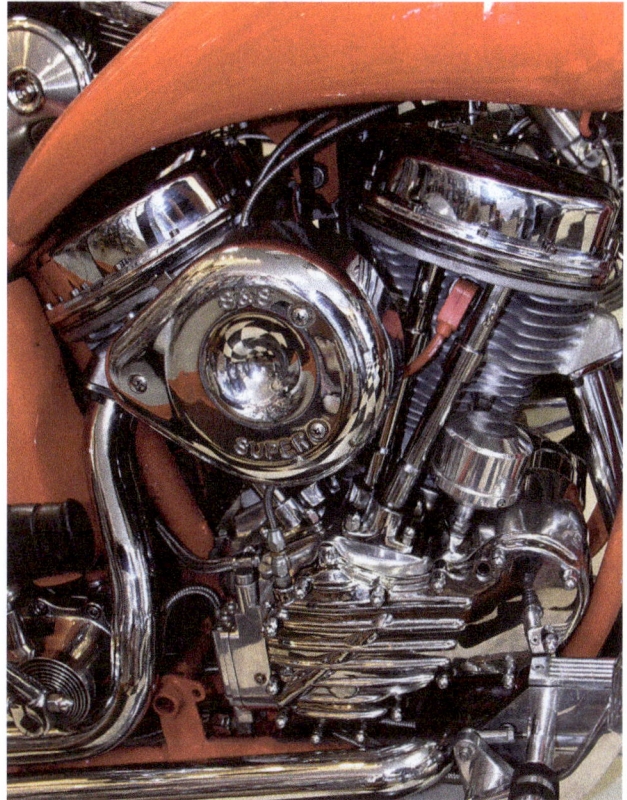

Here is a nice picture of an aftermarket panhead showing the generator side of the engine case. Note the automotive-style distributor in front of the pushrod tube.

A basic point and condenser ignition set. Think twice before replacing the electronic ignition on your V-Twin with a "tried and true" set of points, because they just aren't as good as electronic ignition.

53

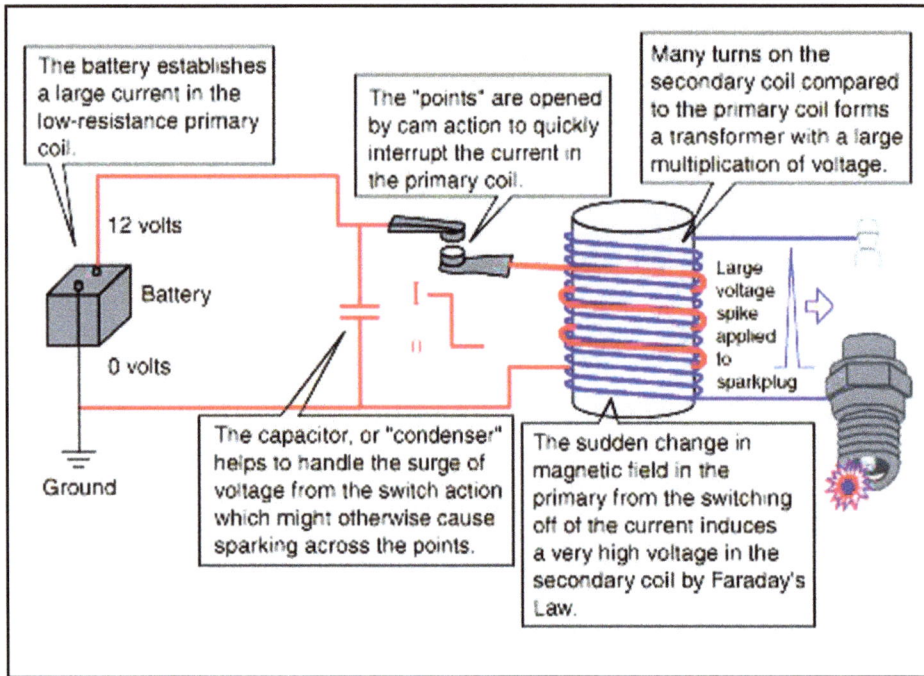

The battery establishes a large current in the low-resistance primary coil.

12 volts

Battery

0 volts

Ground

The "points" are opened by cam action to quickly interrupt the current in the primary coil.

Many turns on the secondary coil compared to the primary coil forms a transformer with a large multiplication of voltage.

Large voltage spike applied to sparkplug

The capacitor, or "condenser" helps to handle the surge of voltage from the switch action which might otherwise cause sparking across the points.

The sudden change in magnetic field in the primary from the switching off of the current induces a very high voltage in the secondary coil by Faraday's Law.

Above you will find the basic wiring diagram that explains how a points style ignition system operates.

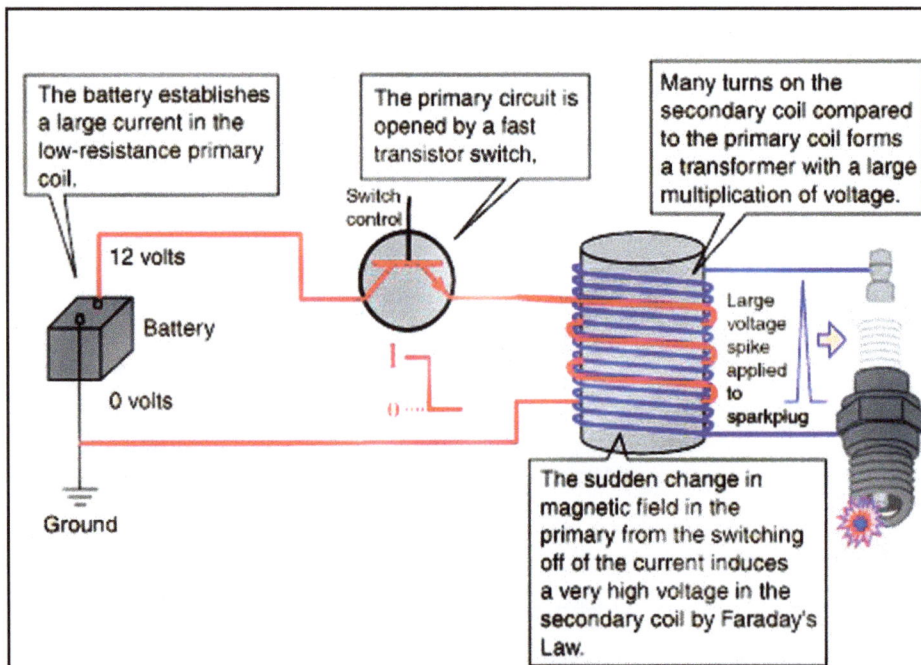

The battery establishes a large current in the low-resistance primary coil.

12 volts

Battery

0 volts

Ground

The primary circuit is opened by a fast transistor switch.

Switch control

Many turns on the secondary coil compared to the primary coil forms a transformer with a large multiplication of voltage.

Large voltage spike applied to sparkplug

The sudden change in magnetic field in the primary from the switching off of the current induces a very high voltage in the secondary coil by Faraday's Law.

This is a basic wiring diagram of how an electronic style ignition system operates. Essentially the transistor switch has replaced the points.

surfaces themselves. Points require regular adjustment to compensate for wear and the contacts are subject to mechanical variations. If the points are burned, voltage in the primary circuit is reduced, which in turn limits the output on the secondary side and affects how the bike runs.

An electronic ignition solves these problems. Instead of a set of points an electronic ignition uses a hall-effect sensor that is stationary while a slotted cup rotates around it. The sensor and slotted cup replace the points and signal the ignition to interrupt current in the primary side.

The rest of the electronic ignition system, (coil and spark plugs) is similar to what's found in mechanical systems. The lack of moving parts compared to the mechanical system leads to greater reliability and longer service intervals. For older motorcycles, it is usually possible to purchase an "electronic ignition" distributor to replace the mechanical one. Starting in 2000, all big twin models did away with the trigger plate entirely. Instead of the trigger plate, the new Twin Cam engine uses a magnetic crank-position sensor mounted on the front of the crankcase to trigger the ignition at the proper time.

DIFFERENCES IN THE VARIOUS SYSTEMS

In late 1979, Harley switched to electronic ignitions. As we said, they are more compact and more reliable than the earlier point-style systems. The electronic ignition uses a coil rated at lower ohm resistance than does the mechanical ignitions. The average mechanical coil is rated at 5 ohms while electronic coils are rated at 3 ohms of resistance. The spark plugs, for the most part, are are the same. One major difference is the addition of an ignition module to the electronic ignition system. These were created for multiple reasons. First, the circuitry in the module acts as a rev limiter. This prevents engines from over-revving and reduces the chance for catastrophic engine failure. Second, the module acts as a computer for the trigger plate and coil. This is where the current in the primary side of the coil is actually interrupted.

Where as the mechanical systems use springs and centrifugal weights to create an advance curve, electronic systems have the ignition curve programmed into the module. Electronic ignition modules are located under the seat or under side covers depending on the model. Coils are generally found on the left side of the bike mounted to a bracket welded to the frame. Some models also

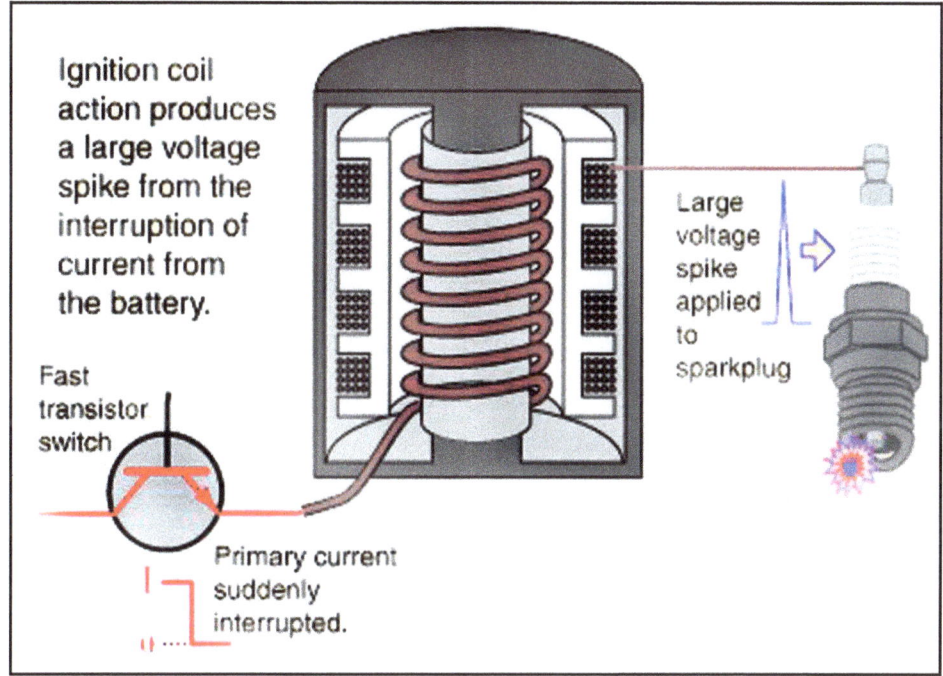

Here is a good diagram showing the basic operation of an ignition coil.

The above picture shows two styles of ignition coils. The one on the left is a dual fire coil and the one on the right is a single fire coil.

55

mounted the coil off of the top motor mount. This was a very clean look and enabled owners to use two, equal length, spark plug wires.

SPECIFIC COMPONENT DIFFERENCES

We discussed briefly some of the differences between ignitions in different model years. In this section we go into more detail so you can be an expert. Early models beginning in 1936 up to 1964 used a coil that was generally rated at 5-ohms of resistance. Models from 1965 up to 1978 used coils rated between 4.2 and 4.7 ohms of resistance. You would find coils rated between 2.8 and 3 ohms of resistance for Big Twins beginning in 1979 up to 1999 and up to 2003 for Sportster models. With the introduction of the Twin Cam engine, Harley went to a single fire ignition. There was also a coil difference between carbureted and fuel injected Twin Cam models from late 1999 and up. Fuel injected models used a coil that was rated at .5 ohms of resistance and carbureted models used a coil with a rating 2.8 ohms.

Here is a close up of a single fire coil that would be found on all Harley Davidson twin cam models starting in 1999.

SINGLE AND DUAL FIRE

So what is the difference between single and dual fire ignitions? Lets take a look. The concept of a dual-fire ignition is simple: the spark plugs operate together, not independently. When the coil fires the plug and tells it to spark it simultaneously fires the other spark plug, even though that piston is not perfectly positioned for combustion. This is referred to as the "wasted spark." A dual-fire system needs only one pickup signal to the module, one signal from the module to the coil, and one coil. A single-fire system needs either two separate pickups or a different module and two coils. It is also possible to have a single coil and still be a single fire ignition. It is wired the same way as using two separate coils with two independent feeds from the trigger plate.

There are people who claim that "wasted spark" can cause a loss of power and will add unnecessary vibration. A single-fire ignition can be nice for "motor heads" since most aftermarket systems offer programming options so the end user can fine tune the timing and ignition curve with the use of a computer. This is all well and good if you're into the performance end of motorcycling, but it you are not a dual fire will get the job done all day long. It boils down to personal preference, either system has advantages and disadvantages. But if you're looking for low maintenance and simple reliability you can't go wrong with a dual-fire system.

TROUBLE SHOOTING

How do you know if your system is bad? This is an area, like many on a motorcycle, that can get tricky. You have to have patience and the ability to diagnose the problem. Words of advice, look at the simplest things first. Example one: look at the spark plugs to be sure they are not broken, cracked or worn. If the spark plug(s) are very white and look like they were baked in an oven then it's safe to say the engine is running lean. This is generally caused when a new high flow air filter is installed without re-jetting the carburetor or recalibrating the fuel injection. If you introduce more air into your fuel system you also need to increase the amount of fuel to counteract the increase of air. Fuel and air always have to maintain a certain balance in order to maintain optimum performance. If the plugs are very dark your engine is getting too much fuel. This generally happens when a carburetor dumps too much fuel due to an incorrect or oversized jet, or running the engine for a long period of time with the choke on. The dark plugs are essentially covered in carbon or unburned gas, which is a by-product of an overly rich fuel mixture.

Example two: check your spark plug wires to be sure that they are connected and in good working condition. Use a meter to verify you have continuity between either end of the wire. Example three: use a meter to test the power at the coil. Be sure that

one side of the coil registers a minimum of 12-volts with the key switch on. The other side of the coil will be receiving voltage from the ignition module. If you have a stock Harley Davidson, you could also check the fuse panel for a blown fuse. Keep in mind, if you find a

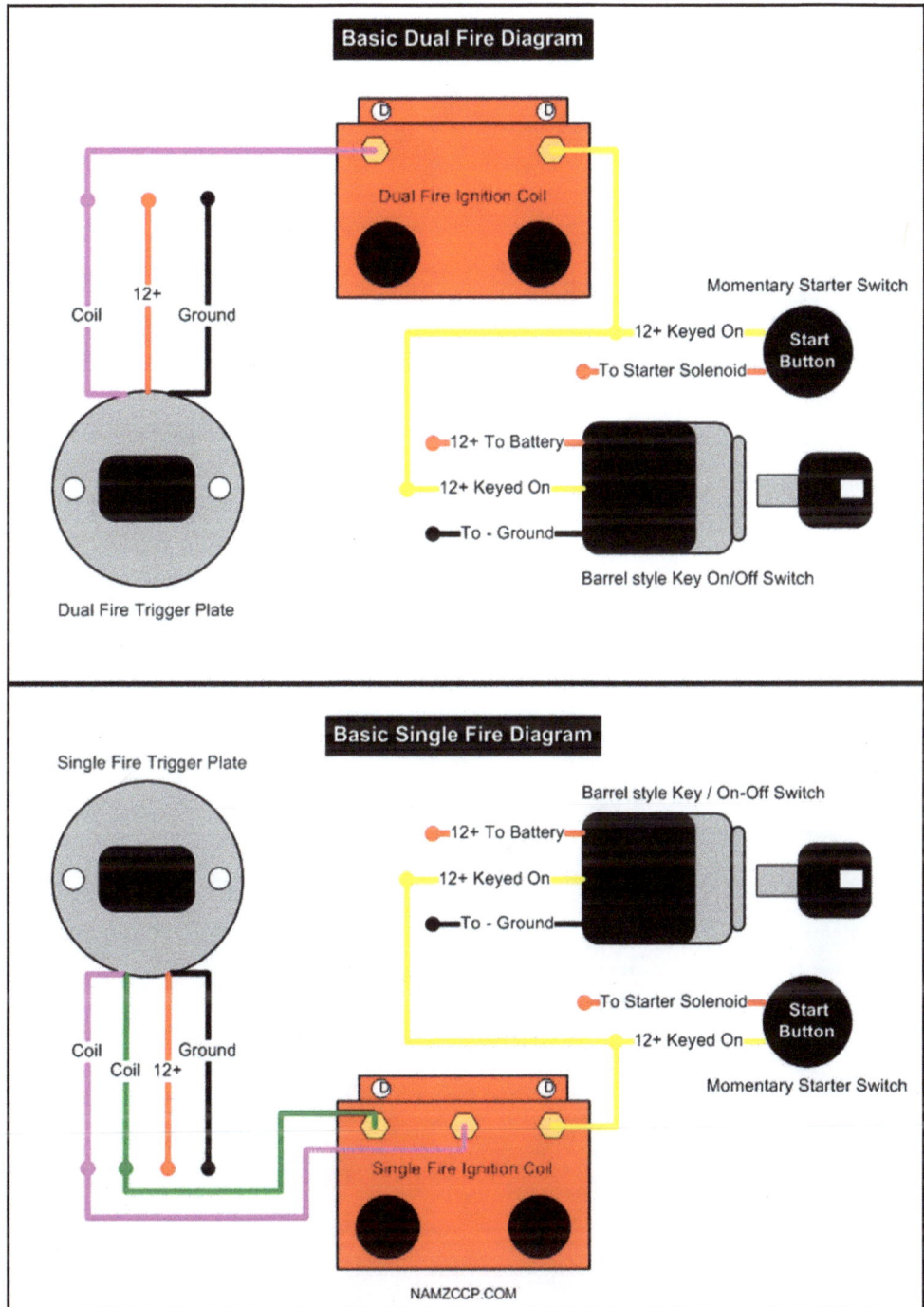

A basic wiring diagram showing the operation and wiring differences between a single and dual fire ignition system.

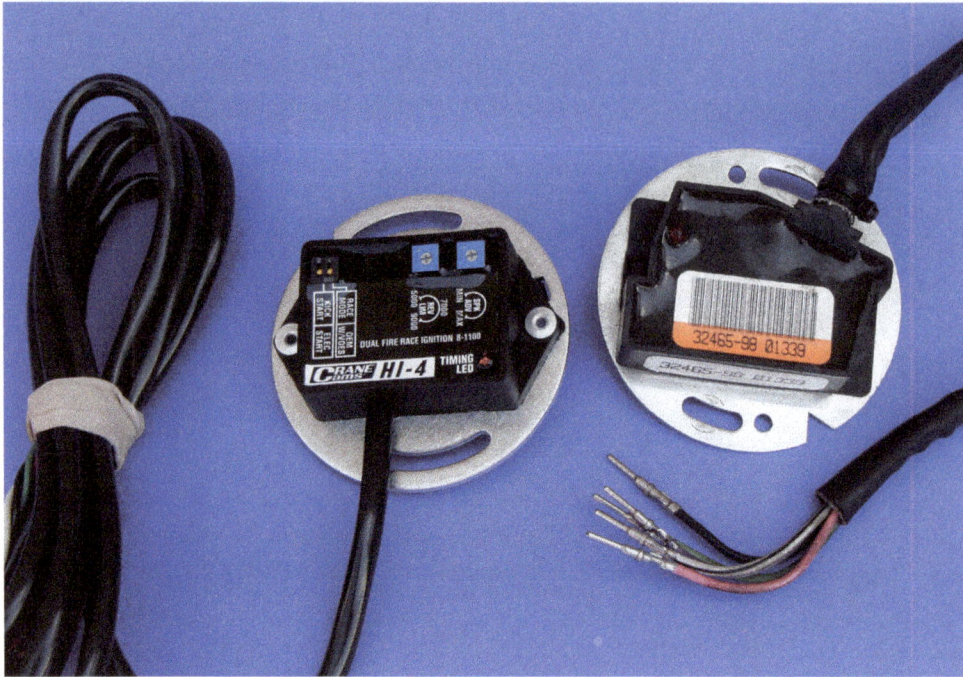

Here is a pair of ignition sensors or trigger plates. The unit on the left allows the user to adjust the rev limiter and ignition curve.

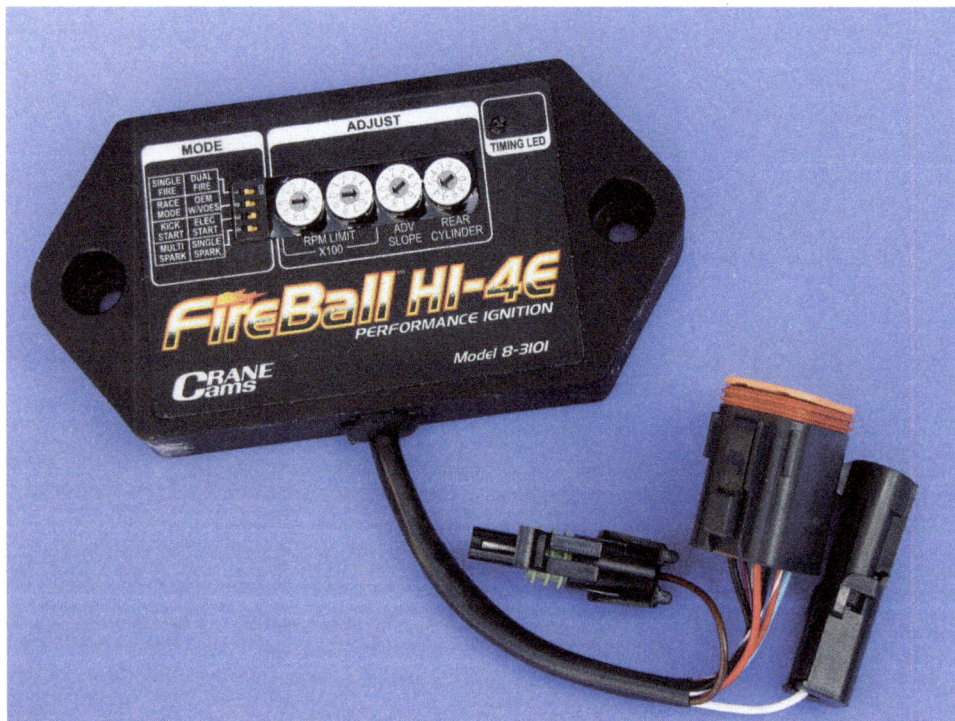

Here is a picture of a high performance ignition module similar to units found on all Evolution style engines. Note the Deutsch connector.

blown fuse, you need to find what caused it. Example four: there is a tool that can be purchased that installs inline with the plug wires that shows if a spark is generated. This tool will light up when a spark is present. If you have a spark on both sides, it is safe to say the problem is not with your ignition system.

Example five: if your test did not produce a spark, check to be sure that the ignition module is plugged into the wiring harness. Sounds silly but you never know until you know. If the module is OK, then it's time to check the connection of the 3-position Deutsch connector under the frame on the right side of the motorcycle. This connects the trigger plate to the coil and module. Be sure to test continuity and that you have at least 12-volts at the connection.

After you have looked at all of these simple and obvious scenarios, it is recommended that you pull out the old service manual. The factory manual lists several tests that can be performed in order to determine where your electrical problem is. Since there are several tests and many things that could be wrong, the service manual is the best solution in order to find the problem. Some other problems to look for are loose battery cables, bad cell in the battery, short circuit in the on/off switch, excessive heat at the trigger plate/cam position sensor or any of the other ignition components like a bad coil or module.

HOW TO REMOVE AND REPLACE

Once you have determined that you have a bad component in the ignition system, removing and replacing these components is very easy to do. The situations described here refer to a Harley Davidson FXST Big Twin model with an Evolution engine. The trigger plate is located in the cam cover on the right side of the engine. Before you do anything, disconnect the battery. In order to access the trigger plate, you will need to drill out the aluminum rivets holding on the factory cover, aftermarket covers generally are bolted on using machine screws. Either way, remove the cover in order to access the sensor. The two threaded standoffs that hold the plate in place are slotted so they may be removed using a flat head screwdriver. Once they are removed the plate can be freed from the engine, but you still need to deal with the wiring. First you will need to disconnect the 3-position Deutsch connector which is mounted on the bottom frame rail under the oil pump. Once the sensor harness is free, remove the green wedge-lock from the connector. This will give you access to the locking tabs that secure the crimp terminals in the connector. In order to remove the wire from the connector slide the locking tabs away from the termi-nals and pull the wire out. Now that the connector is removed the harness will slip through the hole in the cam cover for easy removal. Simply reverse these same steps when reinstalling the new unit.

In order to access the ignition module the seat needs to be removed. The ignition module is located on a plastic fender insert on later models. Simply unplug the 8-position Deutsch connector and unscrew the module from its mounting position. Replace following the same steps. Last to be replaced is the ignition coil, which is located on the right side of the motorcycle. The coil cover is held on with two small machine screws located on the back and bottom of the chrome cover. Once these screws are out you will have access to remove the plug wires and the power wires that feed the coil. Be sure to remove and replace one wire at a time when reinstalling the new coil. This will prevent you from second guessing yourself later on down the road.

Some early motors, like this K model seen in the Shadley Brothers shop, use a magneto ignition.

Chapter Five

Lighting

Headlights, Blinkers and Taillights

Now that we've covered all of the boring stuff, it's time to go through the easy part of this program. Over the years the factory has changed the style or functionality of their lighting systems. Taillights are meant to be a running light, license plate illuminator, and a brake light, all in one. The headlight is always a high and low beam, sometimes with a high beam indicator built in. Though the wattage of the bulbs can vary the housing itself has stayed the same for many years. Finally, the turn signals have changed the most over the years. Their actual size, mounting capabilities and shape

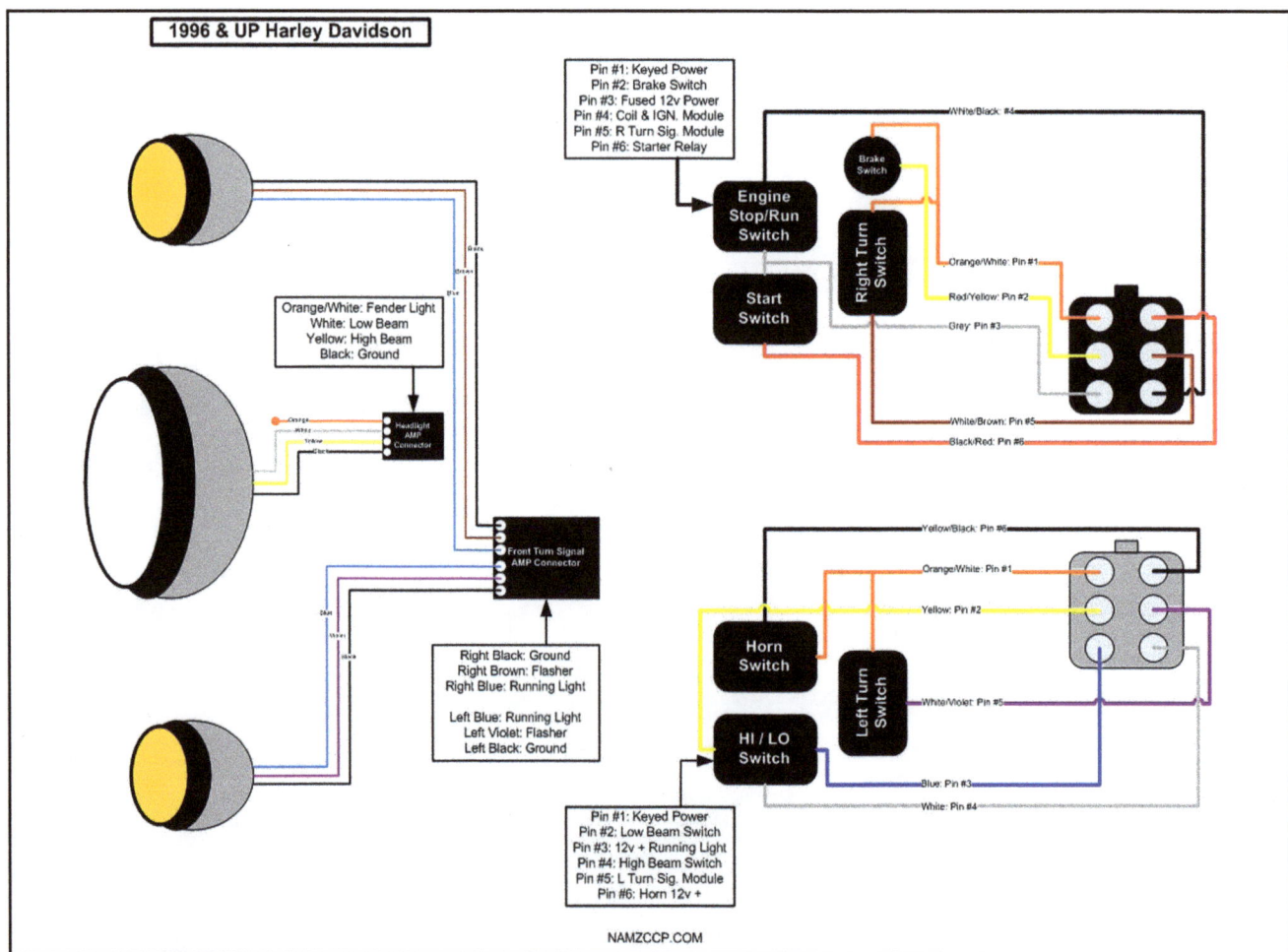

The schematic is for a front turn signal and headlight wiring configuration on a '96 and up model. The handlebar switches show you the factory color for each switch and also how they are connected to the Deutsch connectors.

all have been modified at one time or another. In this section, we will go through most of the basics and then discuss some custom lighting options for a factory Harley Davidson. Keep in mind, there are differences between most models.

HEADLIGHTS

All factory motorcycles come with a headlight, though it may not be the most appealing version you have ever seen. That's the excitement of buying a stock bike and having the freedom to customize it any way you want. A Harley headlight is often different depending on the model. For example, the headlight found on a Dyna, as long as it is bottom mounted, is the same as the light on a Softail. Dyna Superglides and Low Riders use the same top mounted headlights as all Sportster's, except the Custom models. The top mounted style light is a nightmare if you ever have to work on one, all of the wiring from the turn signal and handlebar switches is routed into the headlight bucket which makes it a real treat to service.

Heritage and Fatboy models use the same, larger, headlight bucket. All other FL models, except for the Road Glide, use the same headlight. The Road Glide is the only twin headlight in the Harley lineup. Lastly, the V-Rod uses a very unique headlight that is now becoming a popular choice for custom builders.

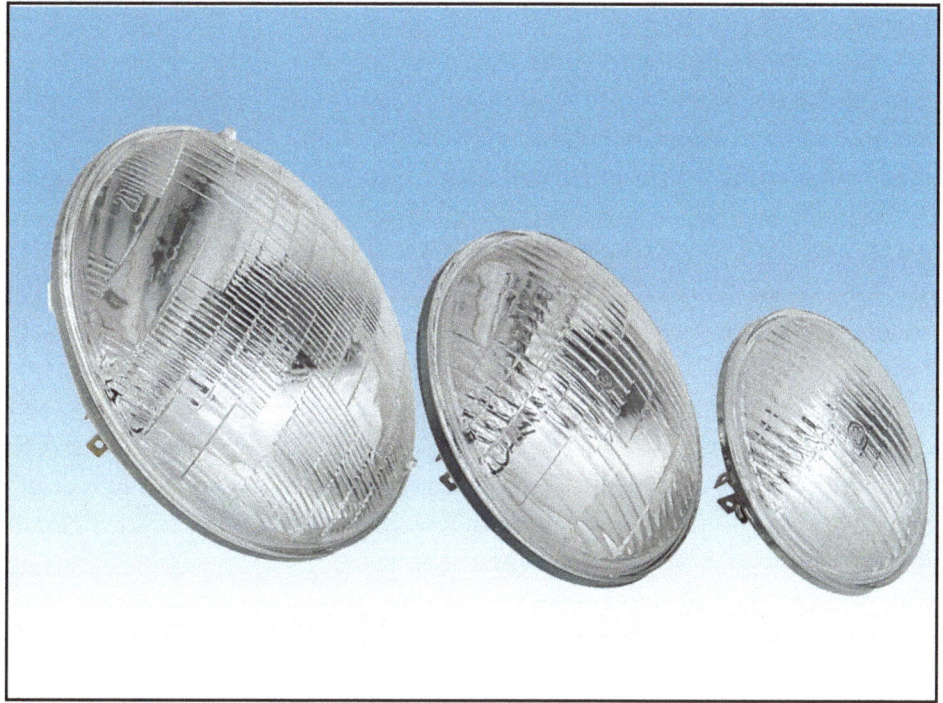

Sealed beams have been around forever, and are still offered in a variety of sizes to fit nearly any spot or headlight housing.

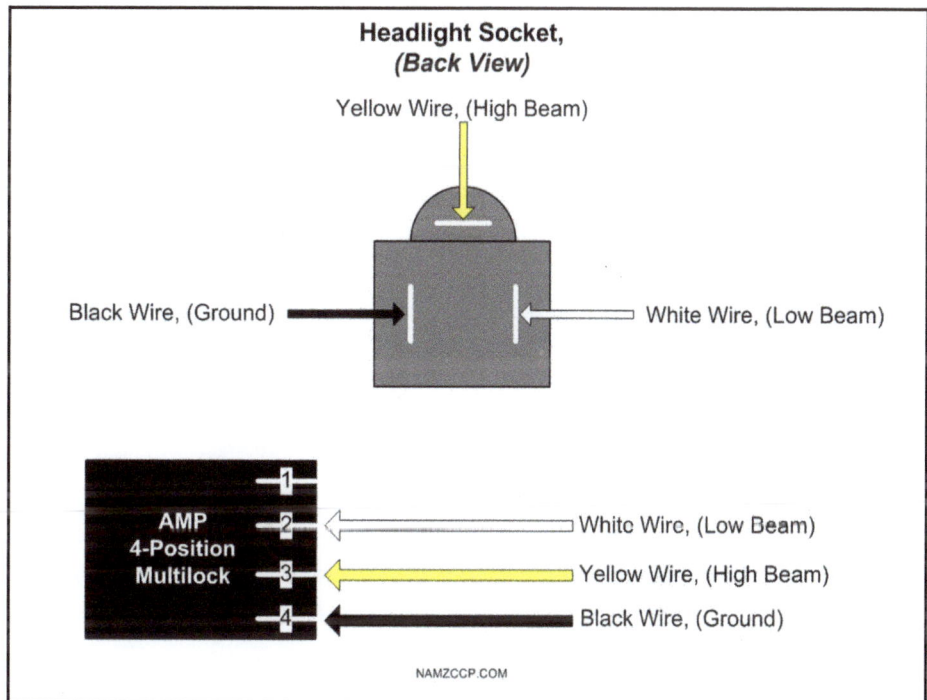

Whether the headlight is halogen or not, the plug on the back is the same 3-wire unit, wired as shown. If you are using a halogen be sure the plug and wire are able to handle the amperage that a halogen draws.

HIGH AND LOW BEAM

Most custom headlights come with dual filament bulbs and every factory built motorcycle is required to have a high and low beam. Older Harley models used a dual filament, sealed beam. These bulbs are reliable and inexpensive but not that bright. When the halogen bulbs arrived, riders had a choice of wattage combinations to choose from. This was a nice safety feature when riding at night. Today, you can even find Xenon bulbs in some customs headlights. One thing to always keep in mind is to use the bulb that is recommended in the user manual. Many people may not realize how important this really is. The reason it is so important is because the wire and connectors that are attached to the bulb are rated to handle only so much amperage. For example, a standard Harley bulb is 55-watts on low beam and 60-watts on high beam. When the high beam is on the draw on that particular circuit is 5 amps. If you were to replace the factory halogen bulb with

a 100-watt low beam and a 130-watt high beam, the draw would be closer to 11-amps. At this high amperage it is possible to blow a fuse or trip a circuit breaker since the lighting circuit on a Harley is rated at 15-amps. You may also risk melting the headlight wiring socket or the wiring harness itself.

DIFFERENCES

As mentioned above, headlights vary, not only in size and style, but in the type of bulb and wattage. If you decide to change out your stock headlight, there are some things to consider. Most custom aftermarket headlights are bottom mounted and may require a custom-mounting block in order to fit. Before you do anything, determine exactly how your headlight is mounted on your motorcycle.

Headlight lenses/bulbs are generally found in three different sizes: 4-1/2 inch, 5-1/2 inch and seven inch. The seven inch is the size found on a factory Harley Davidson Fatboy and every FL Touring model except the Road Glide. This larger

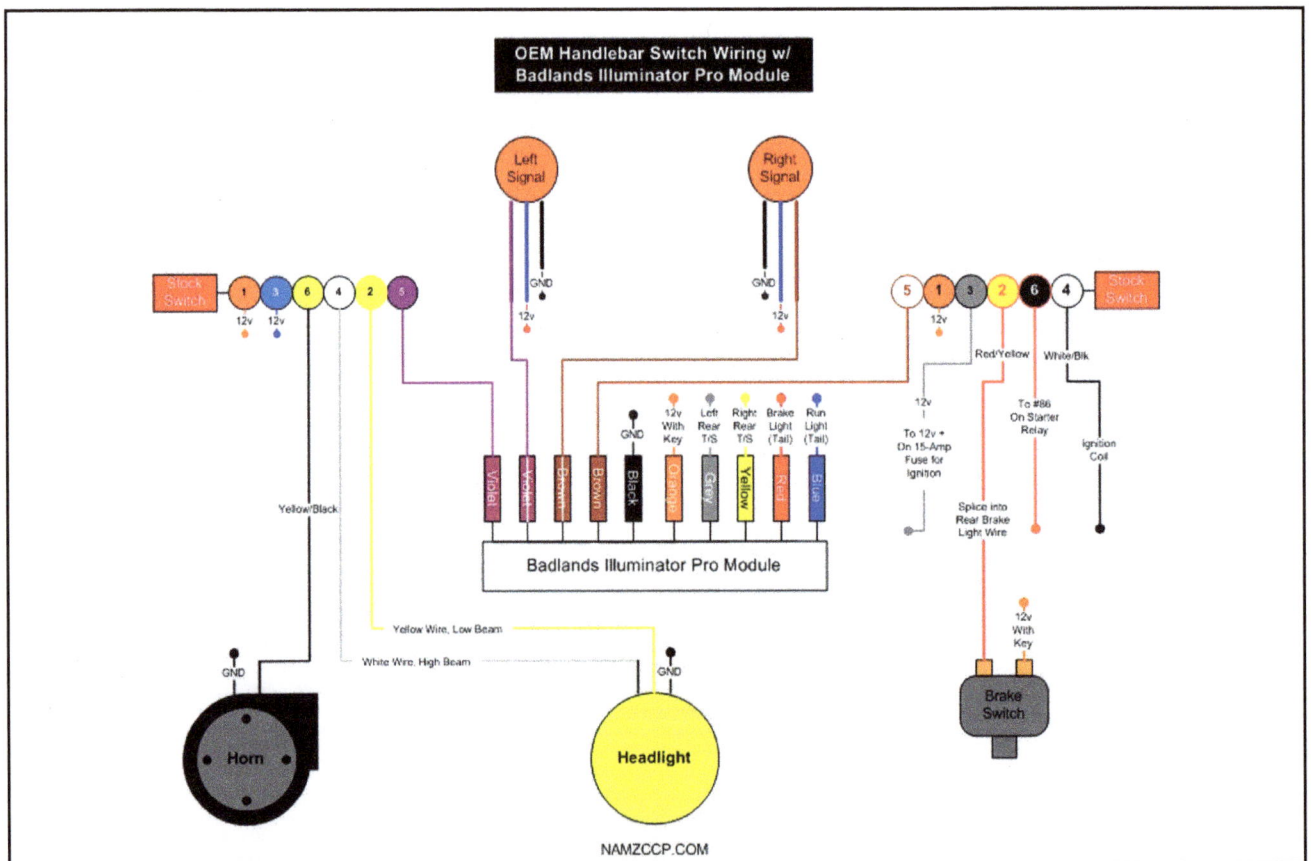

This schematic is for a pair of OEM handlebar switches using a Badlands Illuminator Pro module. This is a great idea for a custom bike built using stock style switches.

light looks nice on a Fatboy front-end but can look rather bulky on a slick pro-street or chopper model. The 5 inch version is found on every other Harley Davidson model. Another decision you need to make before you purchase a new headlight is its depth. You can find small narrow headlight buckets or long billet versions. Both providing a nice look, but you need to pick what's right for your bike.

When you're ready to install your new headlight, it is recommended to use the same terminals and connectors as the factory model. In most cases, the 4-position AMP MultiLock connector can be removed from the harness and pulled through the factory headlight bucket. Whatever road you choose, do not overlook the importance of installing the right connectors. There is nothing worse then having to cut your harness apart to replace a damaged electrical part. Do it right from the beginning and remember that you, or someone else, will at some point have to service what you installed. Make it easier on them and yourself!

BULBS

Before you replace a stock bulb be sure you know the maximum wattage rated for the housing and the circuit, and consult your users manual to check the factory recommendations. It is very important that you do not exceed the maximum wattage rating in order to protect your wiring. As mentioned, using a bulb with a wattage higher than that recommended can cause damage to the headlight harness, headlamp socket or other wiring components on the motorcycle. Most bulbs will note the wattage and amperage draw on the packaging. Remember, amps X volts = watts. Or: watts/volts = amps. So a 60 watt bulb draws 5 amps.

HOW TO REMOVE & REPLACE A STOCK BULB

Most factory bulbs are very easy to access. On all models except for Road Glides, you find a small machine screw and nut located on the headlight bezel. The bezel is the small trim ring located on the front of the headlight bucket. Its purpose is to hold the headlight lens in place on the bucket. Once this screw is removed, the lens should come out very easily providing you have access to the electrical socket. Simply unplug the 3-wire socket, release the spring-loaded bulb latch and pull out the halogen bulb and replace with a new bulb.

With Halogen bulbs, be sure you do not touch the glass with your fingers since the oil from your skin can cause premature bulb failure.

TAILLIGHTS

A motorcycle taillight can be one of the most important life saving items on a motorcycle. It is a fact that most motorcycle accidents involving an automobile are due to a lack of visibility. If this is the case, you want to be sure you're seen. Most states also have laws regarding the positioning of taillights. The Department of Transportation has set guidelines stating the required size of the reflector/lens and lumens power or wattage of the bulb. These requirements are particularly impor-

A host of specialized "H4" bulbs are available, like these Xenon bulbs said to keep the light on the rider's side of the road and reduce glare to oncoming traffic. Can be purchased in either a typical 60/55 or 100/55 watt configuration.

tant in states that have vehicle inspections. Even if you build your own motorcycle, it does have to meet certain regulations on order to be legal. Keep in mind these requirements are all about safety.

Just like headlights, there are a ton of different styles of taillights. Most stock style taillights are made up of a red lens and an incandescent bulb. The bulb is set up as a running light and a brake light. On a factory model, the brake light can be activated when either the front or rear brake is applied. The taillight bulb is referred to as an 1157, commonly found at any automotive supply store. Many aftermarket companies are using LEDs in their taillight assemblies. The use of LEDs continues to grow and they do have some advantages over standard bulbs (see the information on LEDs farther along in this chapter). Besides the lighting styles, there are an array of different mounting positions, housings, shapes and finishes. Side mounts, fender mounts, axle mounts, frame mounts, chrome, polished or painted. You can even find lights in different shapes, like figures, dice, crosses, diamonds, teardrops, cat eyes just to name a few. No matter what you choose over your stock light, be sure it is DOT approved.

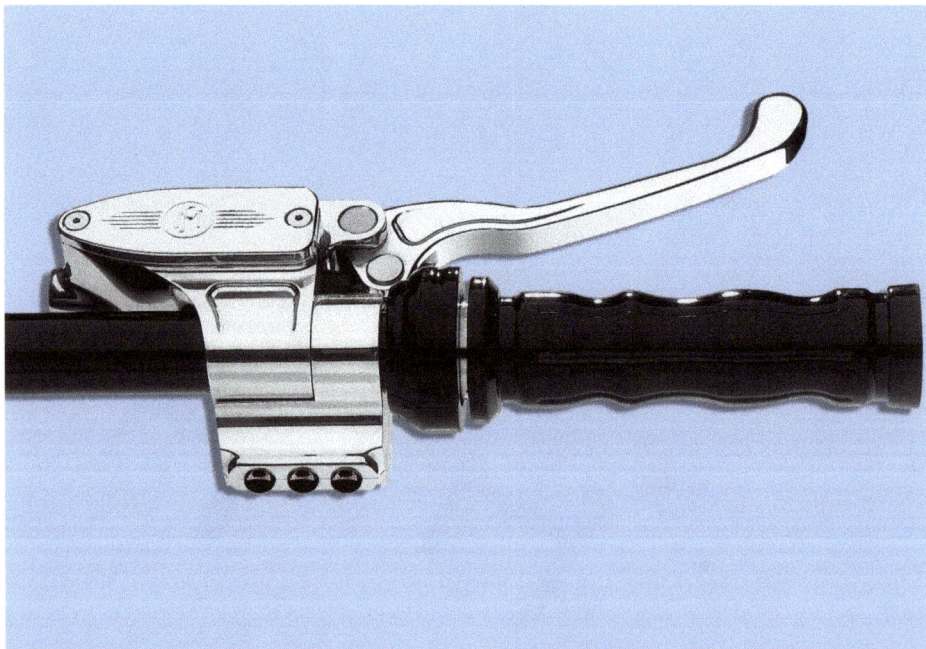

HOW DO THEY WORK?

A taillight is a very simple circuit. It is made up of a keyed 12-volt power source and a wire that is triggered by a switch. The brakelight switch is activated when hydraulic pressure is increased due to depressing the front or rear brake lever. This pressure causes the hydraulic switch to make contact thus closing the circuit and illuminating the brake light. Since a stock motorcycle has a front and rear brake switch, either switch can illuminate the brake light. The running light circuit uses the same protected circuit as the headlight and turn signals. Taillights typically use an 1157, industry standard, dual-filament incandescent bulb. Each of the filaments in the bulb operates independently of one another. The brighter filament is used for the brake light and the lower wattage filament is used for the running light. The difference in lumens power between the filaments is to make it easy for the person behind you to distinguish between the tail and the brake light.

TESTING

The easiest way to test a non-functioning taillight is to remove the lens and visually inspect the bulb. In most cases, if the bulb is burnt out you will notice a dark section on the glass. Sometimes you will need to test the bulb to be sure it is indeed blown. Simply replace the defective bulb with a new 1157. It is also recommended to apply dielectric grease to the socket before installing the new bulb. The grease is made for electrical components and prevents water from corroding the light socket.

If your brakelight is not working, be sure to check the front lever and the rear pedal independently. If one works and the other does not the problem is with either the switch, or the wiring to that switch. Lastly,

Quality front brake master cylinder assemblies come with or without a brake light switch. Though it's more work to utilize a front-brake light switch, it means the brake light comes on no matter which brake you use. PM

check the wiring harness in the rear fender to be sure that it has not been damaged. On 1996 and up models, you will find an 8-position MultiLock connector positioned under the seat that supplies power to the rear turn signals and taillight. The brakelight wire is red and in the number 6 position. Be sure the wires in the connector are intact and not damaged in any way. Test the wires between the connector to be sure there is voltage on both sides. This is the best way to determine that there is a good connection. If the running light is inoperable check the bulb first. If the bulb tests OK then check the same 8-position connector under the seat to be sure there is voltage on both sides. The running light wire is blue and in the number 7 position. The key is to be sure you have power at the 8-position connector and that it makes it back to the taillight. If you do not have power, there is a break in the wire somewhere else on the motorcycle. Refer to your factory user manual for a more detailed schematic.

INCANDESCENT VERSUS LED

There are several differences between standard bulbs and LED's. Probably the most appealing difference between the two is the amount of room that an LED takes up. You can construct a PCB or printed circuit board in almost any shape or style imaginable. Since LED's are attached to a PCB in order for them to operate, you can imagine the endless possibilities. A standard incandescent bulb is what it is. They are large and need a good amount of free space around them for heat dissipation. On the other hand, LED's are usually brighter, which increases visibility. Second, they will last much longer than a normal bulb. Since LED's do not draw nearly as much amperage, the wire feeding them can be smaller. There are some

downsides to LEDs, because they are attached to a printed circuit board, water is an LED's worst enemy. If they are exposed to water they can become damaged or ruined. Another downside comes up when the LED stops working, most are not standardized like typical automotive bulbs and it may be impossible to find an exact replacement. If this is the case, your LED taillight will be worthless and need to be replaced with a new unit.

TURN SIGNALS

They have to be one of the most often changed items on a factory bike. Besides the obvious grips, mirrors or other small chrome do-dads, stock turn signals are not that cool. They are available in many different styles, shapes and finishes. Harley changed over to its current "bullet" style in 2000 with the introduction of the Softail Deuce. These are smaller than previous years and are much more appealing. As nice as the turn signals are, Harley Davidson owners still love to change them.

Do You Need Them? That is a difficult question. We can start off by saying your bike does not need them in order to operate properly. The bike will still run. Is it legal not to have them? In most

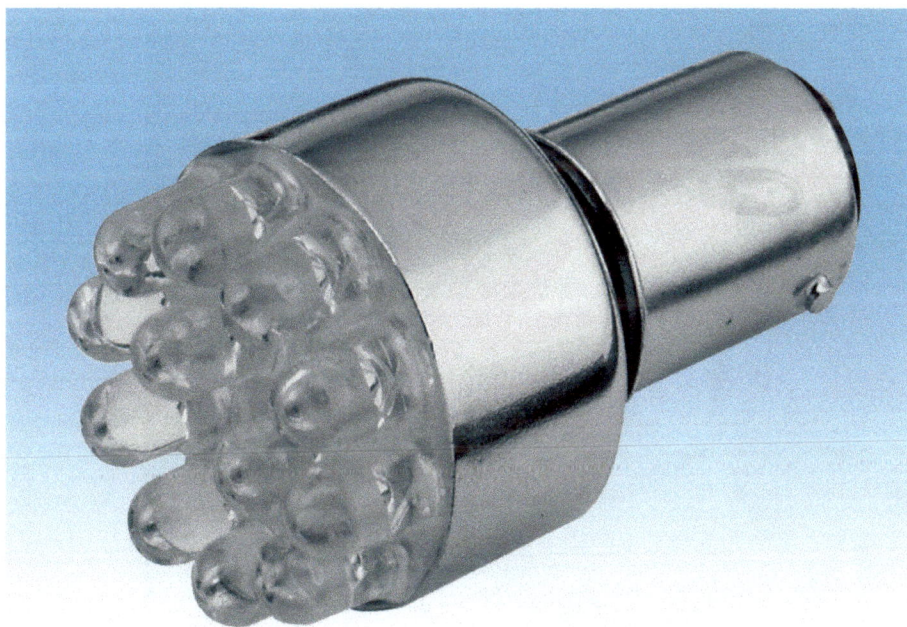

Typical motorcycle and automotive bulbs, both single and dual filament, can now be purchased as brighter and longer-lasting LEDs.

A pair of small silver bullets from Kuryakyn, mounted off the headlight pivot bolt as shown, make for a nice unobtrusive set of turn signals.

The fender from Russ Wernimont (RWD) includes this light assembly which incorporates tail, turn and brakelights into one housing.

states it is considered illegal not to have turn signals. You're not going to get arrested but you could very well get pulled over and fined. You would also have a difficult time passing a state mandated vehicle inspection without them. Before you go through the effort of removing them check to see what your state requires and save yourself some time.

DIFFERENT STYLES & SIZES

If there is only one good thing about turn signals, it's the ability to change them to a different style. There are so many different types of aftermarket turn signals to choose from. Big, small, chrome, polished, painted, LED, whatever you want, they are out there. You can purchase single or dual filament meaning just a flashing signal or a running lamp and a flashing signal respectively. Most stock motorcycles have dual filament bulbs on the front and single filament turn signals on the rear. LED turn signals, big and small have become very popular over the last 5 years. These signals tend to offer more lumens power, or a brighter light, making them more visible.

Why DOT Approved? It is important to know that not all turn signals are D.O.T. approved. Most states will tell you what the minimum exposed reflector size can be. (This is the limit on how small the actual colored lens can be per D.O.T. requirements.) This will help you to purchase not only what is legal but also what are the brightest and safest turn signals available.

MOUNTING

Positioning of turn signals can be a hassle. Not only are the turn signals themselves obtrusive and sometimes unappealing but trying to find a good spot to mount them can be a real chore. There are many different styles to choose from which makes the job a bit easier. You still have to pick out a pair that fits, physically and visually. OEM signals found in flush or bracket-mounted styles are a safe bet, but some of the custom models include mirror mounted signals, built-in signal grips or even handlebar levers with integral signals. Before you buy, be sure that they fit your theme and that they're legal.

HOW DO THEY WORK

There have been some differences in turn signal operation over the years. Early model Harley Davidson's did not have the self-canceling feature. This meant the rider pushed the button to activate the turn signal and had to push it again to turn it off. In 1989, Harley first introduced self-canceling turn signals only on one model. It was not until 1991 that all factory motorcycles had the new self-canceling feature. It was a big step forward. How it all works is quite simple, though there are a few ways to make it happen. Harley used a self-contained electronic module that was mounted under the dash on most models. The module was activated when the left or right turn signal switch was pressed. This action sent power to the module, which acted as a relay, momentarily turning the lights on and off. On all '95 and earlier models, turn signals would automatically turn off when the motorcycle reached a particular speed measured by the distance traveled. This was accomplished via a reed switch that was located in the speedometer. Starting in 1996, all factory models went to an electronic speedometer but with the exception of the connector used, the self-canceling

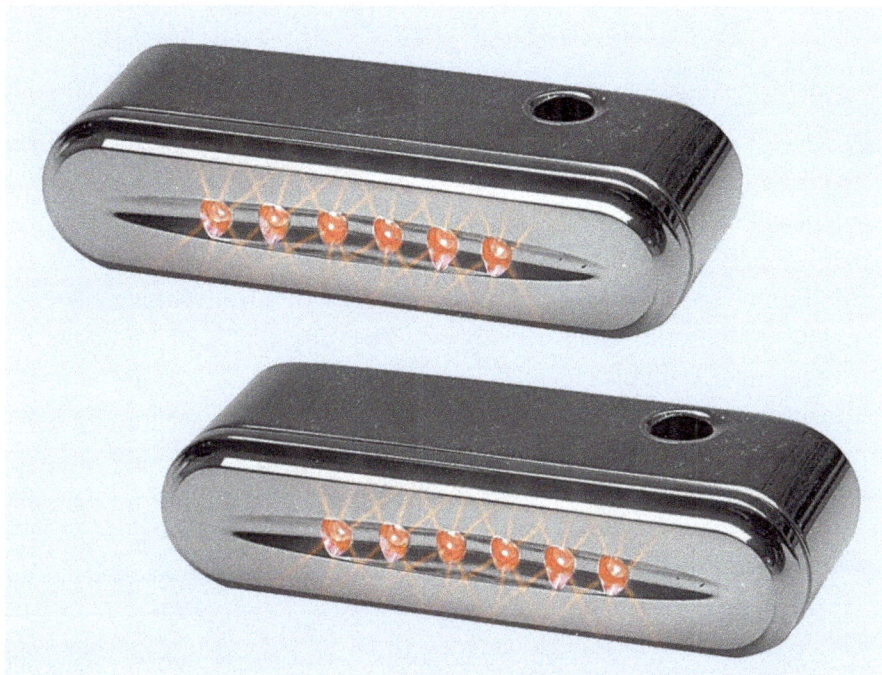

These LED light assemblies provide one more way to create unobtrusive, yet bright, turn signals and/or marker lights. Biker's Choice

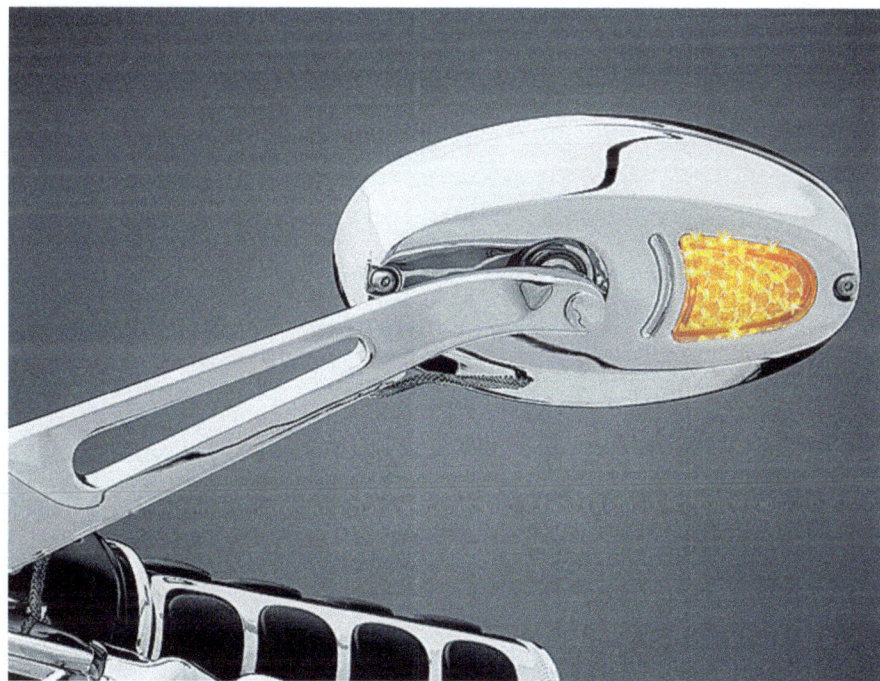

Another Kuryakyn design, these mirrors with integral lights work great as front blinker lights.

modules are the same. As a safety feature, the factory added a four-way hazard flasher activated when both the left and right side buttons were pressed at the same time.

TESTING AND REPAIR

Lets say you're out for a ride and when you go to use your left side turn signal, it rapidly flashes off and on. This is the very same scenario that happens in your automobile. It is saying that one or both turn signal bulbs are burnt out. Simply remove the lens and replace the defective bulb. If your bulbs are OK then it's time to look for loose wires or bad socket connections. Check to be sure that the socket is clean, and free from corrosion or debris. If you have a 12-volt test light, use that in place of the bulb to see if you are getting power to the light assembly. Also check the wire in the turn signal housing, be sure it is tight and intact. Look for a cut or break in the wiring harness that leads from the housing to under the tank. You may need to remove the fuel tank in order to access the 6-position MultiLock connector. Use a multi meter to test for voltage on either side of the connector. This will confirm if you have a good connection. If you still do not have power at the connector, you would want to test the self-canceling module for power. If there is power at the module, then you know the problem is somewhere in the wiring to the turn signals. If there is not power, you may have a bad module. At this point, you want to also use a multi meter to test the handlebar switch wiring for a short. Be sure to review your factory service manual or visit your local Harley Davidson dealer for more technical information.

Factory turn signals are not always the easiest thing to change. Since there are several styles, you need to be sure that the replacement signal has the same or similar mounting capabilities. For example, Heritage Softails have the same turn signal mounting bracket that most FL models have. A Fatboy has the same mounting style that most all other models use. It is safe to say that most aftermarket companies have this figured out as well. When looking for a turn signal and you find one you like, be sure that it has your year, make and model listed. This will confirm a direct fit.

Let's say, however, that you're going for a different look all together and you're not concerned with fitment. There are several companies out there that make custom mounting hardware. This can help you to reposition the lights wherever you want. Keep in mind, the further you move them away

"We created the filler panels, extended the rear fender and then designed the exhaust to exit between the fender and the bags - the whole thing is what I call, 'street rod smooth.'" Brian Klock

from the stock location, the better the chance the wires will need to be extended. Either way, the first thing you need to do is to remove the fuel tank(s) and locate the 6-position MultiLock connector found on the left side of the motorcycle.

It is recommended that you mark where each wire is positioned in the connector before removing. You will notice if you look carefully, that each wire position is marked with a number. This will help you keep track of the colors as well. Some turn signals come with the factory style wiring and crimp terminals already in place. This will make reinstalling the new signals much easier. For the signals that are not ready to install, you may want to purchase the factory style crimp terminals from a Harley Dealer or an aftermarket catalog. This will help you install the aftermarket turn signal as if it were wired as stock. Anytime you have a plug-n-play device, you will be much better off if you have to service them down the road. Once the terminals are crimped in place, the wires should be placed back into the connector before you start on the other side. When both sides are complete, plug the connector back into the main harness and test both turn signals.

INCANDESCENT BULBS OR LED?

Just like taillights, there are several differences between standard bulbs and LEDs. Since LEDs take up less space then a standard bulb, you can construct smaller turn signal housings. Just because it is smaller does not make it better. Most aftermarket small turn signals are not DOT approved and would not be considered safe to use as the only means for a turn signal. Companies that manufacture non-DOT approved signals protect themselves by adding a disclaimer that states they are to be used as a supplemental light source only. Before you install a new set of LED turn

signals, there is one thing you should know. Your motorcycle will not operate a combination of LED and incandescent signals, or all LED signals, without the assistance of a load equalizer. This is because LED's draw less current than incandescent bulbs, and the factory module will not recognize the LED and will react with a rapid flash - the same as if you had a blown bulb or disconnected turn signal.

The best available load equalizer available is a Badlands unit. They are inexpensive and they work flawlessly. Their sole purpose is to allow a smaller draw or lower amperage light used in a turn signal circuit to work the same as an incandescent bulb. If you have gone as far as replacing the front and rear turn signals, you should also decide if you would like the rear signals to act as running and brake lights. Badlands also has a module that will perform this involved function with a simple, low cost plug-n-play device. The all-in-one, run, brake and turn signal module with a built-in load equalizer simply plugs in between the 8-position MultiLock connector that is found under the seat on most models. There is also a version of this module designed for Sportster models.

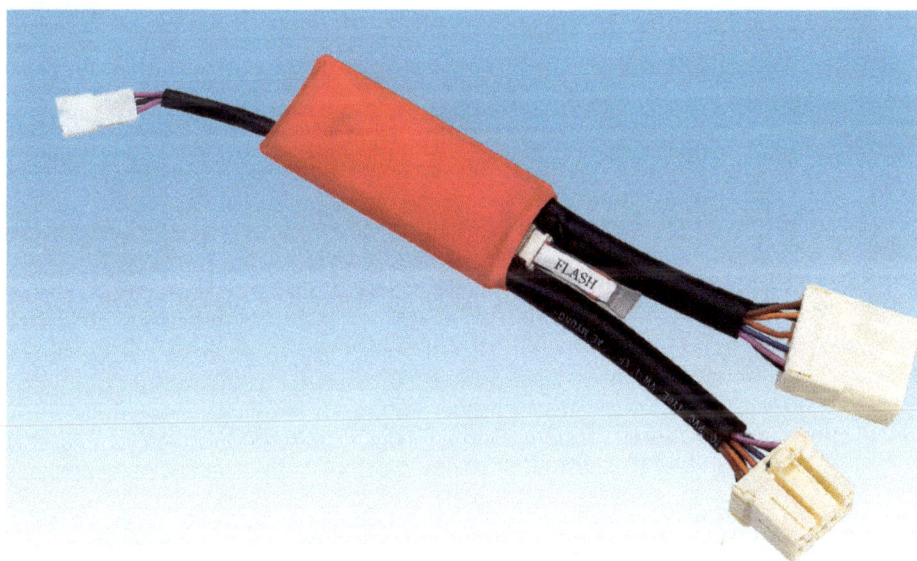

The Flasher is a plug-in module that adds a rapid three time "flash" when breaking, and a run/turn/brake function to existing single filament OEM and halogen lights. Fits 96 & up Softails, 97 & up Dyna & FLH models, and 99 - 03 XL's. Cycle Vision

Chapter Six

Gauges & Switches

Turn it on, Turn it up

Now that you understand the basics of factory lighting circuits, how to swap out components, and even some trouble shooting techniques, it seems only fitting that in this chapter we discuss all there is to know about gauges and switches. Since all factory built motorcycles have a speedometer, we will talk about the differences between mechanical drive, electronic, analog or digital speedos and the numerous sizes and shapes available. We will also discuss the pros and

The Ultra Classics come with a truly full set of gauges, from L to R: fuel, speed, tach, volts, air pressure, oil pressure.

cons of tachometers, the importance of indicator lights and understand the operations of handlebar switches.

SPEEDOMETERS

All factory built motorcycles have one, that's a fact and it's the law according to the DOT. Since it's inception back in 1936, the speedometer has been used as the focal point on Harley dash panels. Over the years the faceplate has changed, with different number styles, background patterns and colors. There are aftermarket companies that make speedometer faceplates with custom graphics, colors and flames just to name a few.

Beginning in 1936 and running all the way up to 1995, all factory speedometers are mechanically driven, usually off the front wheel, except for some bagger models. As mentioned earlier, the speedometer drive is generally located at the front axle on the same side as the brake rotor.

One of the drawbacks of a mechanical or cable-driven speedometer happens when the drive decides to stop working. Nine times out of ten, the drive will cause the cable to break as well. It's imperative to keep the drive and cable lubed regularly to prevent this problem. Servicing the drive meant removing the front axle on most models. Not the most fun but necessary.

When the new electronic speedometer was introduced, the improvement in technology was very noticeable. Transmissions now have an area machined into them that enabled the mounting of a hall effect sensor that measured the rotations of the gears and sent that data to the speedometer.

Another positive note is the ability to change to an electronic speedometer. If you have an older, pre '96 model you could change over from your mechanical speedo. You could buy a newer style transmission with the speedo plug, or purchase a variety of other electronic pickups to do the job. Companies like Dakota Digital have pioneered the science behind speedometers, tachometers and other gauges. These use inductive sensors that measure the rotation of the transmission sprocket, and axle mounted sensors that provide accurate speed-readings to the speedometer. No matter which option you choose, there are plenty of possibilities available.

One area of concern for the electronic speedometer is the sensor - is it covered with sludge from transmission fluid or are there metal chips on the sensor. The sensor is magnetic and a new transmission can create a small amount of metal shavings as the gears begin to mesh with one another. These two scenarios would cause the speedometer not to operate or to operate erratically. The fix is easy. Simply remove the Allen head bolt from the sensor, wipe it clean and secure it in place.

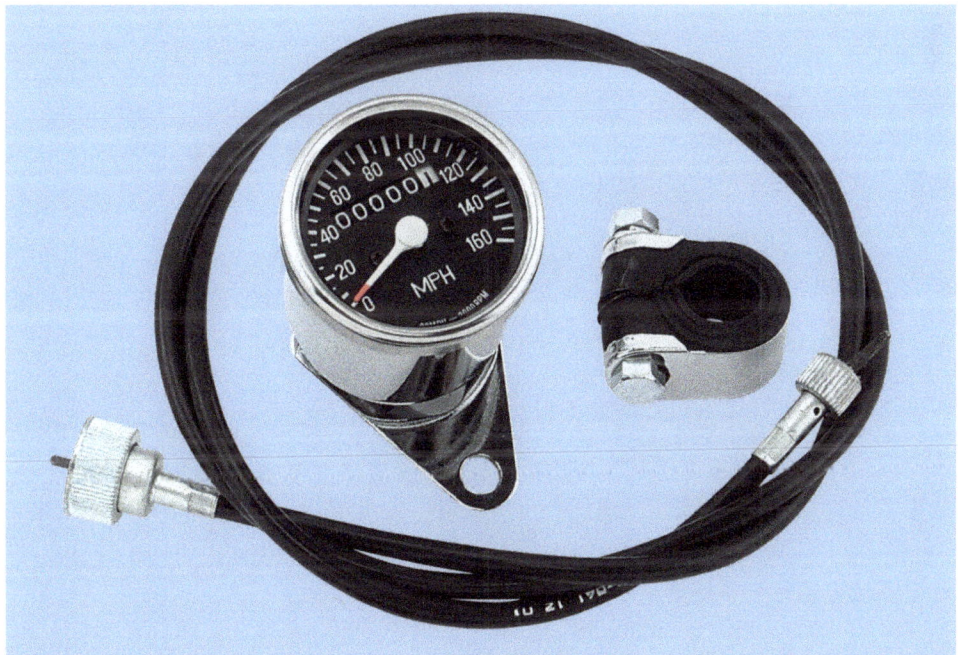

Small, mechanical speedometers are still available. There are two gear ratios commonly used, be sure the speedo drive, cable and speedometer itself are all compatible.

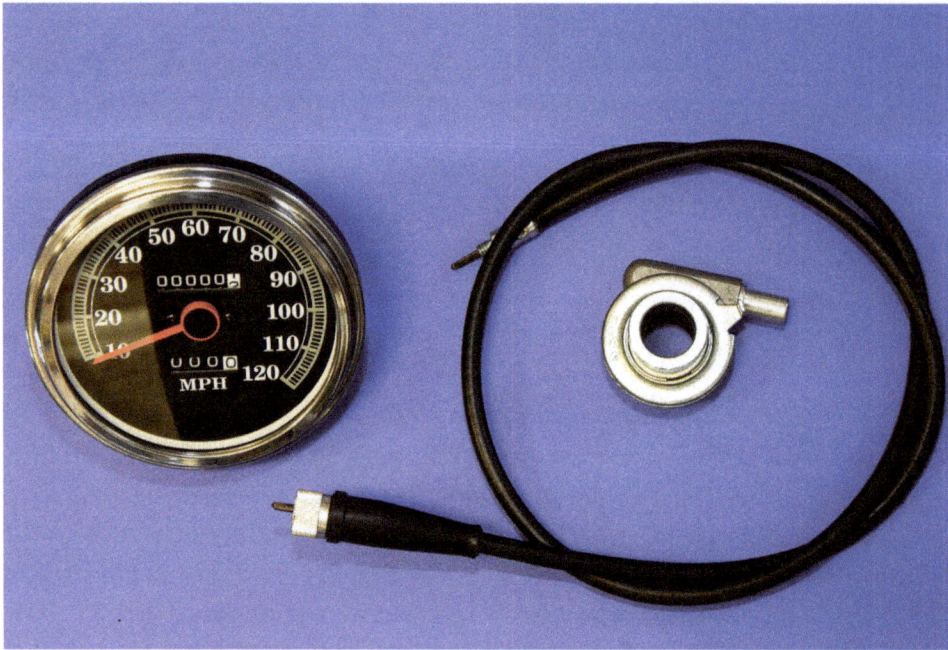

Drive units meant for the front fork come in different ratios and also different styles depending on the type of fork (narrow or wide-glide). Again, you have to ensure the drive, cable and speedo are all meant to work together.

The classic Harley-Davidson dash with speedo and ignition switch is used on pre-'96 models.

Both electronic and mechanical speedometers beginning in 1989 also worked in conjunction with a reed switch that aided the self-canceling turn signal module. As mentioned earlier in the book, the purpose of the reed switch is to tell the turn signal module to stop flashing. What's a reed switch? A reed switch is an electrical switch operated by an applied magnetic field. The switch consists of a pair of contacts on ferrous metal reeds in a hermetically sealed glass envelope. On a motorcycle, the contacts are normally open, closing when a magnetic field is present. The closing of these contacts is what shuts off the flashing turn signals and occurs when the motorcycle reaches a particular speed measured by the distance traveled.

When the custom Harley market was beginning it's skyward travel, aftermarket companies began outdoing each other by redesigning factory components making them more unique. One way to get the attention of consumers was to make things smaller. Speedometers are one of those items that has been reduced in size allowing for so many other dash and fuel tank possibilities. If you wanted to modify your Harley and use a custom fuel tank, moving the speedo was one of the first things you needed to do. Since most models also had indicator lights and an ignition switch mounted along with the speedometer, moving all of them was not an easy task.

Before you dive into changing the location of these items, be sure to understand what is involved. A small speedometer gives you many different mounting options: You can mount it on the handlebars, off of a motor mounted bracket, on the font fork, in the gas tank and many others. The smallest electronic speedometer measures 1.875 inches in diameter and the largest speedo (stock factory size) measures 4-1/4 inches in diameter. Along with a small speedometer are the varieties of finished speedo housings with numerous mounting positions. The possibilities are endless for electronic models but when you a have a mechanical, cable-driven speedo you are somewhat restricted due to the flexibility of the cable itself. Most '95 and earlier models had a dash mounted four inch mechanical speedometer located on top of the fuel tanks. The cable driven speedo also has a mechanical trip mileage indicator mounted on the right side of the unit. Once Harley switched to electronic speedometers in 1996, they were still located in the same spot on most models, but the trip mileage reset was also changed over to an electronic version and moved to the left side of the speedometer unit.

Manufactured in an OEM size, the Dakota Digital speedo comes with turn signal and high beam indicators, and the tachometer comes complete with a built in shift light.

Auto Meter makes these matching and modern gauge sets with an electronic speedometer. A variety of brackets are also available.

These Auto Meter gauges are designed to replace stock, factory gauges...

TACHOMETERS AND REV-LIMITERS

There always seems to be a real debate over the benefits of a tachometer. The old school riders don't think you need them, unless you plan on drag racing. Many of today's riders add them to their rides, whether they need them or not is up for the individual. The true definition of a tachometer according to a dictionary is: a device for measuring rotation speed, a device used to determine speed of rotation, typically of a vehicle's crankshaft, usually measured in revolutions per minute. As you can see from the definition above, tachometers measure the RPM or revolutions per minute of the engine's crankshaft. Now if you think about it, knowing the RPM of your engine is pretty darn important.

Speedometers and tachometers come in many different sizes, shapes, colors, backlighting and finishes. There are also manufacturers out there offering many different options. For example, Auto Meter, known more for automotive hot rod style gauges, produces a line of motorcycle gauges with built in shift lights. This is a nice option for those of you that like to drag race. The shift light is a visual rev limiter that is manually set by the rider. Most riders "dyno" their bike to see where in the RPM range peak horsepower and torque occur. Once the data has been collected, the

...and offer the stylish black on white faces, along with a sexy nite-time glow.

shift light and/or rev limiter can be set accordingly.

There are many different mounting possibilities, allowing the rider to be creative. Most factory tachometers are designed to mount at the handlebar risers. Some mounts are machined along with a top riser clamp built in giving you a clean and subtle look. Since tachometer sizes vary, you can virtually place the tachometer wherever you want to put it. In the aftermarket world there are motor-mounted, handlebar-mounted and even fork-mounted housings available. Before you choose what works best for you, remember that you will need to wire the tachometer to your ignition so placement is important.

For anyone with true fat bob tanks, the aftermarket makes complete dash kits in a variety of styles.

INDICATOR LIGHTS

One of the first things most people think about when they hear the term indicator lights is their other name, idiot lights. Though it seems derogatory it is kind of funny. Indicator lights are very useful to riders so maybe they will get the last laugh. The purpose of the light cluster is to inform the rider of individual component functions. For example, the far left and far right light represents each turn signal. When you press either signal, the appropriate indicator light will also flash. This is nice to know when you're at a stoplight so you can be sure that motorists in front and back of you are aware of

A pair of small, 1-7/8 inch gauges. On the left a mechanical speedometer and on the right an electronic tachometer.

For a very simple wiring set up you can use a coil mount with ignition and hi-low switch. Just use an ignition switch with a spring-loaded start position.

your next move. Going from left to right, the second light is the high beam indicator. This light will illuminate blue when the high beam is on. Like the turn signal indicator, this is nice to know so you don't blind other motorists while riding at night. The center light in the cluster is for the neutral indicator light. This light will illuminate a green "N" when the transmission is in neutral. Do we even need to discuss why this is important? Even the most seasoned rider has made a complete fool of themselves at one time or another.

Although it seems funny watching someone try to start his or her motorcycle while in gear, it can be very dangerous. It has happened at least once to all of us, and can put a world of hurt on your body and your bank account. Dropping your bike or running into someone else's is definitely not a laughing matter. Do yourself a favor and make sure the light works so

YOU don't look like the idiot! The second to last light from the left is for oil pressure. The little wire that connects to the oil-sending unit is what feeds this indicator light. This light will illuminate red when your engine's oil pressure is low. Now I don't know about you, but if my engine's oil pressure is low I want to know about it right away and in a way that can't be ignored. So now you see why calling indicator lights idiot lights may be a complete oxymoron.

All factory motorcycles come equipped with indicator lights. If you were to look at Harley Davidson models, you would find that Sportsters and most Dynas have their lighting cluster installed in the area at the top handlebar riser clamp or on the speedometer bracket. Most touring models have an indicator cluster located above the ignition switch located in front of the dash panel. All other models with a speedometer positioned in the dash panel have an instrument cluster directly under the speedometer. Servicing these lights is rather simple. The most important thing to keep in mind is that the lights will only operate when a switch is engaged. The high beam, left or right turn signals, hydraulic oil sending unit or the neutral safety switch are all momentary switches that trigger their appropriate indicator light when triggered. If you ever decide to go the custom route and get rid of your dash, you will need to rewire the ignition switch and move the indicator lights as needed. For example, if you have a carbureted Softail model and you choose to replace the tank with a stretched version the dash panel and its components will need to be removed. There are several aftermarket companies manufacturing ignition switch relocation brackets that mount to a motor mount or any other custom location. Many people unplug the indicator lights and never reinstall them, but if you still want to use them there are self-contained aftermarket units available in universal or custom mounting styles. Whichever direction you decide, be sure to do the research and purchase the right products for the job.

HANDLEBAR SWITCHES

Q&A, Kevin Wheeler @ Dakota Digital

Kevin, give us a little background on you?

I started here right after high school. Seven years later I've worked in most of the departments including the machine shop, trouble shooting, and the design area. After high school I went to college and received a degree in electrical engineering.

What's the minimum gauge package you would recommend on a motorcycle?

Most people want at least a speedo and all the idiot lights for neutral, high beam, oil pressure, check engine and the turn signals. A lot of people also want a tachometer and either an oil pressure or oil temperature gauge.

First, let's break the gauges down into two groups: speedo/tach and then what might be called the engine or auxiliary gauges. The oil pressure, temperature, gas gauge and voltmeter.

How do I pick a speedometer and tachometer?

Look for gauges designed for a motorcycle application. They have to be weather proof, a lot of the cheap ones are not. Next pick one that's right for your application. Older set ups have cables, Most 1996 and up factory bikes are set up for electronic speedometers.

Electronic speedos are the most popular now. Even most of the aftermarket transmissions like a Baker tranny are setup to accept an electronic sensor. Our electronic speedometer, as well as many others, has an auto-calibrate feature. All you have to do is go out and ride a measured mile to setup your speedometer regardless of tire size or gearing.

You can still run a cable driven speedo with the drive off the front wheel and an older analog gauge, but it's harder to calibrate and not as neat because of the cable. Even if the bike came with a cable set up you can run an electronic speedometer. We make a universal inductive sensor that read any ferrous metal. The teeth on a sprocket or the bolt heads in a hub will create a pulse, which will trigger the speedometer, and the auto-calibration feature will allow you to adjust the speedometer. So the electronic speedometers will work on nearly any bike as long as it's a 12-volt system.

Tachometers often confuse people. Basically, it's a three-wire system. One ground, one hot and one wire that connects either to the negative side of the ignition coil or the tach output wire from the ECM or ignition module.

How do I pick the auxiliary gauges?

A lot of it depends on preference. Do you want oil pressure or oil temperature, for example? We make a package for a dresser with voltmeter, fuel, oil pressure and oil temperature. There are also clocks and outside temperature gauges. Most aftermarket gauges use a proprietary sensor. For instance, the oil pressure gauge will use a sensor supplied by the same company as the gauge, make sure you get a sensor with the gauge if required. Our oil pressure sensors, and temp sensors, are 1/8-inch pipe so they are pretty universal and easily "T-ed" into existing lines and fittings. A benefit to aftermarket gauges is that they are usually more accurate than factory and have better resolution.

What are the mistakes people make buying or installing gauges and how can they be avoided?

One common mistake in bike wiring is bad grounds, it's a huge deal. You have to provide the gauges with a good ground, most of time running a dedicated ground wire to the negative side of the battery is recommended. Be sure there isn't any paint under the ground connection where it attaches to the engine or the frame.

Be sure to use a fuse where it's appropriate. A lot of the gauges don't draw much, so you can run all the gauges off one power wire, but be sure to put a fuse in the circuit. You also need to be careful with bundling too many wires together. You can't route the speedo signal wire right next to the main ignition wire or one of the spark plug wires - this will cause erratic readings on your speedometer. When you're working on the wiring, try not to molest the stock harness, don't cut off one of the stock plugs and then re-solder it, use the harness as it's intended. And don't use a speedometer meant for a bicycle, they're little and neat, but they generally won't stand up to the abuse.

If we look back over the years Harley-Davidson as made very few changes to their handlebar switch assemblies. Before 1982 the switches used were very small, round micro switches that were more often broken than working. Changing the overall appearance in 1983 proved to be a big step in the right direction for the motor company. These switches were made of three larger, but more ergonomic switches that were indeed heavy duty compared to earlier years. The larger switch used a heavy, 16-gauge wire that connected into a 12-position AMP connector.

Though the switches were nice they were still prone to breakdown since they were not watertight. That all changed in 1996 when the factory changed the switches again. The new and current versions are watertight, sealed with epoxy housings to prevent corrosion. Harley also began using 6-position Deutsch connectors that were top notch and also watertight. This was a huge improvement and it was sure to cut down on wiring and component failures. Switches used in '96 and up were also easier to service. The factory began using gray Deutsch connectors for the left side switch harness and black for right to separate each side.

It's safe to say that every aftermarket V-Twin catalog offers custom or OEM style switches, with or without housings, available in black or chrome. OEM switches are commonly listed as 1982 to 1995, or 1996 and up. Although the only real major differences are the housings and the connections to the main harness, it is not possible to mix and match these years. Harley switches are manufactured in Japan and 99% of all other aftermarket switches are also produced over seas. With that being said, there is not much difference between stock/OEM or aftermarket switch assemblies. Before you buy, look at the quality of the switch and wire attached to them. It should be a minimum of 18-gauge and sealed where it enters the back of the switch.

If the stock or stock-style aftermarket switch is not your speed you may want to look at the custom style switches available on the market today. There are several companies out there making custom switches and housings in every style. Most of the switches available are designed using the factory style micro switch that was popular in the 1970s and early 1980s. The switch is called a micro switch because of its size. The drawback to a small switch is its ability to handle high amperage. For example, many of the aftermarket companies manufacture switch assemblies with 22-gauge wire leads that are soldered to the switch contacts. First, if you ever need to remove the wire from the switch too much heat from your iron will melt the switch housing. Second, small wires generally need a

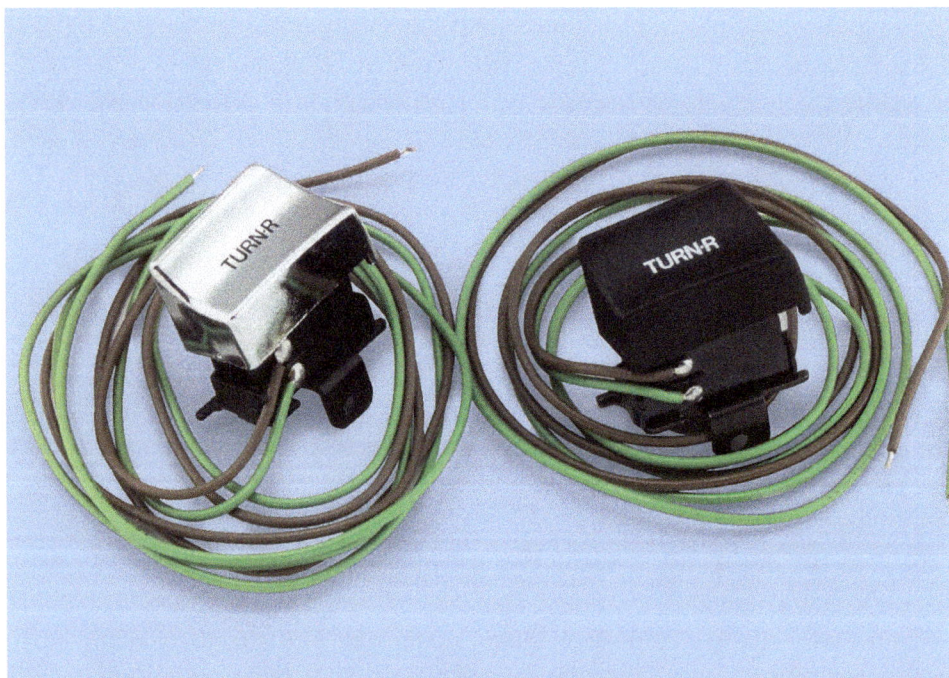

These '82 to '95 handlebar switches come in black or chrome - late model switches are likewise available in either finish.

relay to handle the required power. As we mentioned earlier, the power needed to supply a standard Harley headlight, using a 55/60-watt bulb, is a minimum of 5-amps and the minimum wire gauge to safely handle 5-amps is 18-gauge wire. Anything less than 18-gauge wire will require the use of a relay. If you still want the custom switch be sure you have the room to mount a relay. The positive side to the aftermarket switch assembly is its size. Smaller in this case is better, but of course there are pros and cons that you need to consider.

Whether you go to aftermarket style mini switch housings or you want to get away from handlebar-mounted switches, there are many options to choose from. If you are designing a custom bike from scratch you may want to go a different route. Many custom builders are using the motor mount for barrel key switches and a toggle switch for high/low beam. This is a nice way to keep the handlebar area clean of wiring and provides an easy access location for electrical components. A simple watertight toggle or micro toggle switch is a slick and affordable method for a high/low beam switch.

If you don't like the motor-mount locations, put the high/low toggle in the headlight bucket or anywhere else you can think of. A single pole, dual throw switch will enable 12-volt power to be sent to one of two outputs, either to the high beam or the low beam. Be sure that the switch you purchase is rated no less than 5 Amps.

There are key switches available that mimic stock factory applications such as the barrel on/off style found on Sportsters and Big Twins, as well as cus-

tom starter style switches that resemble an automotive switch. With any of these options the appropriate mounting tabs and brackets are also available from several manufacturers. In a custom application the key-start switch is very nice to have. It makes it nice and easy to start the motorcycle in one location, as apposed to an on/off key switch. The key start switch is a double throw switch, where the first position turns on the electricity and the second position engages the starter relay, then the solenoid and then starter motor (some installations eliminate the starter relay). A simple on/off switch is just that. It is a single throw switch that will only turn the power off and on with a key. There is key start switch that has all the bells and whistles and manufactured by Bob McKay in Canada. His switch has all of the normal positions, on/off, start and when the key is pushed inward it is a momentary horn button. If you want a really nice, all-in-one style switch, this is a great choice.

NOTE: We've added information on the new H-D switches, including the CAN-bus system, all of which can be found in Chapters 10 - 11.

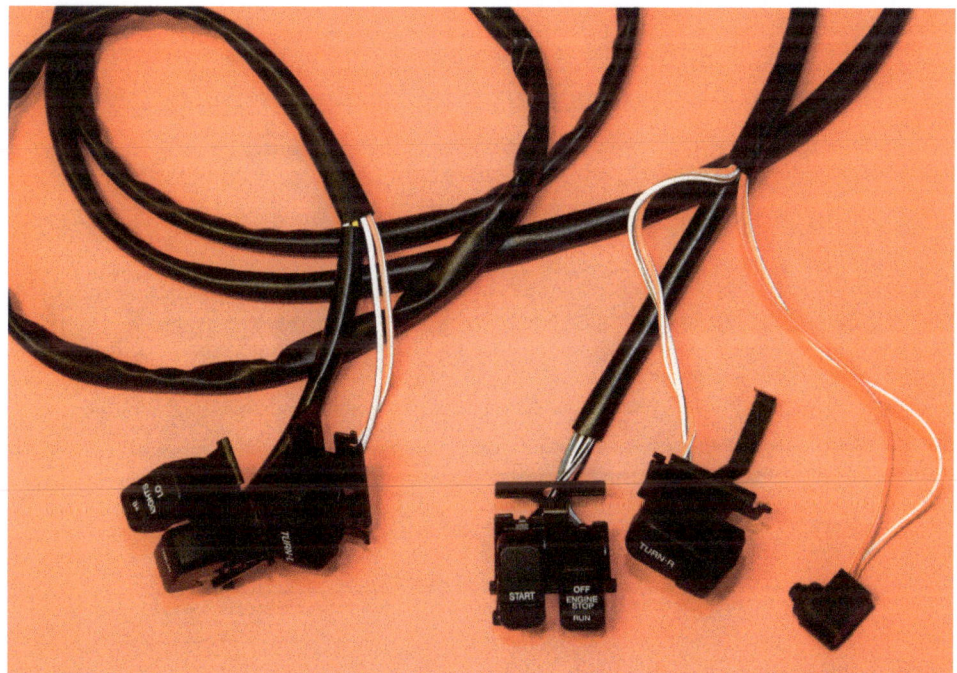

Factory style handle bar switches come in black or chrome. Though they're bigger than small custom switches, they are generally very durable and come with color coded wires.

Chapter Seven

Harness Kits

Pick the Best Aftermarket Solution

You should be feeling less like a novice by now with all the information you've learned from this book. We've talked about so many of the little things that make up a harness, now we are going to discuss the main harness itself. After reading this section, you will be able to determine which is best for your application: factory or aftermarket. We will also discuss the pros and cons of both harnesses and some of the options available to you when you buy a complete wiring harness kit.

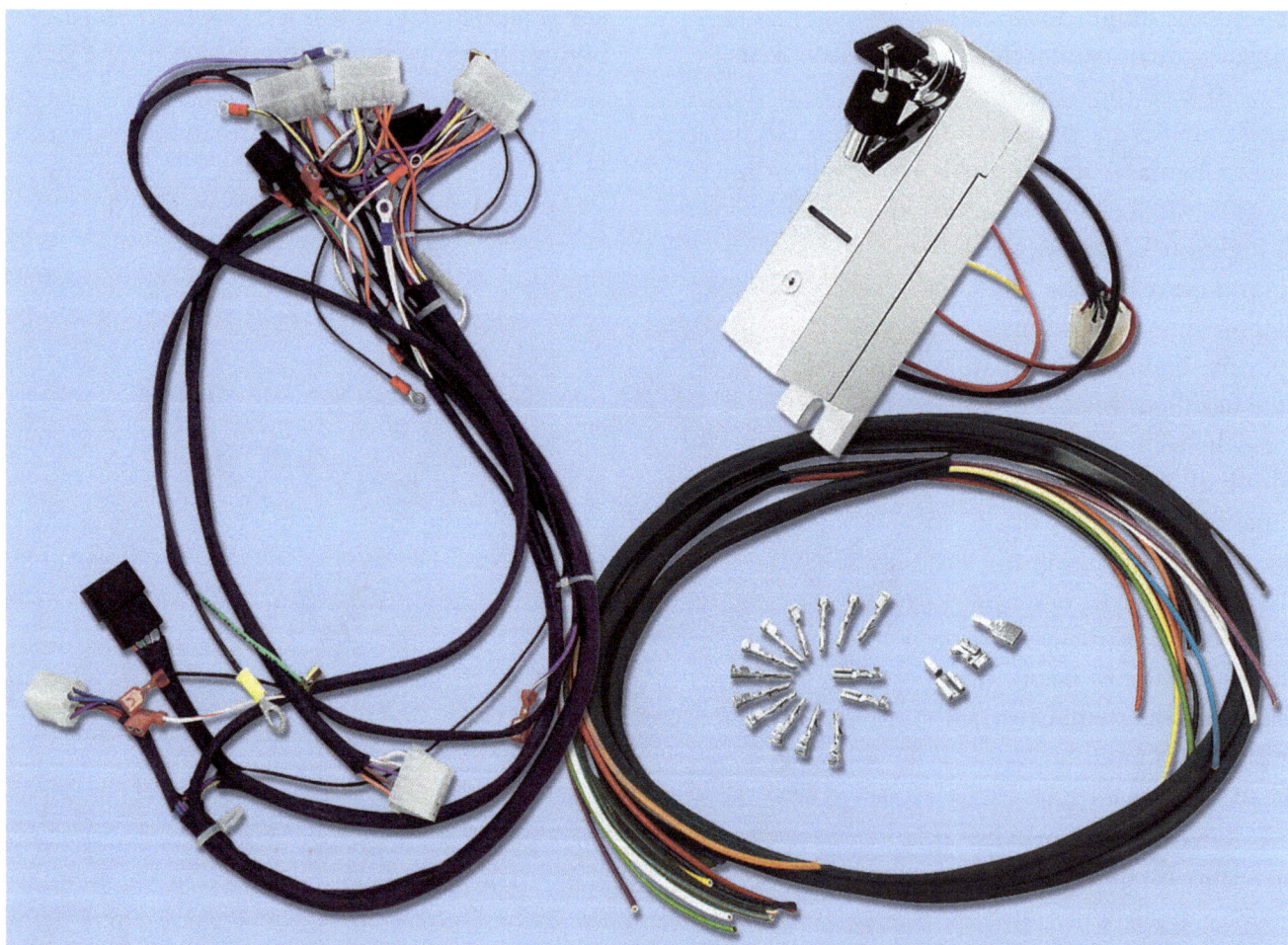

Wiring harness kits include everything from simple "chopper" kits to full-function kits with provisions for turn signals and handlebar switches.

80

COMPLETE WIRING HARNESS KITS

If you are attempting to build you very own custom motorcycle from scratch, there are some things you should know before you get too far along. Besides the obvious - motor, transmission, front end, wheels and tires - you need to decide what type of electrical items you want to have? For example, do you want turn signals, a horn, and stock style handlebar switches? These are important decisions that need to be made. The project will go together much more easily if you decide the location and style of the major electrical components during the mock up stage, instead of waiting to figure all this out during final assembly.

FACTORY OR AFTERMARKET

If you buy or build your wiring harness there are a couple of things to consider. First and foremost you should think about safety and your state transportation laws. When you're riding a motorcycle, especially at night, you want to be seen. The brighter the better the light, the better off you'll be (and less likely to get run over from behind).

From the legal aspect, most states require turn signals, especially on a custom built motorcycle with a state assigned Vehicle Identification Number, (VIN). So, if you need to have turn signals they must be D.O.T. approved and be strategically placed on the motorcycle. If this is the case, you will need a harness that supports switches and turn signals. Keep in mind that if your state also requires a mandated vehicle inspection, all items must operate properly in order for the bike to pass. Before you get started you may want to take a ride to your nearest D.O.T. office or look online to find out all the requirements. If you are more the rebellious type and choose not to use turn signals or your state does not require them, you should think about your safety on the road.

An OEM or factory wiring harness is an easy way to make sure you get the wiring job done right. Since all of the main wiring harness connections are installed for you, it will make your job much easier. Connecting a headlight, turn signals, taillight, ignition and fuse panel will be virtually plug-n-play if your components were equipped with factory style mating connectors. Most aftermarket catalogs offer factory-style replacement self-canceling turn signal units, brake switches and circuit breakers. So having to go to your local Harley Dealer is not the only way to stay "factory". One drawback to a factory harness is the size of the wiring itself. It is rather big and bulky, it can take up a lot of room on a sleek custom motorcycle. There are also many taps underneath the vinyl protective jacket on a factory harness. If you want to get super clean and take the minimalist approach to your wiring harness, a factory harness may not be a good choice. That's not to say you couldn't cut it up and make it your own but for an average cost of

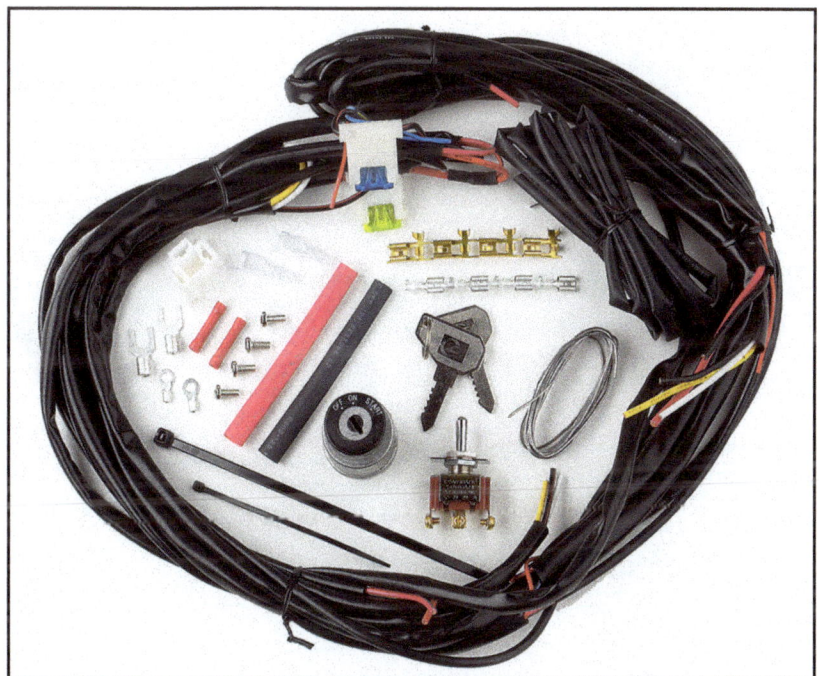

The Chopper Custom Wiring harness from Cycle Visions is designed to ease the job of wiring a simple no-blinkers bike and comes with a toggle hi-low switch and an ignition switch with a start position.

$400 that's a lot of money to spend to only be half way done.

A BASIC HARNESS

A basic wiring harness can be easily made from scratch. The main components to a basic harness are a key switch, high/low beam switch, brake switch, starter relay, one 30-Amp and one 15-Amp circuit breaker. The key switch will turn the bike on and off, act like a kill switch and activate the starter relay. High/low beam and brake switches perform their perspective duties. The 30-Amp circuit breaker is for your charging system and the 15-Amp is for your lighting circuit. Of course you will need to wire in your ignition system, coil and charging system. With a bunch of watertight connectors, heat shrink, a minimum of 18-gauge color-coded wire, you are in business. Sounds simple, right? For anyone who wants to go this route, there is a no-blinkers, basic wiring schematic farther along in the book.

COMPLETE WIRING HARNESS

Now lets say that you decide to make your own main wiring harness using OEM style turn signals. In order to make the turn signals operate you will need a flasher unit and a set of switches. A Wagner 552 flasher relay is the cheapest method for making a light flash off and on. The Wagner relay is inexpensive, but not self-canceling. If you would rather have the self-canceling feature, spend the extra money and purchase a Badlands self-canceling module. The average retail of a Badlands all-in-one module is about $100.00 and it offers quite a bit for the money. Not only will your turn signals cancel after 7-seconds but these modules also have a built-in load equalizer. This is an important feature if you are running a mixture of incandescent bulbs and LEDs or LED turn signals by themselves. The load equalizer will adjust the load/amperage regardless of the actual wattage of the bulb. This will allow different styles of lights to work with one another without conflicts.

If you decide to purchase an aftermarket harness and you want to use OEM style handlebar switches be sure to have the appropriate connectors. For example, 1995 and earlier Harley Davidson's used AMP Mate-n-Lock connectors throughout the entire bike. This is important to know because many of the less expensive "stock-style" aftermarket complete harness kits still use the older style connectors. Make sure you know what you are buying. As mentioned earlier, starting in 1996, Harley changed most of their AMP Mate-n-Lock main harness connections over to Deutsch connectors. You will also find a different style AMP Multi-Lock connector being used on headlights, turn signals and a few other main harness connections. Since most aftermarket catalogs have a variety of OEM electrical

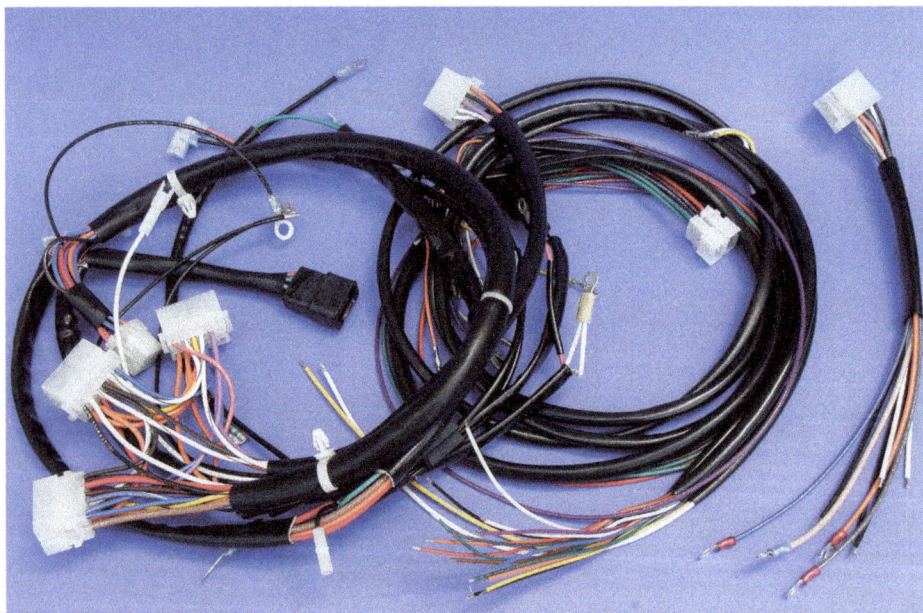

An early style factory harness, compete with the pre-Deutsch connectors. If you're building a custom, especially one without blinkers and switches on the bars, the factory harness like this contains way more wire and circuits than you will ever use.

parts available you should always be able to find exactly what you need for your build.

QUALITY AND RELIABILITY

Wiring is one of the most important, but yet overlooked areas of a customized or custom-built motorcycle. When you hear the word quality, some of the first things you think of is long lasting, built well, good reputation and so on. A quality-wiring product is all of those thoughts put together. The last thing you need to do is to install an inferior wiring product on a motorcycle that you will be riding all over God's earth. Saving a couple of bucks on an electrical product is not always a good thing. You want to use the best there is, a good brand name, solid reputation and proven product that you know works.

Now, a good product is only as good as the person installing it.

The best products in the world do not install themselves. They require someone with skill, patience and understanding. Lets look at the basics. Do you know the most important part of a motorcycle's wiring harness? A good ground, that's right. Without it, you and your motorcycle are doomed. The first bike I ever built did not have a solid ground between the motor and the frame and this simple oversight smoked a couple of batteries, starters, relays and wiring harnesses. As we have learned throughout this book, a bad connection or loose ground causes resistance, which builds up heat. Heat will cause many components to fail, melt or even catch fire. It is really that simple. Make sure you have a bare metal grounding post on your frame for your wiring har-ness, battery ground cable and bare metal where the motor mounts onto the frame.

Build your custom or customize your stock bike to the point where it is still reliable. Don't outdo yourself because that's when most people get caught focusing only on form and forgetting about function. If you want a reliable motorcycle don't take any short cuts. Use the best electrical connectors. Remember that your ride will have to come apart at some point so keep it serviceable. There are some many "builders" that hardwire handlebar switches and headlights. This is a really bad method when wiring your motorcycle since the only way to remove or replace these components is to cut the wires. If a male/female connector were installed from the beginning, cutting the harness would not be necessary. Use your factory service manual as a starting point. If you're going full-blown custom, there are so many good ideas to choose from in the service manual. Don't try to reinvent the wheel. The factory has been building electrical systems for over a hundred years and they know what they're doing.

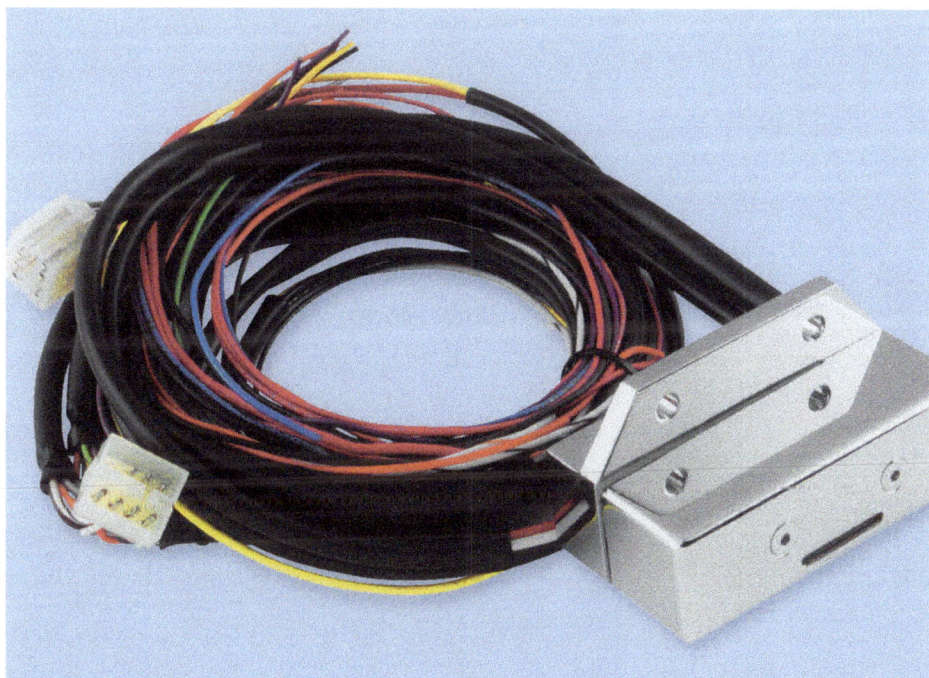

Wire Plus makes harness kits with an integral module. Different models are designed to place the module in different locations depending on your preference.

Chapter Eight

Tools

An Essential Part of the Job

You can't weld without a welder and you can't overhaul an engine without a good set of hand tools. And you can't install or repair a wiring harness without some specific wiring tools. From a soldering iron to a high-quality crimper, there are a few things you've just got to have. Shown here are tools used in two different "Harley" shops. You don't have to have everything seen here, but you do need most of the items. And even if you absolutely, positively don't have to have all of these, you know you can't have too many tools.

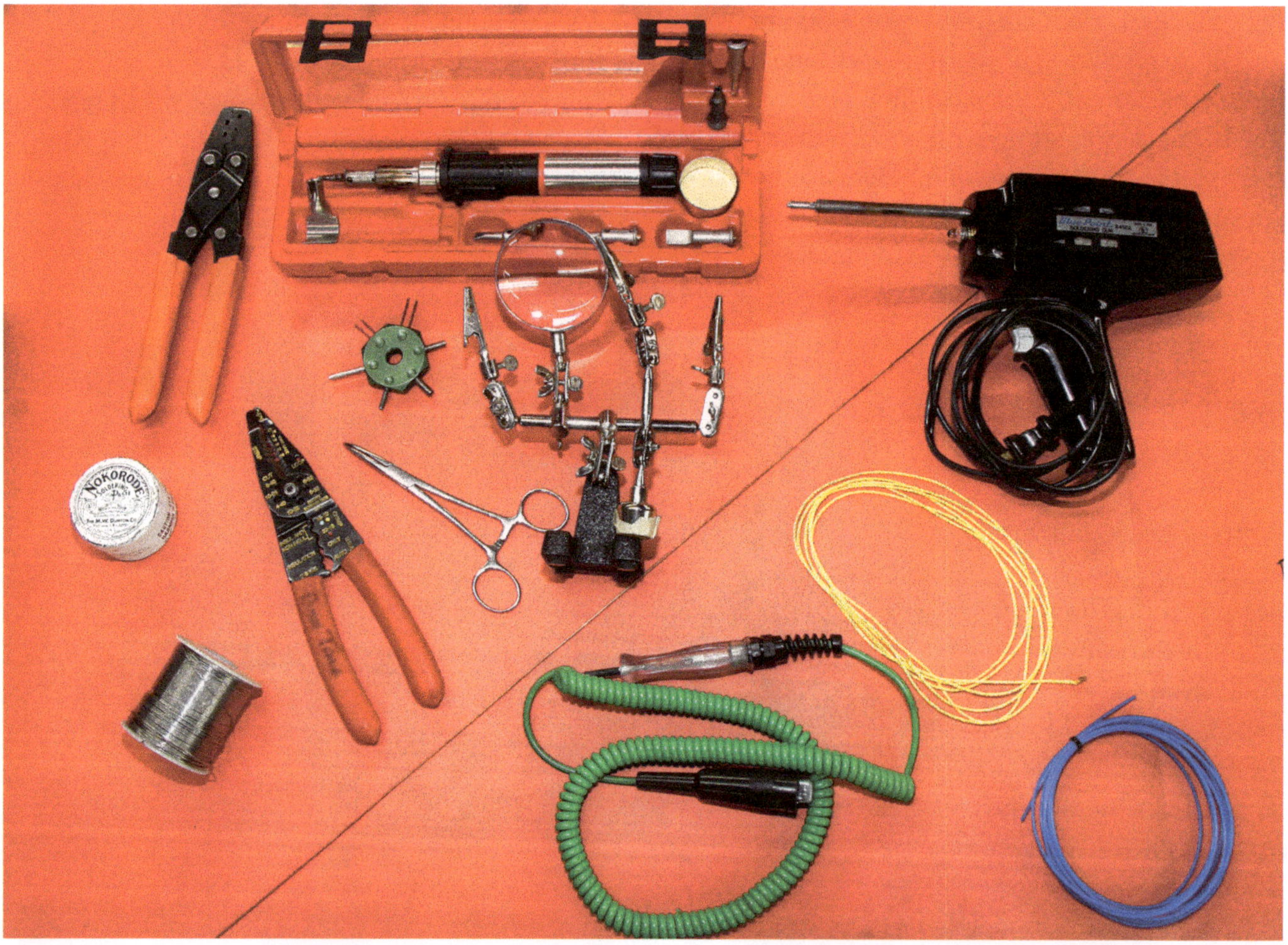

A look at the variety of tools Don Tima used to assemble the scratch-built harness seen in Chapter Nine.

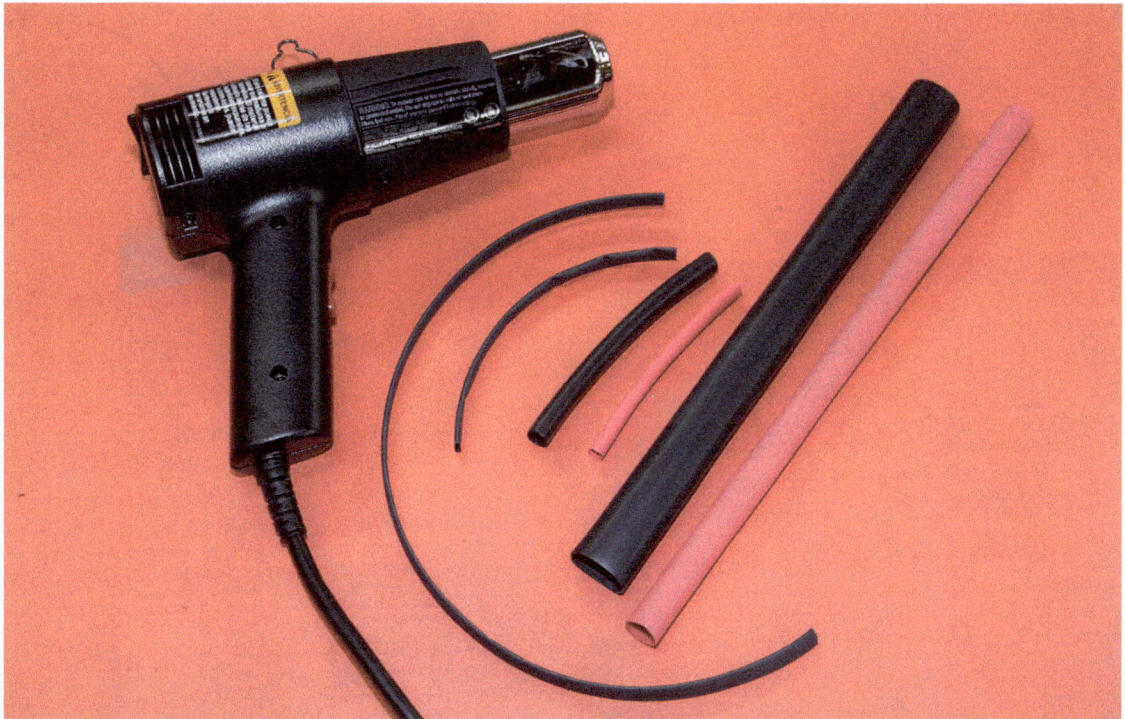

Some people use hair dryers or cigar lighters, but a true heat gun is the tool of choice for shrinking the shrink tubing.

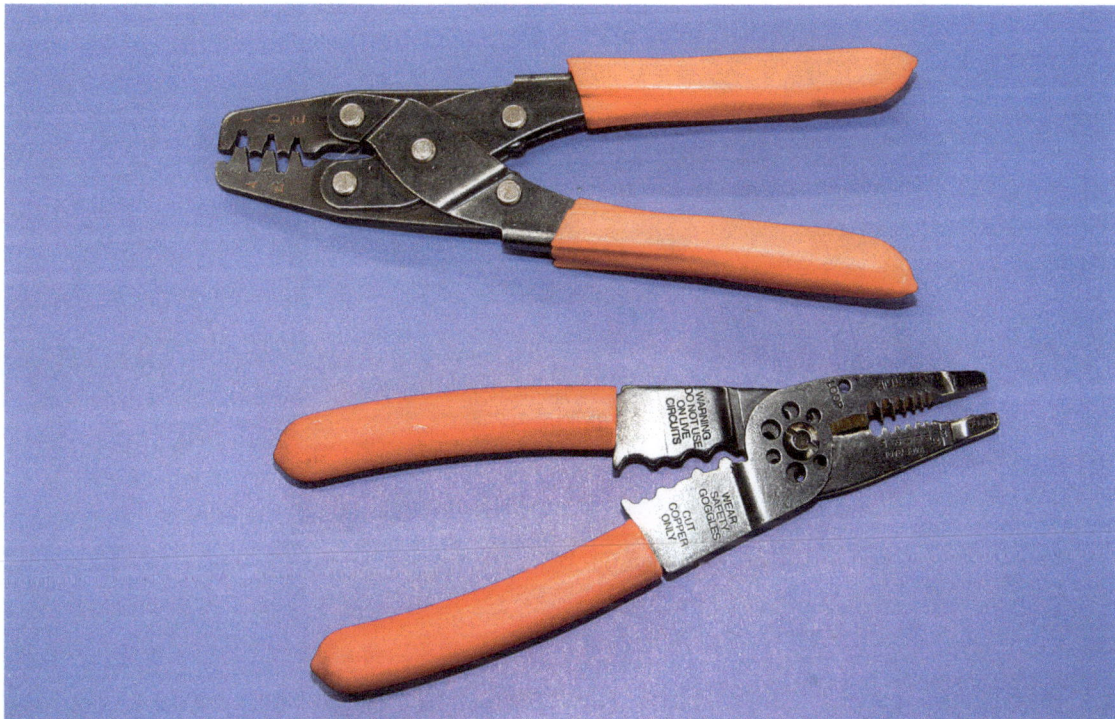

You need a wire striper, seen on the bottom, and a good quality crimper. As always, you can go cheap on these items and wish later you hadn't.

At least one good multi meter is a very nice thing to have in the tool box. The better ones have more scales, and include an inductive pickup to measure the amount of amperage moving though circuits - even those like a starter circuit with heavy draw.

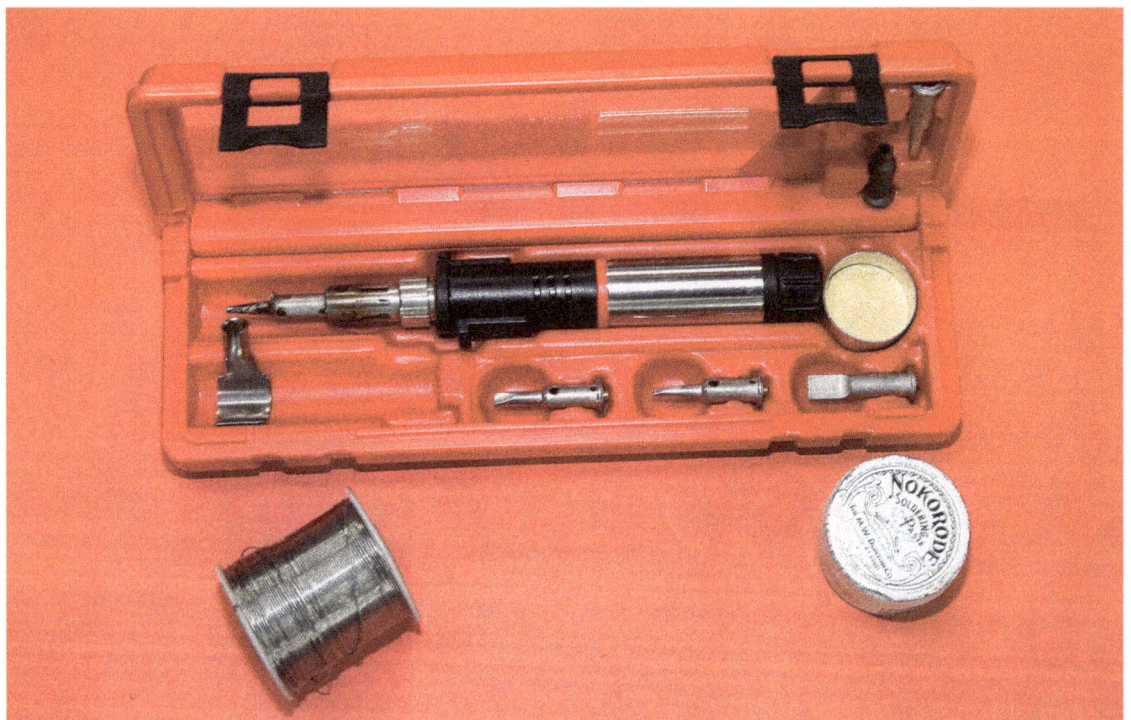

Though it might seem extravagant, this little butane-fired soldering iron has two huge advantages: lots of heat and no power cord.

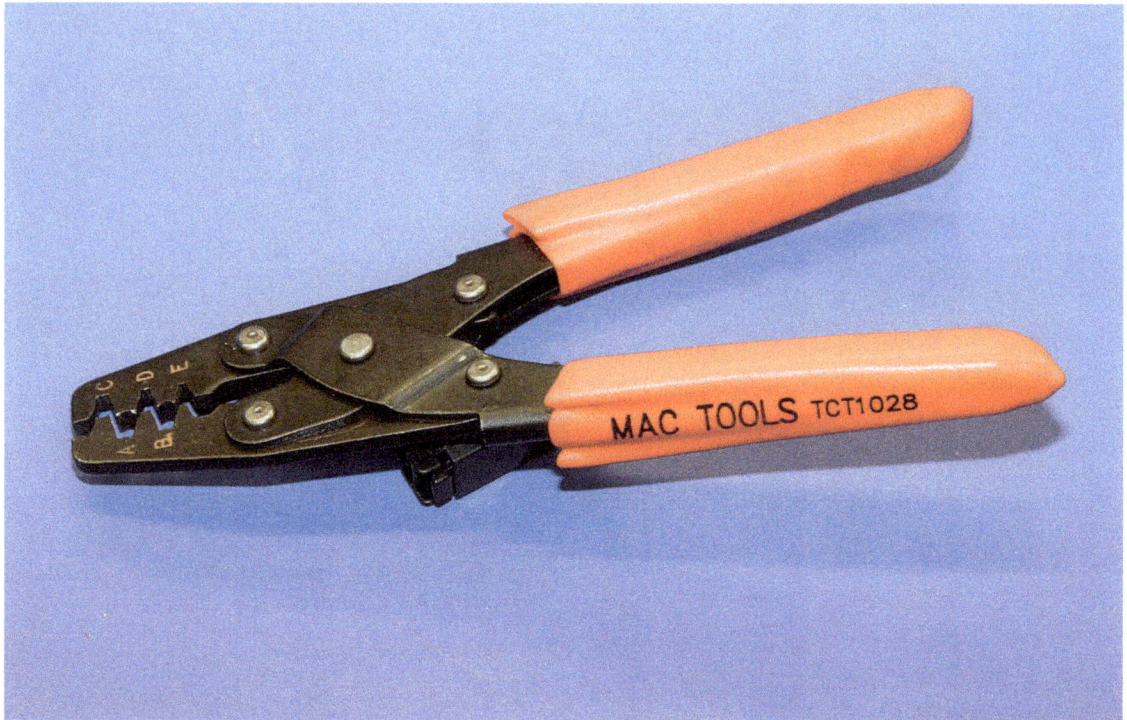

You can't do the nice double-crimp required of most electrical pins without a really good crimper. This particular model is easy to find and works with both Deutsch and earlier-style systems.

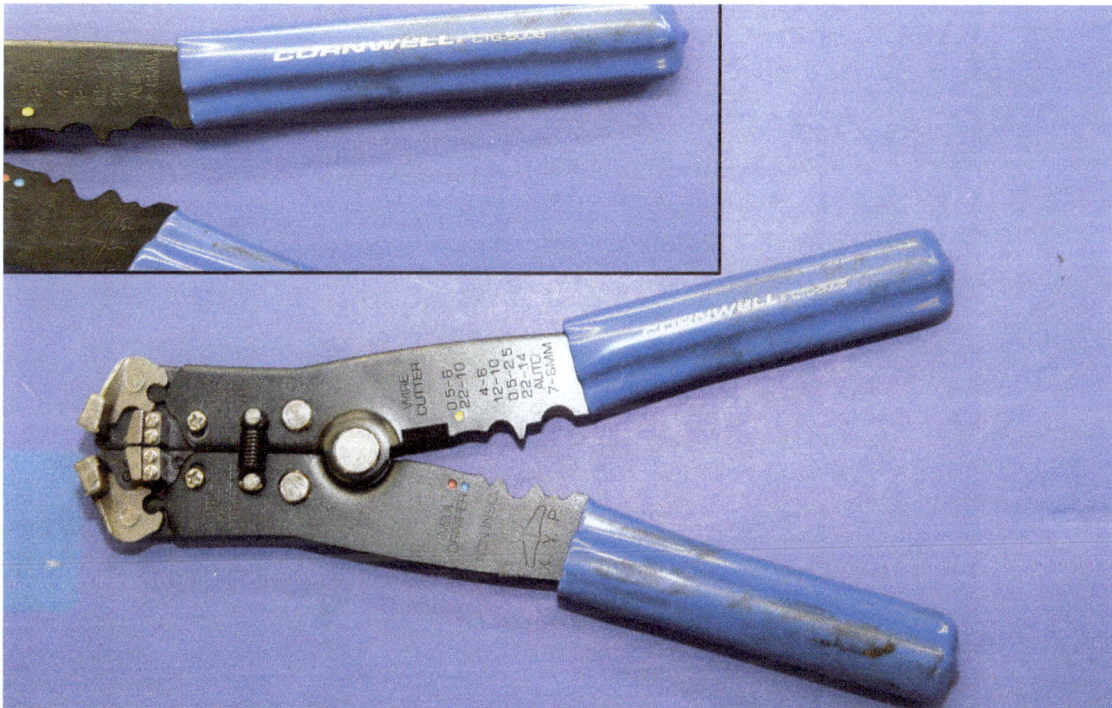

Even with a good pliers-style stripper you have to be careful when stripping the insulation off the wires so you don't cut any of the small copper conductors. This little tool will strip the insulation off most of the common smaller gauge wires with no muss and no fuss, and way quicker than the old-style strippers we all have on our tool boxes.

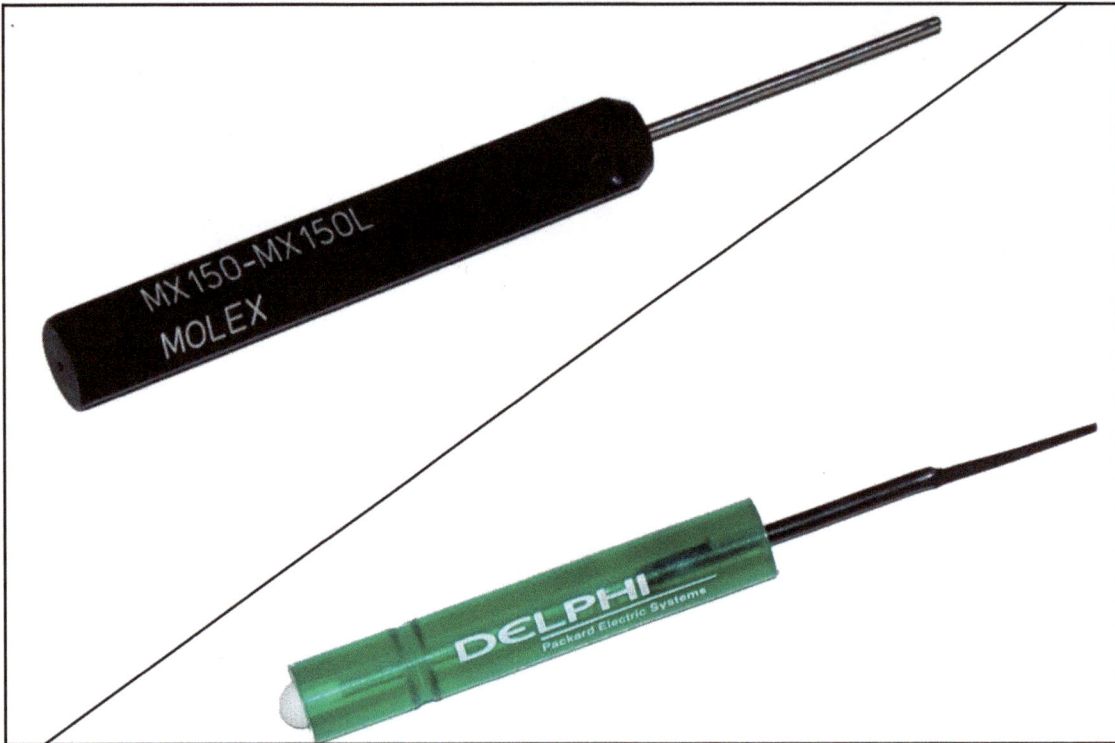

Top: This Molex removal tool is key when servicing any '07-up factory models. There's no better way to de-pin a male or female connector. Bottom: The NDP-422 is a universal removal tool that works with AMP Mulitilock and the entire Delphi lineup of connectors. NAMZ

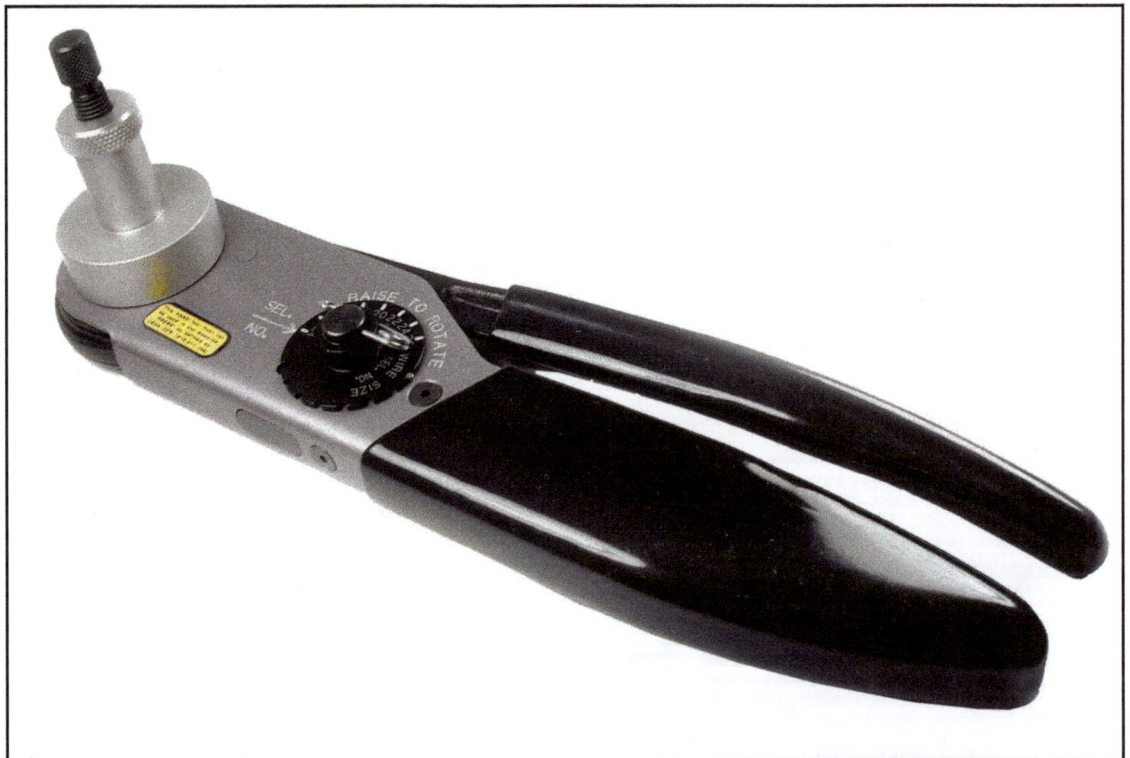

The once impossible to find Deutsch crimp tool has been found and NAMZ has it! This crimping tool will work with ALL Deutsch solid terminals for many wiregauges. Made by Deutsch so you'll get a perfect crimp everytime! DPCT-01. Use for solid pins. NAMZ

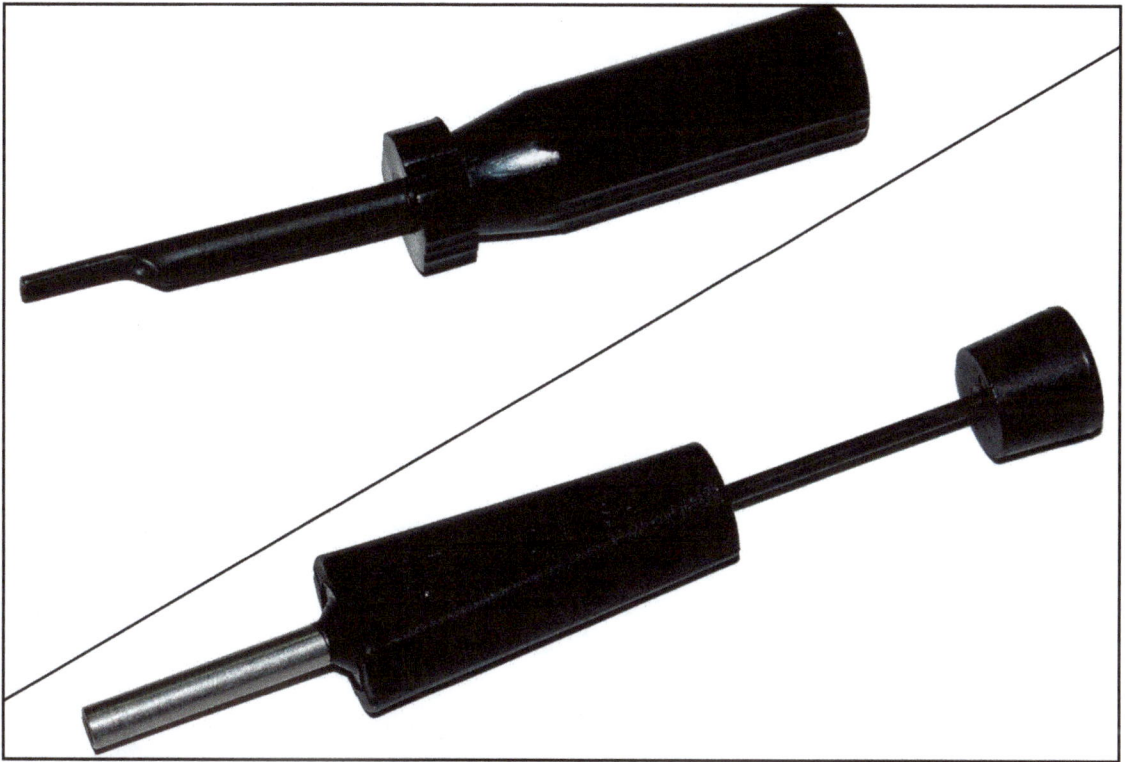

You have used other tools for AMP connectors on '84-'95 bikes, and they probably didn't work so well. These OEM removal tools are 100% perfect for the entire line of Mate-n-Lock Connectors! NMLRT-01 (Top) Female, NMLRT-02 (Bottom), male removal tool. NAMZ

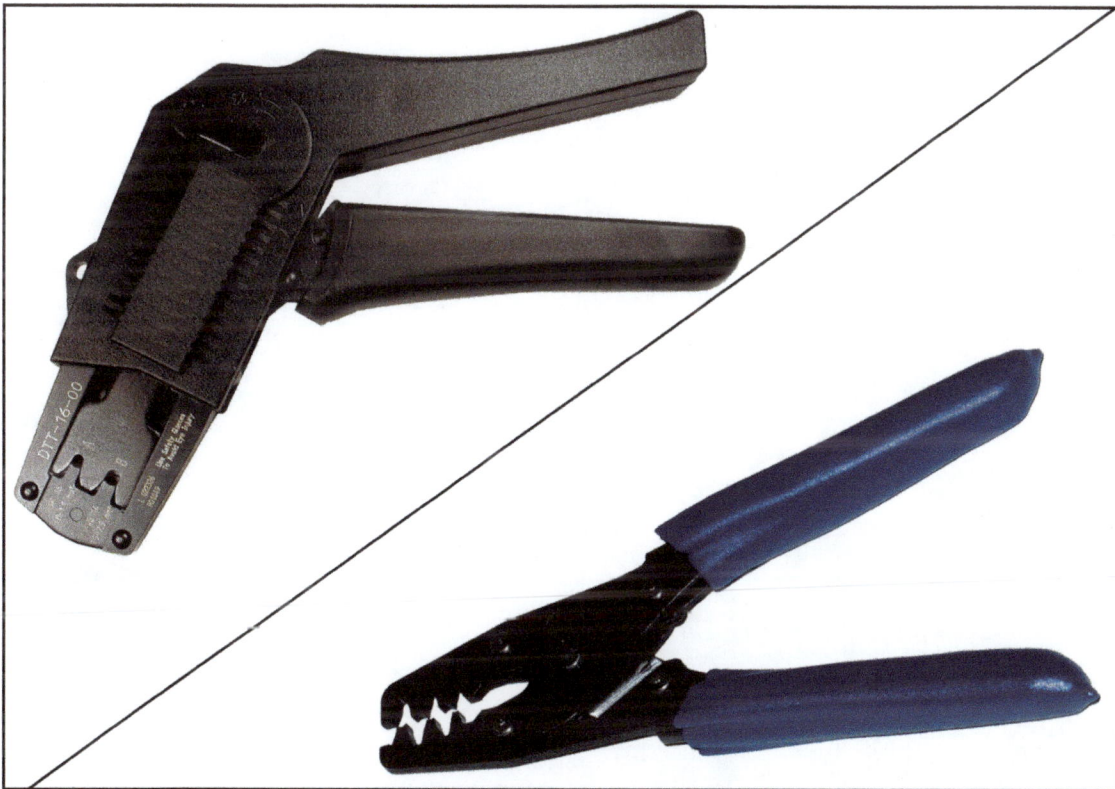

Top: made by Deutsch, this stamped crimp tool is designed for their stamped and formed terminals, and 14 - 16 gauge wires. Bottom: If you're working with Delphi crimp terminals or any other open style, U-barrel terminal, our universal crimp tool will do a perfect job every time. NAMZ

Chapter Nine

A Minimalist Harness

From Design to Installation

To document a complete start-to-finish scratch-built harness installation we made a visit to the Donnie Smith Custom Cycles shop in Blaine, Minnesota. When we arrived, Don Tima, ace mechanic for Donnie, was starting to build a harness for Dave Bodell's custom hardtail.

As we've discussed earlier in the book, the first step, and also one of the most important, is to plan out the job. This means you need not only a schematic but also a "map" that includes the location of each of the various electrical components.

The project seen here is the same project described in the text - a custom hardtail wired from scratch in the Donnie Smith Custom Cycles shop outside Minneapolis, Minnesota by resident mechanic Don Tima.

To quote Don Tima: "The person doing the wiring needs to decide what components will be used and where they will be located. What type of headlight will be used, if it's a halogen you need a good electrical plug because they draw more current. And if it's an LED taillight in back, then you can run lighter wires because they draw less current than a conventional bulb. You need to know things like, will the brake light switch be a banjo-style switch mounted off the rear master cylinder or a more typical pressure sensitive switch mounted on a T someplace between the master cylinder and the rear brake caliper? And will there be a front brake light switch?"

"You also have to know if the bike will use turn signals, and whether or not it uses idiot lights for oil pressure, hi beam and all the rest. If

it uses idiot lights then you need a neutral switch and oil press sender, and a wire for the hi beam indicator."

"Next, you need to know what kind of coil(s) you're using and where they will mount. Are you using an ignition switch with a start position, or do you want to a small starter button on the bars which means you probably want to use a starter relay? If the speedo requires a calibration unit you have to plan for that. And how nice do you want this to be, are all the wires going inside the bars and the frame tubes? If so then you need holes in the frame and the bars, and you want to be sure that the holes don't weaken the tubing. Any holes that are drilled need to be de-burred, so the wiring isn't cut by those sharp edges."

This particular bike uses no blinkers, one

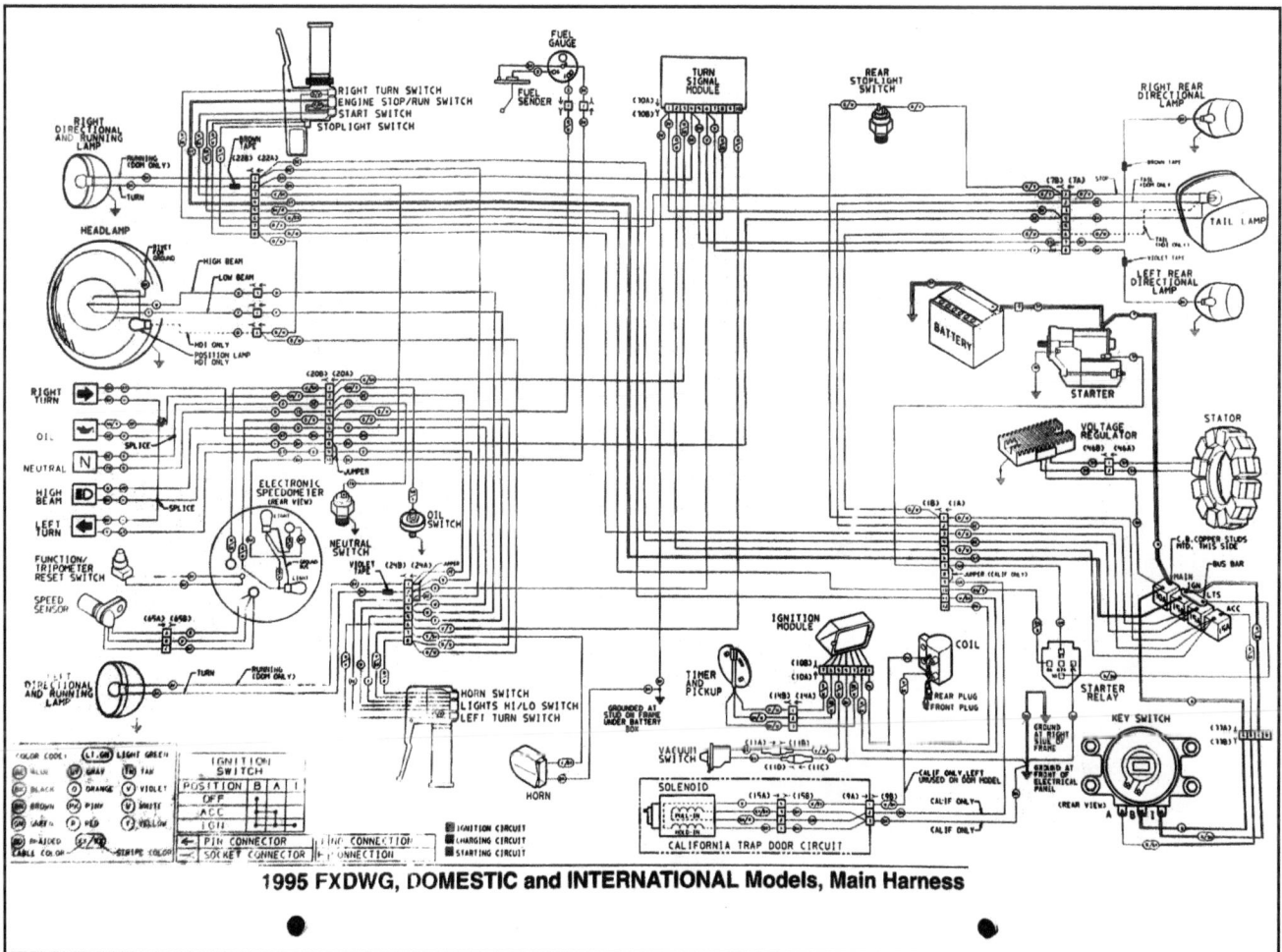

For his basic schematic, Don Tima uses the factory wiring diagram for an Evo-powered Dyna. Don's harness is, however, simpler than the harness represented here.

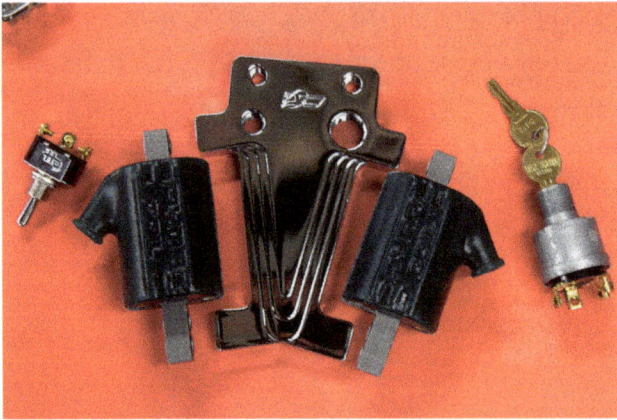

This bike puts the ignition switch and hi-low switch on the coil bracket. This particular switch has a start position, one that cancels power to the Acc terminal during cranking for better voltage to the solenoid.

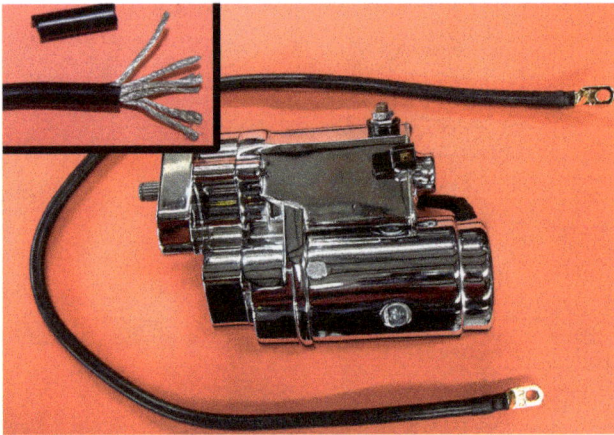

The cables are from Terry Components. Note how the cable itself is made up of small bundles of very fine wire - which means good flexibility and high current carrying capacity.

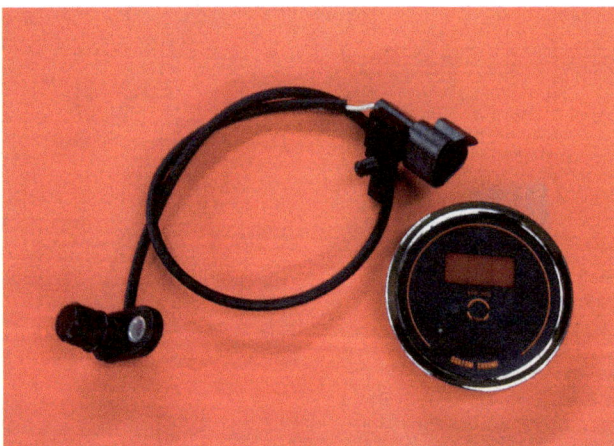

The speedometer is an aftermarket digital unit "driven" by the electronic sensor in the transmission.

multi-task digital gauge from Custom Chrome mounted to the handlebars, a standard halogen headlight, and an LED-style cat's eye taillight assembly mounted chopper style on the right side of the bike. The Dyna coils are mounted in a Donnie Smith bracket that hangs on the left side of the engine. This same bracket houses the ignition switch and the hi-low switch for the headlight. The ignition is a single-fire HI-4 from Crane. To protect the wiring the plan calls for three circuit breakers: one 30-amp breaker mounted in the battery box; and two, 15-amp breakers (one for the ignition, and one for "accessories" which includes the lights) mounted on the inside of the coil bracket.

THE WIRING BEGINS

Don starts the actual wiring at the headlight. Once the headlight is mounted, the three wires coming out of the housing are enclosed in shrink wrap. A lot of builders run only two wires to the headlight, one hi beam and one low beam. In these situations the headlight grounds to the triple trees and through the neck bearings to the main frame. At Donnie's shop they like to have a third wire on the headlight that runs all the way back to a good ground point on the main frame or all the way to the negative terminal on the battery. As Don Tima says, "a bad ground can cause all kinds of problems, including a melted headlight plug.

There are two sub-harnesses that begin at the front of the bike, one is the 3-wire headlight harness and the other comes from the gauge unit. The harness that starts at the gauge is routed down the top tube first. Some of these wires run all the way back to the battery box area and some will exit through a hole just above the motor mount on the bike's left side (page 130).

Routing the wires down the main frame tube is done by a variety of means. In some cases Don just tapes the wires together and pushes them down the tube until he can see them at the next hole. Then it's just a matter of reaching up into the tube with the hemostat to grab the wires and pull them out at the coil area.

92

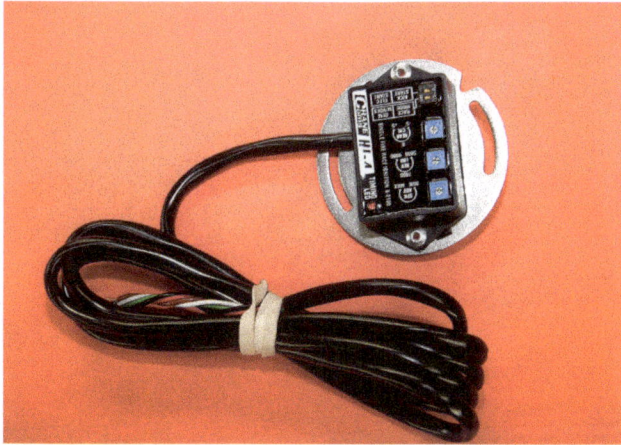

Don likes the Crane HI 4 because it's been proven to be very durable and trouble free.

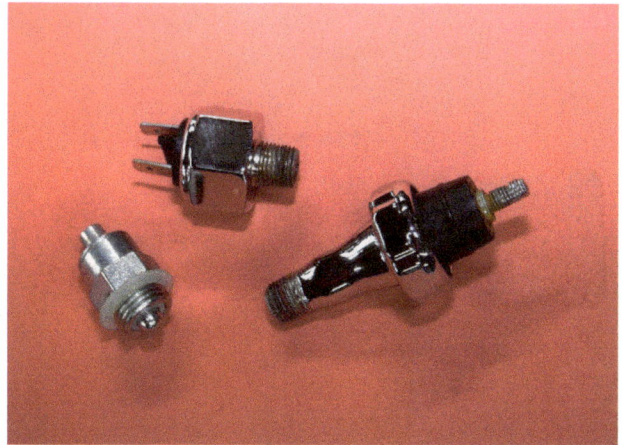

The "senders" used on this bike include the neutral indicator for the transmission, the pressure sensor for the brake light and the oil pressure sender.

The headlight is a standard H4 halogen unit.

Chopper style taillight is a LED version of the popular cat's eye light, which means long life and low current draw.

The complete charging circuit, a typical 32 amp aftermarket system. Note the bracket for mounting of the regulator.

Don uses 2, 15 amp breakers as shown, one for the ignition, and one for accessories - which means lights in this case. There will also be a main, 30A breaker.

1. Here Don runs the wires from the gauge unit into the top tube. These wires are broken down into 2 groups...

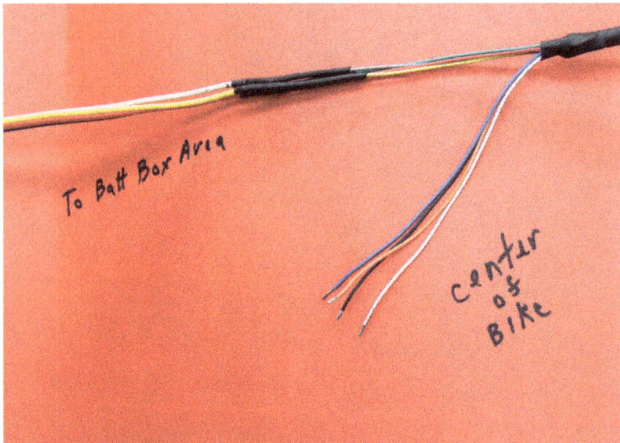

To Batt Box Area

center of Bike

2. ...one group that goes all the way back to the battery box area, and another that will exit near the top motor mount.

4. Once all the wires from the gauge have been pulled through the top tube and out the hole, Don attaches another pull wire to get the longer wires all the way back to the battery box.

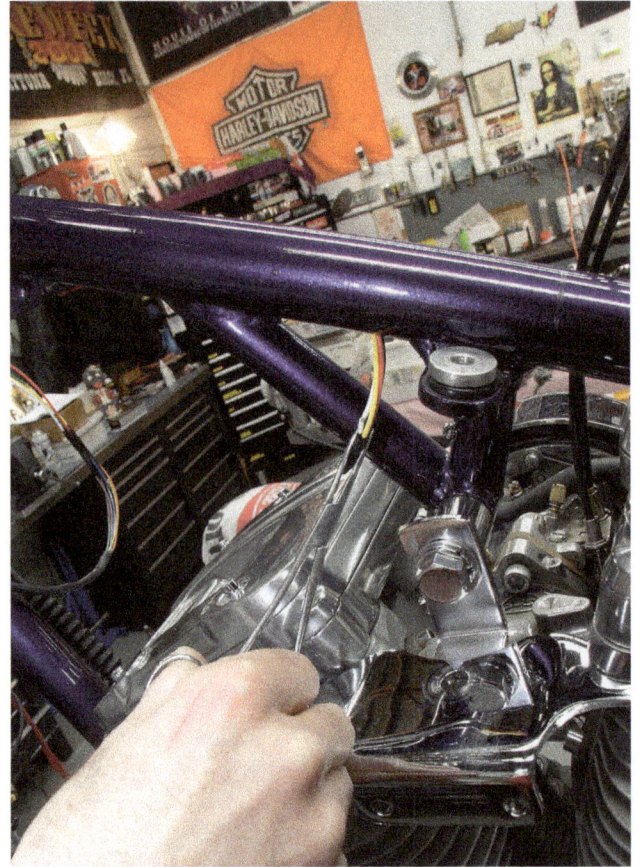

3. Here you can see Don pull all the wires from the gauge out of the hole just above the motor mount.

In the case of the harness coming from the gauge, some of the wires are long enough to go all the way to the battery box area while others are shorter, meant to reach only as far as the coil area. Don pulls the whole harness through to the coil area, then separates the ones that go farther back from those that will be attached to the ignition and lighting switches. Those that are meant to go back to the battery box area are grouped together, and with the help of a pull wire (made from a light piece of welding rod), are routed though the top tube to exit just above the oil tank.

The next harness to be fed into the top tube is the three-wire headlight harness. Because there's already one harness in the tube, Don uses the pull wire to ensure the harness exits at the coil area without any hassles.

1. Here you can see the wires as they exit just above the oil tank and battery box.

2. Now Don gathers up the wires from the headlight...

4. You can see the gauge wires already in place and pulled snug, and the headlight wires just ready to be pulled into place.

3. ...slides them into the top tube. Don did decide to use a pull wire for this task (not shown here).

Here are the headlight wires as they exit the top tube. Because both the ignition switch and the hi-low switch mount to the coil bracket, this is where these wires need to be.

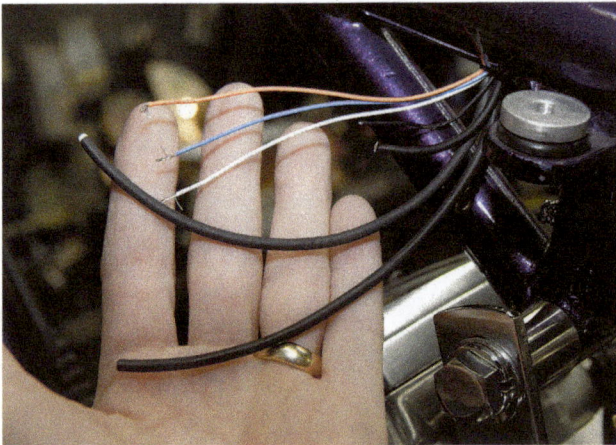

Inventory, here are the light gauge wires, and the heavier headlight wires. Sometimes it's necessary to peel back part of the shrink wrap to see the color code.

Don tapped the frame and will ground the headlight and gauge here. The other screw is for a wire that will run all the way back to the negative battery post.

A Good Ground

To make sure the electrical system is well grounded Don combines the ground wire coming from the headlight with the ground wire for the gauge unit and solders both wires into one terminal. This terminal is then attached to the frame under one of the screws that thread into the frame tubing that supports the upper motor mount. There are two screws in this area, the other one will be used to run a ground wire back to the negative battery terminal. As Don keeps repeating, "good grounds are an essential part of a good wiring job."

After a group of wires are pulled through a hole in the frame Don makes sure they are protected by shrink-wrap tube, "If the wires aren't already in shrink wrap, I like to push shrink tubing onto the wires far enough that it will protect the wire where it comes through the frame hole, especially if the hole has any roughness at the edges. And when you heat the tubing you do have to be careful with the heat gun that you don't blister the paint."

The next harness to be routed into the top tube is the three-wire harness that runs from the battery box to the coil area. The three wires are: one wire that runs from the main 30-amp breaker to feed the ignition switch (the B terminal), one that runs from the starter "trigger" terminal on the starter, to the ignition switch (the S terminal). And one that will be used to power the taillight and hot side of the brake light switch that runs to the Acc position on the ignition switch. These three wires are pulled through from the battery box area to the coil area with a pull wire that Don solders to the wires.

The Other Harness

There is another harness already installed in the bike, and that is the (mostly) ignition harness that comes from the Crane HI-4 ignition, out the bottom of the cone cover, then up the center frame post where the wires exit just above the oil tank. The Crane harness contains five wires, though some of the wires won't be needed

continued page 99

4. Here are the wires that go to the back side of the coil bracket before Don installs pins and a terminal.

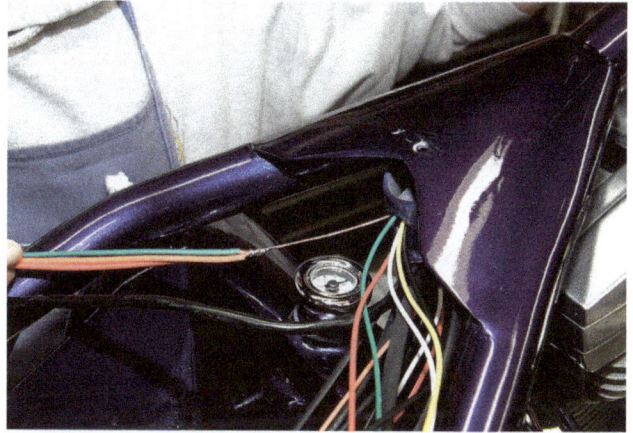

1. Next, Don pulls three wires from the battery box area up through the top tube to the motor mount areas.

2. Here are the same 3 wires exiting the frame at the motor mount. One will bring power from the main breaker, one is from the starter trigger and one goes to Acc position on the ignition switch.

3. After the wires have exited the frame Don puts shrink wrap on each one. He's careful to push it far enough onto the wire that it will act as a chafe protector where the wire exits the hole in the frame tube. If there's any doubt, he puts a second piece of heavy duty shrink tube on the wire where it exits the frame tube.

Soldering

1. To start, strip the insulation off the end of the wire. Next, dip that end into the flux which will help draw the solder into the joint.

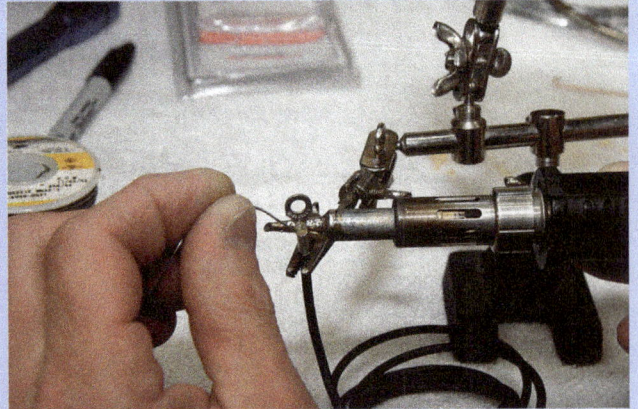

2. Now crimp the connector onto the wire, note there is no insulation on this connector.

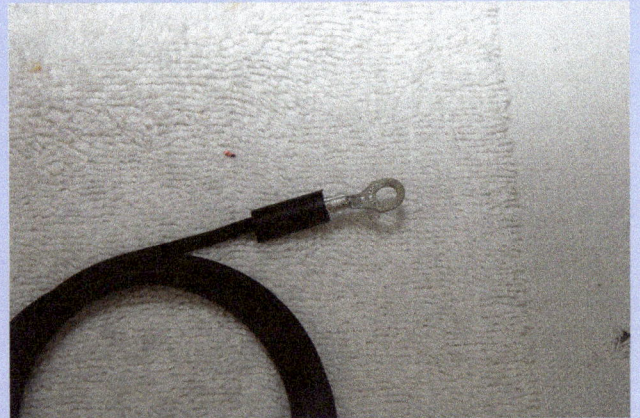

3. Set the crimped connector into the little handy vise, what Don Tima calls his, "extra set of hands."

4. Heat the connector from the back side and allow the solder to be drawn into the connection. Try not to over-do it, just solder the connection.

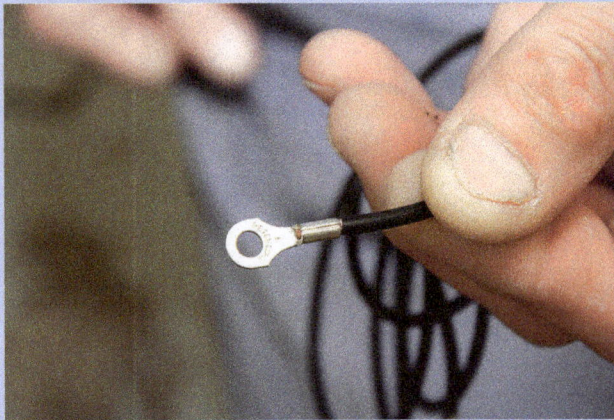

5. Slip the small piece of heat shrink, the one you cut and slid over the wire earlier, up onto the base of the connector.

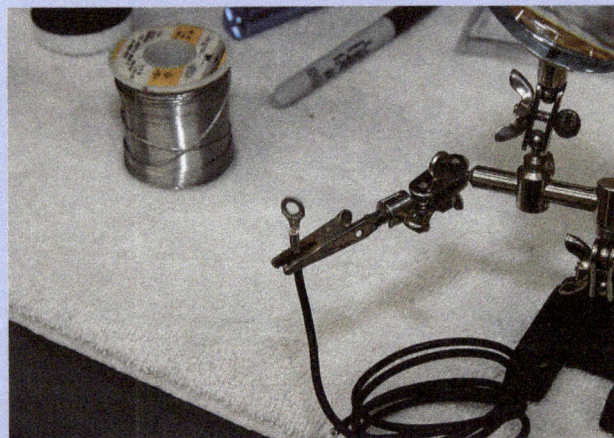

6. A little heat and you're all done. A connection that looks factory fresh.

for this application. This harness is pulled through the top tube to the coil/motor mount area.

THE COIL BRACKET

On this bike the coil bracket also houses the ignition switch, the hi-low headlight switch, and two, 15-amp circuit breakers. In order to make the bike as serviceable as possible Don groups all these wires together into a harness, which runs to a 8-pin terminal block. The other half of the terminal block will be connected to the wires coming out of the frame in the same area. In this way, if the coil bracket needs to come off for any reason, it's an easy matter to just unbolt the two screws that mount the bracket to the top engine mount bracket and unplug the whole affair.

BATTERY AND BATTERY BOX

Most custom bikes take a standard "Softail" battery. Don uses a battery that places the negative terminal on the left when both terminals are pointed forward. There are a couple of interesting things to note about how a professional shop deals with both the battery and the battery box. To make access to the main stud on the solenoid easier, Don already cut a hole in the bottom of the battery box. The cables themselves are very high quality cables from Terry Components, And rather than just buy them in a length that's as close to correct as possible, Don cuts them to length and then solders on a new terminal. The battery itself sits on a cushion pad from Drag Specialties which helps to absorb a measure of vibration and lengthen the battery's life. You also need to use a good tie down strap, again to minimize vibration.

The main, 30-amp, breaker is positioned in the lower right corner of the battery box. Small insulated covers are used on both wires that run to the circuit breakers, so in case someone drops a wrench or screwdriver down into the cavity alongside the battery there will be no sparks or melted wires. Finally, though everyone has their favorites, at the Donnie Smith shop they think the batteries from Milwaukee offer the best bang for the buck.

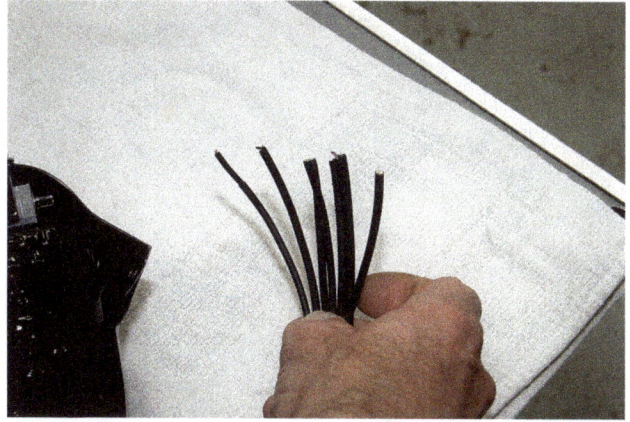

These are the wires from the back side of the coil bracket, each gets a pin and will be inserted in a terminal block to match up with the other half of the terminal (seen on page 136).

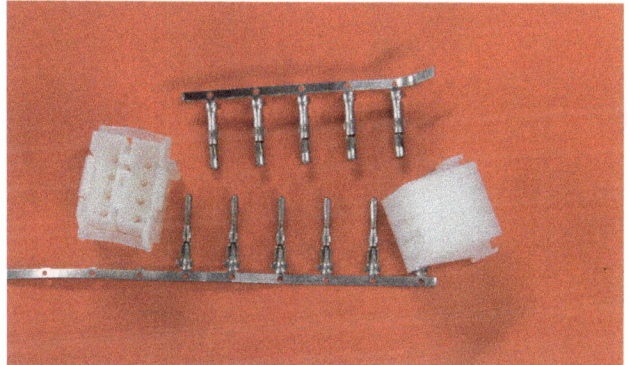

These are the pre-Deutsch connectors and pins that Don used for most of this wiring project. When you insert the pins in the terminal block, be sure the little tabs snap into place so the pin can't back out, "if you listen there's a little 'click' when they seat correctly."

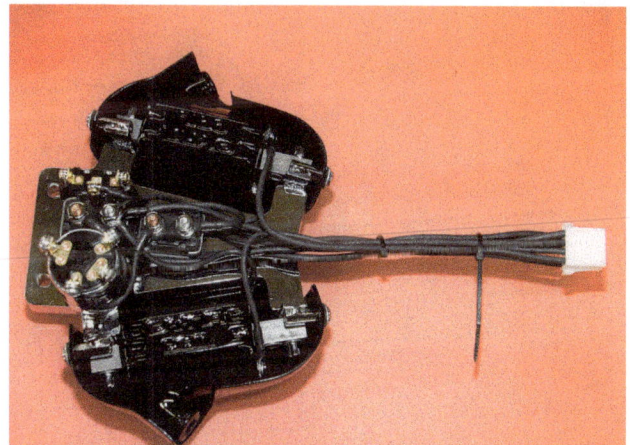

The finished coil bracket, complete with plug-in terminal for easy installation and removal, ignition and hi-low switch, and two circuit breakers.

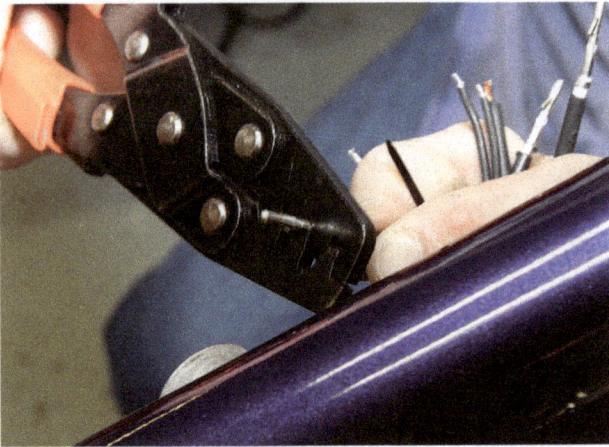

Each of the wires gathered above the motor mount must be stripped and then have a pin crimped on.

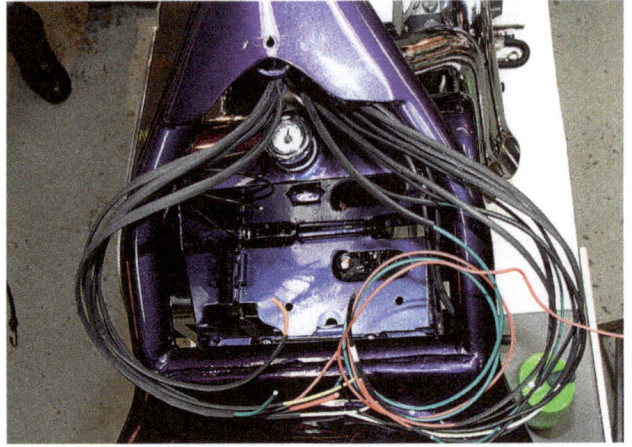

Here you can see how Don has the two main groups of wires grouped and organized on either side of the battery box.

Then each pin is inserted into the terminal block.

Don puts the main, 30 amp, breaker in the lower corner of the battery box.

Small pieces of aluminum are available and can be used to "bridge" two terminals.

He drilled a small hole and used a small machine screw to mount the breaker bracket securely to the battery box. Note the hole in the bottom of the box, which provides access to the starter terminal.

Crimping In Style

Whether the pins and terminals you use are Deutsch or the earlier versions, they must be carefully crimped onto the wire using a two-step crimp - first onto the wire itself and then onto the insulation. Only a high quality crimper will do an adequate job.

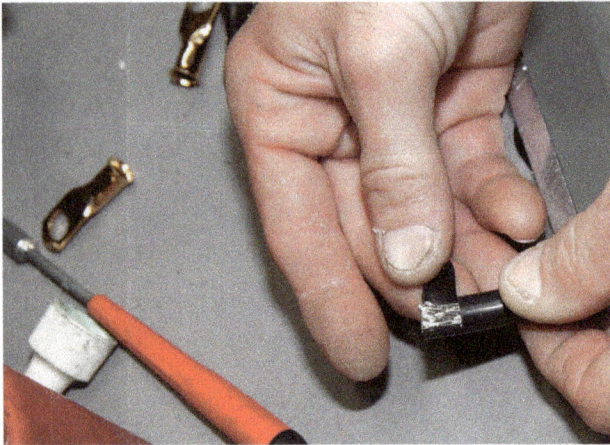

After cutting the battery cable to the correct length Don Strips back just enough insulation.

Followed by a piece of red (this is the positive cable) shrink wrap.

After putting some soldering flux in the terminal Don melts the whole thing full of solder...

Here the wires are connected to the main breaker, and one of the small insulating covers is in place.

...then while keeping it nice and hot he inserts the cable. Don "indexes" the wire and cable so the cable won't be twisted once it's installed.

Time now to connect the wires that come down the top tube (on the rider's left) with those that come up through the center seat post. Again, each will get a pin and be inserted into the terminal block.

CONNECTING THE TWO HARNESSES

At this point the two main sections of harness are in place. One starts at the front: the headlight and gauge harnesses run down the top tube to the coil area and the battery box. And another three-wire group runs up the tube from the battery box area to the coil area (note the photo on the top-right on page 136).

The other main group of wires includes the ignition wires and a few additional wires that come up through the frame's seat tube (or the area just under the oil tank) to the battery box area. This group includes the small harness that runs to the taillight.

Essentially, these two groups of wires, or harnesses, need to be connected. After carefully sorting the wires Don connects them with a male and female terminal block much as he did with the wires that go to the coil and ignition switch.

DETAILS

These two groups of wires are identified as follows (The number refers to the gauge. Colors for the oil pressure sender and neutral wire were chosen to match the gauge-wire color, otherwise the colors are Harley-Davidson colors). The wires coming up from the center tube and those grouped on the right side of the oil tank include:

16 green, from starter trigger, will connect to the ignition switch.

14 black, wire from voltage regulator to the positive post of the battery.

18 green, from neutral light switch, will connect to the gauge.

18 orange, hot wire that runs to the positive side of the hydraulic brake light switch, this same wire powers the taillight.

16 red, to brake lights.

16 red, from the oil pressure sensor, will connect to the gauge.

There are three additional wires from the speedo sensor:

16 white, signal wire.

16 black, ground.

14 red, brings power from ignition switch.

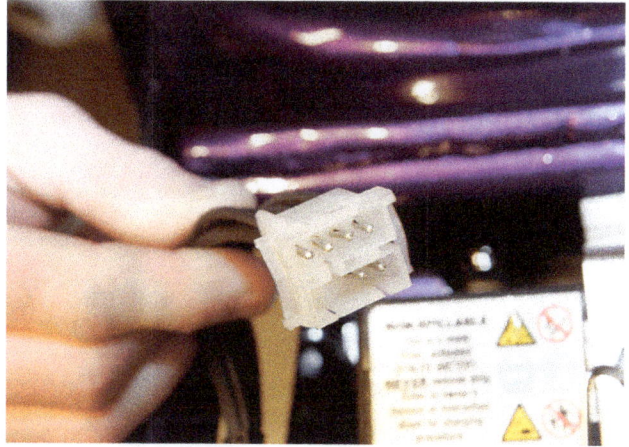

Here's one of the terminal blocks that connect the two "halves" of the harness.

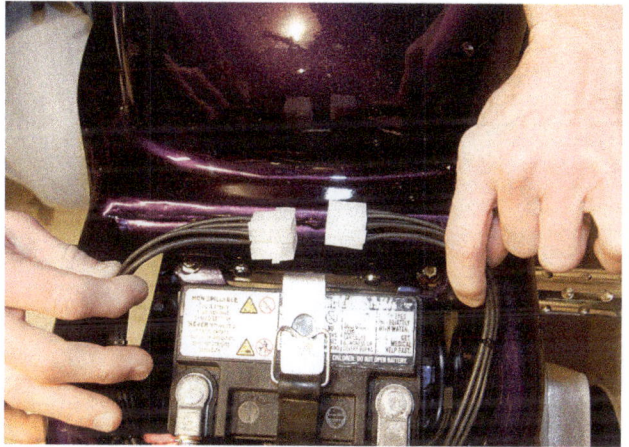

With two terminal blocks in place...

...the two major parts of the harness can be connected. Now the ignition switch is connected to the starter, and to the battery, for example.

Q&A: Andy Anderson

Andy Anderson, and his wife Sherry, run Anderson Studios, where they make T-shirts and other apparel for everyone from Dave Perewitz to Garth Brooks. Hidden away in their building is a full blown motorcycle shop and this is where you're likely to find Andy anytime he's not sleeping or running a T-shirt press. A long-time motorcycle nut and a very talented painter, Andy recently completed the construction of a pro-street custom. What follows is a short interview with Andy, discussing such things as which harness he used and why.

Andy, tell us briefly about the project, the wiring part of it in particular.

Basically we built a pro street bike without a lot of fabrication. We used lots of off-the-shelf products to keep it straightforward. That's why we tried to keep the wiring as simple as we could, I didn't want to build a harness from scratch. Also, this bike has the buttons on the bars, and turn signals and a brake light switch in the front master cylinder, so we were dealing with all of that. A kit seemed easier.

Which wiring harness kit did you use?

We bought a Wire Plus Z-1, in-frame harness. We put the module right behind the oil bag on this soft tail, though you could put it someplace else. The kit is pretty much all inclusive, it has a built in load equalizer, starter relay and breakers, the only thing that's outside the box is the 30 amp main breaker. This kit has provisions for blinkers and han-

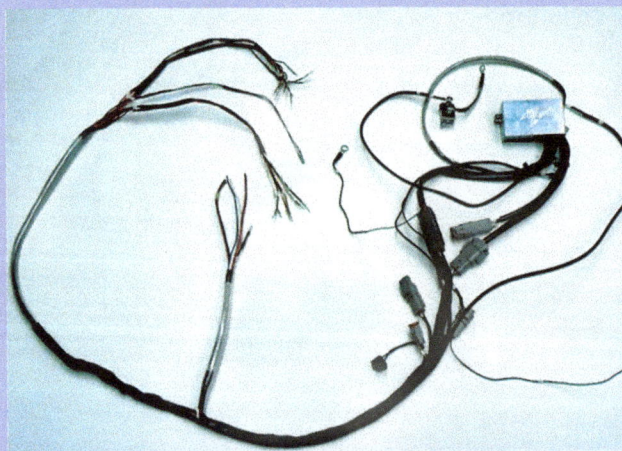

This particular WP harness kit is designed for a bike with blinkers and handlebar switches.

dlebar switches. The wires are color coded and marked. The one we bought had the wires already routed into sub-harnesses in shrink wrap. If I did it over I would buy the one that wasn't wrapped, because we had to open it up due to the location of some of our components.

What other products did you use during the wiring part of the project?

I called Jeff Zielinski from NAMZ and he set us up with some small multi connectors, some Deutsch connectors, the braided stainless covering and some little mini connectors that work really well with the small 22 gauge wires that come off the Russ Wernimont taillight. Jeff also sold us the Accel crimping tool and it works great.

Did you do all the wiring during the mock up?

My friend Clyde McCullough did most of the mock up, during the process we decided where parts would mount and how the wires would run.

What kind of tips can you pass along to anyone else who's going to wire a bike like you did?

The wires that run inside the frame are protected by heat shrink tubing, but we also used the braided stainless to protect the wires where they come out of the frame. The stainless was used for cosmetic reasons and also to protect the wires.

What kind of problems did you encounter?

The main problem was the harness, it wasn't long enough. Our kit was made to have the connections or terminal blocks under the tank, and we made our connections in the headlight bucket. The wires weren't long enough to reach to the headlight. We called them though and they sent an extension kit which was color coded and worked great.

What would your advice be to someone who is installing wiring in a custom bike?

Consider the options available with aftermarket harness kits. There's a chopper wiring kit I looked at recently and it's really small and compact and easy to hide for a simple bike. For a more complex bike you can buy one like we did with provisions for turn signals and anything else. For a guy in his garage a harness kit solves a lot of headaches and makes it painless. You just have to figure out where you're going to mount the module and then just go from there.

The Other Half

The other half of the wiring harness (those grouped on the left side of the battery box) include the following:

14 red, from ignition switch B terminal, will connect to the main, 30 amp, breaker.

16 green, from the ignition switch, S terminal, will connect to the starter trigger.

18 green, from the neutral light on the gauge, will connect to switch on the tranny.

18 red, from oil light on gauge, will connect to the sender.

16 orange, from ignition switch Acc terminal (sometimes called I or Ign) will provide power to brake and taillights.

16 white, (actually grey) from speedo, will connect to the signal wire.

16 black, ground.

FINALLY

The trick now is to connect all these wires. As you can see in the nearby photos, the wires are grouped together and run on either side of the battery. One of the final steps is to put a male or female pin on each wire, insert that pin into the right spot in the terminal block and then plug the two "halves" of the wiring harness together, turn the key and have a running motorcycle.

Final assembly, the fully assembled coil bracket ready to be bolted in place.

With painted coil covers, the finished job makes for a very, very neat installation.

The finished bike with a minimalist wiring harness in place. No blinkers and no handlebar switches. Just an ignition switch with a start position, and a hi-low headlight switch on the coil bracket. Because the ignition switch has a start position, and is designed to carry current to the starter trigger, there is no starter relay used on this bike.

Chapter Ten

Changes

Year by Year Updates

2007 MODEL YEAR CHANGES

Since the initial release of this book back in 2007, there have been many changes throughout the Harley Davidson lineup. It was a great year for Sportster and Big Twin's alike as fuel injection was new for XL models and the 88 cubic inch Twin Cam became a 96 inch cubic inch along with a 6-speed transmission - gaining an extra five-hundred RPM in sixth gear on the highway was in my opinion one of the greatest factory changes next to Delphi fuel injection. Riders have been asking for it and now they got it. Sportster's rubber mounted (since 2004) and fuel injected engine was a serious upgrade for Harley's entry-level model. A much

If there's one bike, one model, that represents the factory's willingness and ability to continually tweak the product line to produce bikes that are hugely popular, it has to be the Street Glide. Harley-Davidson

more comfortable and smooth ride made the Sportster a bit more desirable for novice riders as well.

Big twins with that sixth gear and larger 1540cc engine helped spike up sales for the factory as *you had to have the latest and greatest* if you were a true HD die hard. But along with the positives also came some negatives, but you knew that, or at least you should have as the first model year for anything usually has some bugs that need to be worked out. The 96 inch motor was no exception. There was a serious heat problem that the engine, or more importantly its owner, needed to contend with. Along with larger cylinders and pistons comes much more heat, and an air-cooled engine needs a lot of air movement to keep cool. Since heat has always been an issue, and all Harley models except for the V-Rod are air cooled, the factory's attempt at a fix was feeble at best. The factory's answer was to have riders bring in their 96 inch model for a download. This quick flash to the ECM basically forced the rear cylinder, (the hottest one) to shut down when the temperature reached 280-degrees. This is also considered "parade mode" and is a user option beginning on 2009 models. Simply roll your throttle backward past idle, hold it there for a few seconds with the bike hot, stopped and the engine idling, watch your cruise control light and it will change from green to yellow (off) or from yellow to green (on).

Progress: though the Twin Cam started out at 88 cubic inches, mated to a five speed tranmission, it soon grew to 96, 103 and 110 cubes, mated to a six-speed tranny.

Look Ma, no throttle cables. Used first on the Bagger models, Throttle By Wire means the elimination of those ugly and hard-to-route cables.

2008 MODEL YEAR CHANGES

In 2008, the factory made some changes that brought them closer in line with the automobile industry. One of the most noticeable changes was the introduction of throttle by wire or TBW. Cars and planes have had a similar version called "fly-by-wire" for years so the technology is proven. The introduction of TBW arrived on the 2008 Glide (Street Glide, Road Glide and Ultra) models and was not a user option. It took some getting used to for most riders as there was a noticeable delay in throttle response - but TBW was definitely a step into the future for the factory.

One of the nicer things about throttle-by-wire is doing away with the ugly pair of push-pull throttle and idle cables. It's hard to believe how many little issues are resolved when the cable are eliminated: no more adjustments, no need to lubricate, no worry that they might break, no need (for some) to replace them with braided stainless steel, and no worry about how to route them to keeping a nice clean look. For most riders however, it is still a change that takes some getting used to.

That being said, the wiring for the TBW is

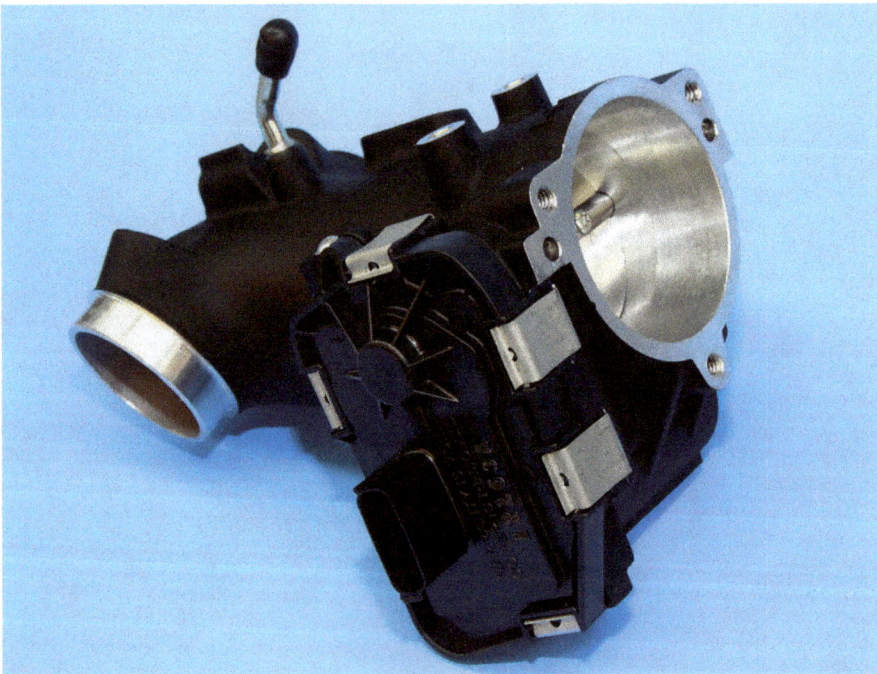

At the other end of the missing throttle cables you will find an electronic throttle body.

routed inside the handlebar and attaches via a black, 6-position Molex MX-150 MALE connector. *NOTE, industry standard states the gender of a connector is based on the TERMINALS inside the connector.* This really cleans up the handlebar area and also keeps the wiring safe from the elements. You can find the Molex connector in the headlight nacelle on a Road King or inside the fairing on Street Glides, Road Glides and Ultra models. There are (6) 22-gauge wires in the TBW harness that are routed from the Molex connector into the handlebars and attach to a twist grip assembly located under the right side grip. The twist grip is held in place by notches that are cut into the bar and an O-ring that keeps it centered. It operates using a spring loaded and grooved end cap that fits into the grip which provides the same feeling of tension that a throttle and idle cable do.

Inside the twist grip assembly is a pair of Hall-effect sensors very similar to a transmission speed sensor. These sensors work together, one measuring zero to five volts and the other measuring five to zero volts. They control the operation of the throttle servo-motor which sends precise amounts of fuel to the engine. The pair of sensors operate in redundancy for safety reasons and are intended to assist with lowering the amount of unburned fuel during deceleration. As with the introduction of fuel injection back in the mid to late 1990's, throttle-by-wire is another way to help lower exhaust emissions.

WHAT ABOUT TALLER HANDLEBARS?

On the custom end of throttle-by-wire, having an extension or longer TBW harness is a must if you want to install taller handlebars. The custom market seems always to have the answer and they did as TBW extensions and a plug-n-play extended TBW harness was available from NAMZ

Custom Cycle Products in January 2008. A simple harness to install with both connectors pre-installed for installation ease and allows for up to 20 inch taller bars. The extensions are a little bit more involved as they require de-pinning the Molex connector, (de-pinning: the method of removing terminals from a connector).

An important fact to know is that CVO or Screaming Eagle Glide models have a different type of twist grip assembly. These models do not use the small green AMP connector found inside the handlebars as they are hard-wired directly into the twist grip assembly. All 2008 non CVO/SE Glide models use this small connector which can make it a real challenge when fishing switch-wiring through the handlebars. A best bet is to use the plug-n-play harness for non CVO/SE models and the extensions on CVO/SE models.

The best method for installing a throttle-by-wire harness is to fish the small green connector up from the bottom to the right side grip of the bars. This will allow more room when installing handlebar switch wiring and prevent damage to the green connector. If you choose to install a CVO/SE throttle-by-wire twist grip assembly, simply de-pin the 6-position Molex connector, cover the male terminals with heat shrink or tape and fish from the right end of the handlebars down to the bottom exit hole near the riser clamp. If you damage the green connector or decide to install extensions, it is recommended that you DO NOT SOLDER your connections. Soldering should be done by a professional as a poor solder joint could cause catastrophic damage or bodily harm.

2009 MODEL YEAR CHANGES

In 2009, the factory was at it again and totally redesigned the "Glide" frame for all Ultra, Street Glide, Road Glide and Road King Models. All of the *other* models were pretty much left alone. The frame boasted a bolt-on rear section that was easier to work on and repair when needed. The swing arm was wider, boasting a much wider 180mm tire, one inch wide final drive belt, new wider rear fender and fender struts. The exhaust system was changed as well. Instead of exiting the rear cylinder above the starter then back under the left side saddle bag, it stays on the right side of the bike and exits under the swing arm pivot before continuing back and out the left side saddle bag. This change makes it much easier for removal and servicing.

As began in 2008, the factory continued the use of larger diameter brake rotors, isolating rear wheel final drive pulley, Brembo front and rear calipers with or without ABS (anti-lock braking system) and non-adjustable engine stabilizers. When you take all of the new features introduced between 2007 and 2009, the factory was clearly looking to make a statement that they were on top of new and better technology, but also new that "Baggers" as they are so often called now were going to be their next hot model for years to come.

The Baggers have come a long way in the last few years. Better brakes, re-routed exhaust, no throttle cables and no conventional taillight. Taken together the changes make for a very clean package. Harley-Davidson

If you haven't ridden a 2009-up Glide model as of yet, you really need to do so. The new frame, swing arm and wider rear tire makes for a much more comfortable and smoother ride. The bike is a bit longer and sits a little higher off the ground. Along with a better suspension, 2009 was a great year for Glide models.

2010 MODEL YEAR CHANGES

After all the changes in 2009, the factory didn't do

Among the many improvements seen on the Bagger line is the use of bigger and bigger rear tires.

For many of the new bikes the very traditional rear light bar is long gone, replaced by "taillights" that function as brake and blinker lights, all thanks to the integral run-brake-turn module.

that much in 2010, though there were some lighting changes on Glide models. Specifically, all Street Glides and Road Glides came without the center taillight on the rear fender. Harley also installed their own version of a run-brake-turn-signal module, the same technology that Badlands Motorcycle Products has been producing and selling for over 10-years. This device enabled the factory to remove the taillight and use red lenses on the rear turn signals allowing them to operate as running lights, turn signals and brake lights which meets DOT approval. Seeing a Street or Road Glide without a taillight takes some getting used to but they are the only models in the 2010 fleet with that factory installed option.

2011 MODEL YEAR CHANGES

Now along comes 2011 and Harley didn't disappoint. The previous several years saw the Glide or Bagger as the guinea pig for Harley's newest advances, but 2011 was different, it was the Softail Model that saw some major changes in the electrics department. It's all in the switches, literally. Harley has been using CAN-Bus (Controller Area Network) technology for many years now most notably on electronic speedometers and tachometers. The technology began back in 1983 at Robert Bosch GmbH and was officially introduced in 1986 in the automotive field. This technology allows several streams of electronic "data" to run across the same wire at the same time without the use of a host computer. This is perfect when you need to reduce the amount of wire used to power or talk to a particular device. Since digital data uses minimal amperage draw, the gauge size of the wire can be much smaller as well. But along with smaller wire gauge size and fewer wires needed in a CAN-Bus device, comes the need for understanding what you can and can't do to it or the attached wiring harness.

While the Bagger models were the first to get the TBW system, the Dyna and Softail lines retain their cables, though they are the first to get the CAN-bus switches.

Now that you understand what CAN-Bus does and why it was implemented, you also need to know that the factory took it to a whole new level in 2011. The handlebar switches used on ALL 2011 FX and FL Softail models use CAN-Bus technology. What does that mean? Well, for starters, the switch housings come apart differently, the top half pops off when the screws are removed as it no longer holds the upper two switches. Once the top clamp is off, you will see a thin plastic box of sorts directly behind the switch buttons. This is where the technology is as this holds a circuit board with a logic chip. The logic chip has the CAN-bus protocol that communicates with the motorcycle and carries out the switch button functions. Instead of having 6 or 8 different colored wires on each switch assembly, the CAN-Bus harness consists of (4) 20-gauge

The elimination of the conventional taillight is slowly making its way across the showroom.

There is a connector for the left and right side handlebar switch wiring. The funny thing is you can insert the left side plug - shown - into the female terminal on the right side and the bike doesn't care. Clever techs can even program switches to do something the factory never intended.

The Screamin' Eagle Road Glide is a good example of modern technology put to good use to improve the product.

wires, orange with a white stripe = 12-volt switched power, black = ground and a twisted pair, white with a red stripe and white with a black stripe. The twisted pair is where the data is transferred from the switches to the ECM (Electric Control Module) / BCM (Body Control Module).

Some of the features are a bit mind bending. For example, since both harnesses for the left and right side switch housings are the same, you can literally disconnect the right side switch harness and plug it into the left side harness connection (under the fuel tank) and that right side switch assembly will still operate the right side functions of right turn signal, on/off and start. This holds true for the left side plugging into the right side as well. I'd say that's pretty cool! Another feature is the access of reading or resetting trouble codes via the left side mode button. This can only happen because of CAN-Bus. Lastly, some models have handlebar-switch-mounted turn signals and those signals are hard-wired into the switch housing connector that mates to the circuit board. If you want to change the location of the turn signals say to the front fork, you simply cut the wire harness, heat shrink them for safety, install female Multi-lock terminals, a 6-position female connector and plug right into the mating turn signal harness which still resides under the fuel tank as it has since 1996.

As for every positive, some of us can always find a negative so now some of the new CAN-Bus handlebar switch drawbacks. Since the new technology is only standard on 2011-up FXST & FLST models and 2012-up Dyna models, the effects are not all that bad considering the bagger market is the trend these days. But for those with a Softail or a Dyna it can be a big deal. When you decide to change out handlebars, which is still one of the first things done after changing pipes, you need to know your options. As of today, the stock CAN-Bus switch assembly is the only way for the system to operate properly so changing switches to an aftermarket style is virtually impossible. I have heard of some customizers going as far as replacing the wiring harness and removing the BCM in order to obtain that custom look they're after. Not for the faint of heart or shady-tree mechanic by any means. But there is always a way around a problem.

Since the factory went with a new supplier for the connectors used on the handlebar switch harness, a new handlebar extension harness was needed. The connectors used are so very small they actually will fit through the stock one inch handlebar. Unlike earlier Deutsch or late model Molex terminals, the JAE terminals are under a half-inch long and require a very special crimp tool to apply them correctly. The very first handlebar switch extension harness was from NAMZ Custom Cycle Products. Our extension harnesses are 100% plug-n-play and come in 4 inch, 8 inch, 12 inch and 15 inch lengths.

Like throttle-by-wire harnesses, it is strongly recommended that you do NOT solder on extensions. Many do not realize that the data carried in the twisted pair of wires can be affected if there is any disruption due to the wires being soldered or untwisted. So before you make a mistake, be sure to not only purchase your favorite custom handlebars but also buy the correct wire extensions so you can complete the job the first time.

Though they look better than ever, the Sportsters are (so far) still left with cables to operate the throttle and conventional, non CAN-bus switches.

Interesting that the factory can combine new ideas and technology without losing the classic looks and feel of models like this Deluxe Softail.

Chapter Eleven

Aftermarket

New Products and Accessories

For those in the motorcycle business, especially the aftermarket parts accessory business, it is safe to say that the general perception of Harley Davidson is not a good one. You can always hear someone saying "because the factory did this or changed that, we had to totally redesign our part to make it fit." On the other hand, there are two sides to that story. Without the Motor Company, the aftermarket side of the two-wheeled business would be a lot smaller if around at all. Another important fact is that sometimes the aftermarket gets too complacent and thinks that things will remain the same forever. That's not a good thing, but keeping the aftermarket on their toes helps

From Brian Klock comes this FLH-style late-model Bagger. Note the Klock rear fender, stretched bags and bag fillers. Oval turn signals are mounted in the filler panels. High-rise bars are another unique Klock-Werks item.

everyone understand that this industry starts with the motorcycle and the sales and service of those motorcycles. So change is a good thing!

Nowadays, when you think Harley Davidson aftermarket, you think Baggers. The Glide, FL, grocery getter or anything else you call a Road King, Street Glide, Road Glide or Ultra is where it's at right now. Stretched saddle bags, huge front wheels, ape hanger bars, outrageous stereo systems and radical paint is now the norm for a high percentage of bagger owners. There are even magazine publications that have monthly releases with the latest and greatest baggers from around the nation plastered from front to back. Like most two wheeled trends, the west coast is usually where custom begins with names like Arlen Ness, Sims and Jesse James. But with the Bagger segment, it really seems to have started in the middle of the country. Names like Fat Baggers, Paul Yaffe and Dave Dupor all have home bases in the mid-west.

Since baggers are dominating the custom market, it doesn't mean that customizing Softails, Dyna's or Sportsters is unheard of, it just means baggers are the most popular bikes right now. Like anything else, the bagger segment may be hot now but something will come around and take its place. It's just a matter of time as most trends are cyclical. Remember five years ago

Klock Werks front fender shows off a nice flare at the lower edge, designed to match he look and shape of the rear fender. Klock Werks covers for the bottom of the floorboards are painted to match the rest of the bike.

When it comes to customizing a late model ride, you are truly limited only by your imagination. Not all Road Kings, or Baggers or Softails have to look similar or use the same design cues. Klock Werks

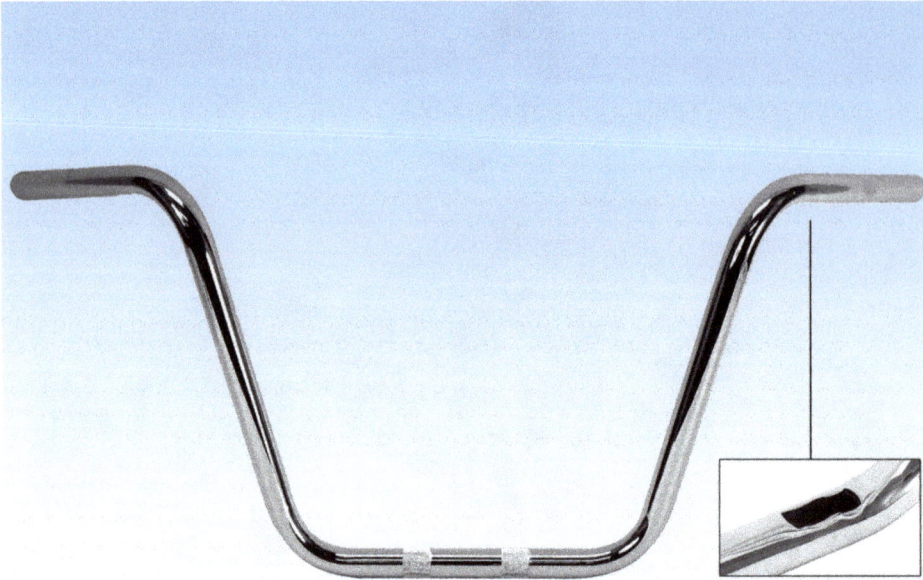

Beautifully chromed 1 inch diameter APE hanger bars with knurled at the riser mounting points to help prevent slipping. Bars are drilled and slotted for hidden wiring and except early, late and custom style controls. Kustom Werks

when building a bike, whether a chopper or bobber, was the thing to do? There were so many companies that sunk a boat load of time and money into their products based on a market of building new bikes that, many of those same companies today have downsized or are out of business altogether. So before you start purchasing accessories for your ride, be sure you come up with a long-term plan.

The best thing to do is come up with a theme. For example, say you like smooth lines and a lot of chrome. When you start buying bolt on parts, be sure to look at all of the choices and find parts that fit your style and plan. Like a derby cover, there are hundreds if not thousands of different styles and colors. If you like smooth lines, maybe a ball milled version is not the right fit. Maybe

T bars lend a nice clean look to the front of the bike with their integral risers, be sure the set you buy are set up for internal wiring. Note the blinkers incorporated into the mirrors, a nice way to make one part do two things.

you're going to change out your handlebars to a tall set of chrome bars. Before you do the bar swap or take it to your local shop or dealership, decide if you're going to change out the black OEM switch housings or upgrade to stainless braided cables so you can do everything at once. This kind of planning will save you a lot of time and money in the long run. Try to envision what parts must come off to complete any given job. Wouldn't it be easier to replace any of those parts once the originals have been removed? Probably so, but sometimes you can only do what the budget will allow.

ADDITIONAL LIGHTING

One of the accessory upgrades that will never go out of style is lighting. With lighting, you can change anything and everything on a factory motorcycle. Harley even offers many different styles and upgrades. One of the most common upgrades is to convert factory turn signals with incandescent bulbs over to LED replacements. This is a simple upgrade to complete for any enthusiast while providing increased visibility and a much better look. Many LED manufacturers make a plug-n-play LED insert that uses the standard incandescent 1156 or 1157 base to make installation a snap. Now, along with the upgraded LED's, install a Badlands Illuminator which will convert your rear turn signals

Available in red, amber and clear, these front, flat-style LED inserts come with a load equalizer and function as both run and turn signals. Kuryakyn

You can easily brighten existing lights with the installation of an LED bulb, available in various colors and for both 1156 and 1157 style bulbs. Kuryakyn

117

With Panacea's Run, Brake, Turn modules and rear turn signal inserts, you get amber turn signals....

... red, LED stop lights on all three lights...

... and slightly dimmer red LED run lights. Kuryakyn

into running lights, turn signals and even a brake light without ANY wiring modifications. Simply disconnect the rear fender harness under the seat and plug their module in between. If you choose this option remember to change your amber lens out for red as that is a DOT regulation.

There are options to convert standard headlights to HID or LED and taillights over to LED as well. These options also provide the same increased visibility as LED turn signals do. But upgrading factory lighting will not satisfy the true custom in some of us, we want more. A perfect example of some trick custom lighting is adding frenched LED's in a fender, saddle bag or fairing. This is a pretty difficult job but when done correctly, the outcome is awesome. The key is securing and finishing the plexi-glass. Painting around it has to be perfect as well to provide that "stealth" look.

A good in-between or safe option is to add surface mounted or through-hole lighting. This is really big in the bagger market and helps set the bike apart from that plain stock look. When the factory introduced the Street Glide, they added a rear fender extension made from urethane and painted to match, it housed additional lighting for added effect at the tip of the rear fender. It made for a sleek look and additional length. The CVO/Screaming Eagle model had a similar fender extension but they had long, vertical strips of LED lighting positioned on either side of the fender. In Harley's eyes, when people saw this look, they knew it was the top of the line model rolling down the road.

You don't need a CVO or SE model to have trick lighting. Many bagger enthusiasts start with a new or used stock bagger then begin to swap out factory saddle bags and rear fenders with custom, stretched versions. These upgrades give you a longer and lower look while still providing the form and function of stock saddle bags. Along with new parts come all the additional expenses like fitting the parts, buying additional parts to make them fit properly, and then the body and paintwork. It can get very expensive so plan accordingly. There are many options available today from manufacturers like Milwaukee Bagger, Paul Yaffe or Sinister Designs, but know that all stretched bags and fenders are not the same. Most stretched fenders allow for the use of any style taillight while others have a molded pocket made for a standard light available with the fender. Due to the added size of the fender you also have more options for custom turn signal designs and placement.

If you choose to place lighting in your saddle bag, be sure you do not disturb the factory gasket on the saddle bag lid or you will end up with a water leak. For the wiring, simply drill a hole on the backside of the bag where it is not visible and use a rubber grommet that will seal itself to the bag and around the wires.

Whether you choose additional or custom lighting on stock or custom bags and fenders, be sure to wire it up correctly with the following in mind. First, plan the whole job on paper making sure you have all of the materials, wire, terminals or connectors, solder, heat shrink, grommets and all the necessary tools. Then, using the new lighting, mock up the placement and routing of the wiring. Be sure to get measurements so you can create a wiring harness later. Now you can install the lighting in the finished product and prepare to build a wiring harness. Remember that saddle bags are removable. In order to keep them that way be sure to install a male and

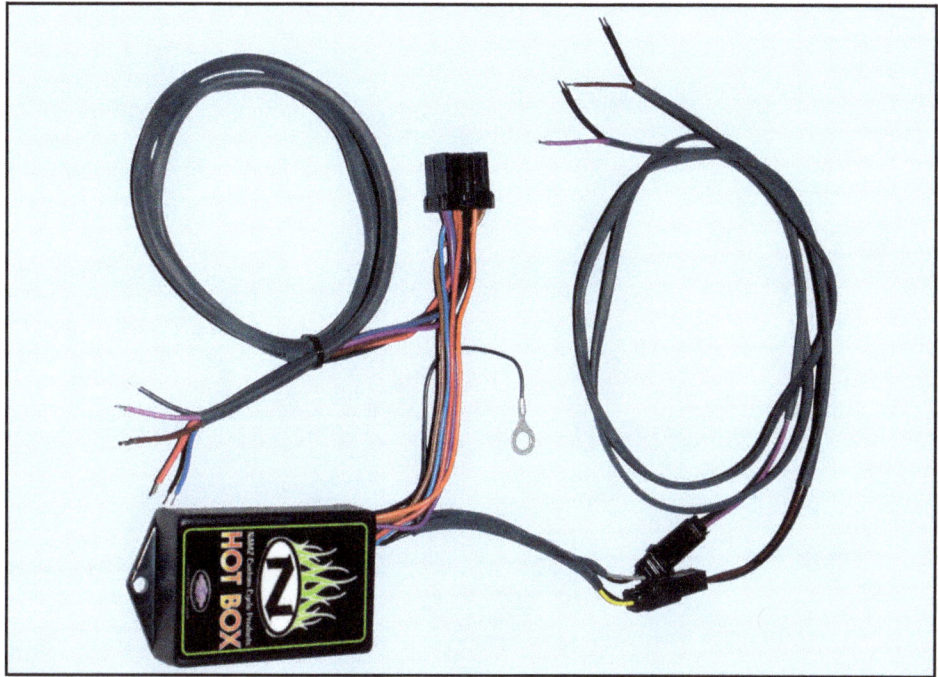

With this harness you can come up with any lighting option imaginable. It adds a RUN, BRAKE and TURN module, detachable saddlebag wiring and a new rear fender wiring harness with turn signal wires. Uses OEM connectors and provides detachable right & left RUN, BRAKE & TURN pigtails. Installs in minutes! NAMZ

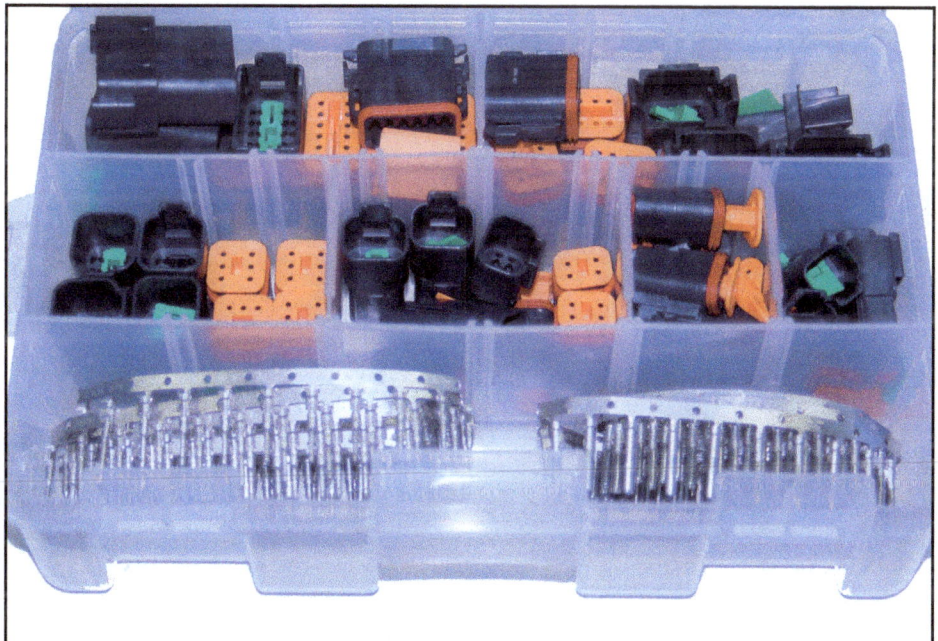

NAMZ Has made it even easier for custom shops or dealerships to get the parts they need! Introducing the NAMZ Deutsch Connector Builders Kit. It comes with an assortment of receptacles, plugs and 100 of each stamped crimp terminal. (Gray or Black).

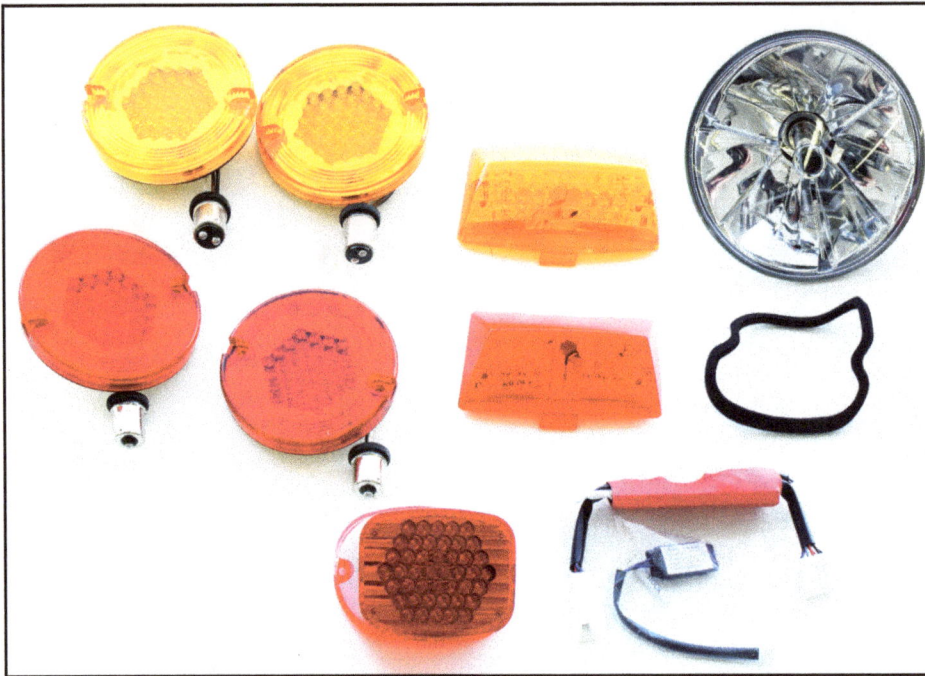

These plug-n-play LED inserts are perfect stock replacement items and simple for any rider to install without difficulty since there is no cutting or splicing involved.

Here is a great example of frenched-in LED turn signals and a custom designed LED logo taillight on a bike with a stretched rear fender and bags.

female connector system on the harness. This will allow you the ease of disconnecting the wires when removing the saddle bag. If the connectors are exposed, use a water-tight connector like Deutsch or Mate-n-Lock or if you can keep them under a side cover or under the seat, any simple connector will do just fine.

Say you don't have a Bagger but you still want some decent LED upgrades, or a change from the factory placement - you have many options available. Turn signal mirrors have been around for over 15-years and allow installation without lighting controllers or load equalizers. They are not DOT approved and are considered supplemental lighting. So having them alone without factory or DOT approved signals is not legal in most states. Regardless, it's safe to say that adding additional lighting, (within reason) especially LED's will work along with the factory turn signals or run/taillights. The factory turn signal module can handle the additional amperage as LED's in particular do not draw much current. One interesting note is that 2012 Dyna and Softail models can swap from factory incandescent bulbs over to LED's without needing a load equalizer. This is not the case with all 2011 and earlier models.

Another craze where many try desperately to outdo one another is adding strips of LED lighting all over their motorcycle. I'm sure you have seen it before, riding down the boulevard and a glowing multi-colored bike rides by looking like a neon sign in Vegas. These are very simple to install and really help to make your bike stand out in the crowd. Most sets come with double faced tape to attach the LED's to any (safe) surface on the motorcycle. The instructions usually tell the installer to run the 12+ power wire directly to the battery with an in-line fuse for safety and the ground to any source. This will allow you to use the low amperage LED's while the key switch is off. Some LED light kits even come with controllers which allow you to change the color and intensity of the lights - and even make the lights go off and on in a pattern. A basic starter kit can sell upwards of $100 so adding these additional lights can really add up!

Before you add any lights to your ride, be sure to know what you're doing. Make a plan, decide if you want LED's or standard bulbs, know what Hot Boxes or modules will do for your application. For example, NAMZ Custom Cycle Products produces several, 100% plug-n-play harnesses with an attached Hot Box module that will provide you endless lighting control, safely and easily. These kits plug in between the rear fender connection under the seat

Replace your standard rear turn signals with bright LED inserts (load equalizer included). These can also be used as multi-function lights with the addition of a run, brake, turn module.

Super lizard lights will have your scooter glowing like Chernobyl before the sarcophagus. Kits come with adhesive pads - lights can be used in a variety of modes and colors. Kuryakyn

or under the side cover on some baggers. They allow simple wiring solutions for additional turn signals, rear fender, or saddlebag lighting. You can keep your stock rear fender and turn signal lighting and add extra LED or bulb style turn signals in your saddle bags that will allow you to install run, brake and turn signals with one power and one ground wire. You can also install a kit that will give you a quick disconnect when removing the seat and allow for easy removal of the tour pack. Another kit will give you the ability to separate the wires in your tour pack and have left and right, run, brake and turn signal functions. Lastly, if you have a really custom bagger and you wanted to remove all the factory rear fender lighting, we have the kit you need. This kit will provide you with a run, brake, ground, left and right side turn signal wire for any style taillight you can imagine. It also has a left and right, two-wired pigtail with installed connectors for each saddle bag, (or anywhere else you can think of) that have run, brake and turn signal functions. There is no need for an additional load equalizer, all the wires are covered in heat shrink and ready for installation.

When it comes to additional lighting and modules there are so many different styles and applications to choose from. Before you make a regretful impulse purchase, however, do your homework and be sure you know what you need to complete the job right the first time.

TALLER HANDLEBARS

Well now you know about the drastic change in 2011-Softail and 2012-up Dyna handle-

Make your bike shine even while at rest with these low-draw, hidden LED lights. Kuryakyn

bar switches. Understanding throttle-by-wire functionality on 2008-up bagger models was simple and you can recognize any factory or custom, incandescent or LED turn signal ever made, this section about taller handlebars should be just as easy to follow. We will talk about all custom bars and most of the important differences between them. As you should already know, there are thousands of different handlebars available. How do you know what works best on your ride?

Handlebars are probably the second most popular thing people change on their stock bike after exhaust of course. There are so many manufacturers out there making handlebars; large companies with years of experience and huge engineering departments, all the way down to small mom and pop shops building one custom handlebar a day. The options are endless. Not only do you have countless manufacturers to choose from, but you also have hundreds of styles, colors, finishes and sizes available as well.

Let's start with 1982 to 1995 models. The handlebar switches were clunky, not sealed and had open solder connections on each button in the switch housing. Like we touched on earlier in this book, these were not the factory's glory years when it came to electrical smarts. The handlebars for these years did not have a dimple pressed into them therefore it was next to

Throttle by wire assembly pulled out of the handle bars, note the cutouts on the end of the bars and the matching tabs on the TBW assembly.

Pre-CAN-bus switch assembly, note the relatively large size of the wiring harness.

The CAN-bus switches are visually very similar to their predecessors.

Inside the switch assembly is a different story, note the relatively small size of the wiring harness.

impossible to run the wiring anywhere other than the outside of the bars. The wiring was then held in place with circular clips that were also pressed into small drilled holes along the handlebar. On 1996-up models, the factory began pressing a dimple in the bar under the switch housing preventing pinched wires and allowing for a logical place to enter into the bar for internal wiring. In the early years, bars where dimpled but not drilled. The aftermarket world fixed that and began drilling all 1996-up model bars to make it easier to fish the switch wires through the bars. Notice I said "easier" not "easy."

Most models still have similarly built handlebars today except for the 2008-up bagger models which have a couple of differences. The most noticeable of these is the right side end of the handlebar which has two notches cut out to allow a tight "one way only fit" of the throttle-by-wire twist grip assembly. This keeps the twist grip in place and prevents it from spinning during operation. But as discussed in the throttle-by-wire section, fishing an additional small, but six-wire, harness along with all of the other switch wires in the handlebar is not easy at all, even for the professionals. Whatever you do, fish the TBW harness first. When adding extensions, fish the stock wiring first, then add the extensions.

The handlebars on 2011-up Softails and 2012-Dyna's are pretty much the same as any earlier model except for the switches and wire harness connected to them. Unlike all other factory switches, these are hard wired into small circuit boards located in the switch housing (CAN-bus technology). The circuit boards reduce the number and size of the wires, making it much easier to fish the wires through the new bars. Handlebar swaps on these models are very easy!

The only set of bars that are different from all the rest are used on Springer models. These models have a wider center-to-center measurement on the riser clamp. Why is that important to know? The knurled area of the bar is also wider and meant to mate with the wider riser mount only found on the Springer front end. Installing these

With the tank off this 2012 Softail, you can see how the main "harness" is now split and runs down either side of the top tube.

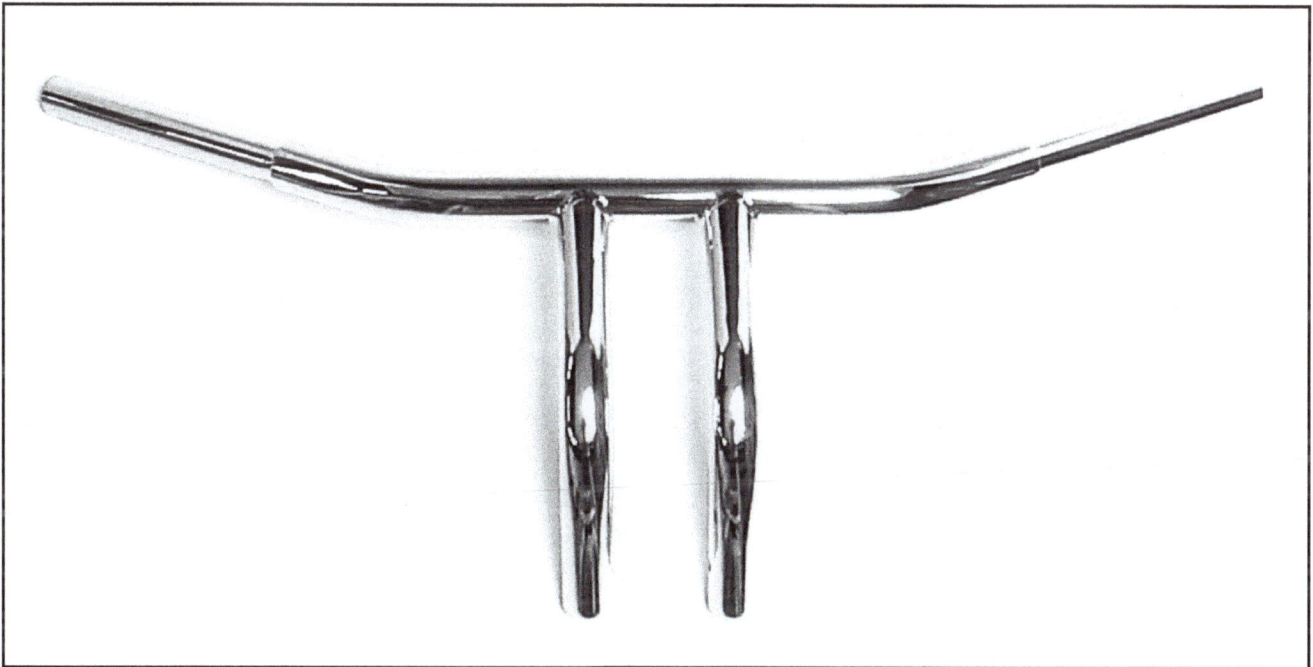

This 31 inch wide, 1-1/4 inch diameter "Beefy" T - Bar has an 8 inch rise and 5 inch pull back. Mounts with 1/2 inch bolts, 3-1/2" between bolt centers - get the fat look popular with todays custom builders. Made in the USA and has a beautiful chrome-plated finish. Kustom Werks

Large diameter Burly bars (1-1/4 inches) come drilled and slotted to make it easy to run the wires internally. Kustom Werks

bars on any other model would make the knurled area exposed on either side of the riser clamp therefore preventing the clamp to have enough bite while clamped down on the bars. If the Springer bar is a 1.125 inch or 1.25 inch outside diameter, the smaller one inch area where the clamp mounts would also stick out past the riser on a non-Springer model.

Now let's talk about taller bars. There are buckhorns, (early stock style bars) drag bars, (no rise, straight and narrow bars) T-bars, (bars with built in risers) beach bars, (very wide and low rise bars) and ape hangers, (tall to very tall bars). Ape hangers put the rider in a contorted look of an ape with arms stretch up high holding on to the bars. For most ape hanger bars, they can be very comfortable unless they're mounted too far forward.

You might think you look cool but after an hour of shoulder swelling and pinched nerves, you will probably change them out for something a little less radical. You may want to find out what your local law on handlebar height is as well. Most states will pull you over and issue a ticket for any handlebar taller than the rider's shoulder. If the bars are too high, it also makes low speed handling a real challenge.

You can purchase ape hangers with or without built in risers, in one inch, 1.125 inch or 1.25 inch diameters, with 90-degree

A very current custom Bagger assembled by the mechanics at St. Paul Harley-Davidson, complete with killer stereo, ape-hanger handle bars, stretched tank and fenders and a "flat" two-tone paint job.

pointed bends or a traditional smooth radius bend. Most if not all handlebars come pre drilled for internal wiring and come off the shelf in black or chrome finishes in almost any height. Speaking from experience, buying an ape hanger handlebar with built-in risers is not the best idea. What you may not have ever thought about is the amount of stress that is put on the welds attaching the risers. Think about the 16 inch or 18 inch tall handlebar mounted on factory style risers, sometimes after tightening them, you can still move them due to the leverage created with the taller bar. Now, add that taller bar to a small welded riser then bolt it to a front end with urethane riser bushings so the bars are even more rigid. That's not a good thing. I had a set just like that, 18 inches tall on a custom bike we built back in 2004. While blasting down the highway during the Myrtle Beach rally, a good friend noticed four cracks in the bar, two on each side of the welded riser. The bottom line, the leverage is too great to put all of that added stress on welded risers.

The only other bar with built in risers is the "T-bar". You can find these bars on most models except baggers but I have seen some on Road King models with a modified top clamp cover. These handlebars were very popular in the 90's as the clean smooth lines from not

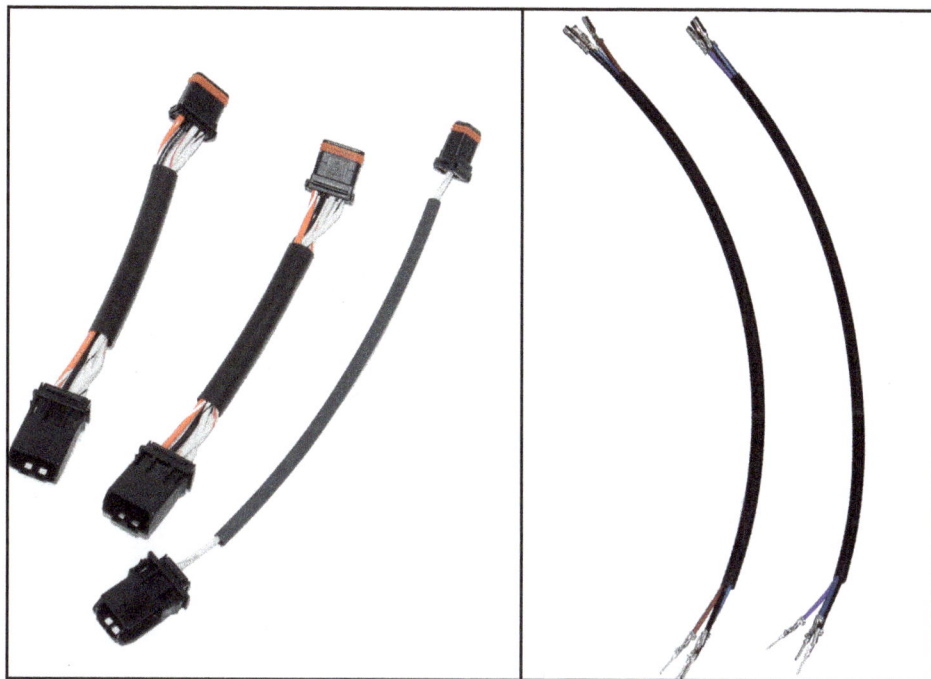

Left: NAMZ plug-n-play CAN-Bus handlebar wiring extensions are perfect when installing taller bars on a 2011-FXST/FLST or a 2012-Dyna model. No cutting, splicing or de-pining.
Right: NAMZ also produces front turn signal extensions when you're going to taller bars on any model using handlebar mounted turn signals.

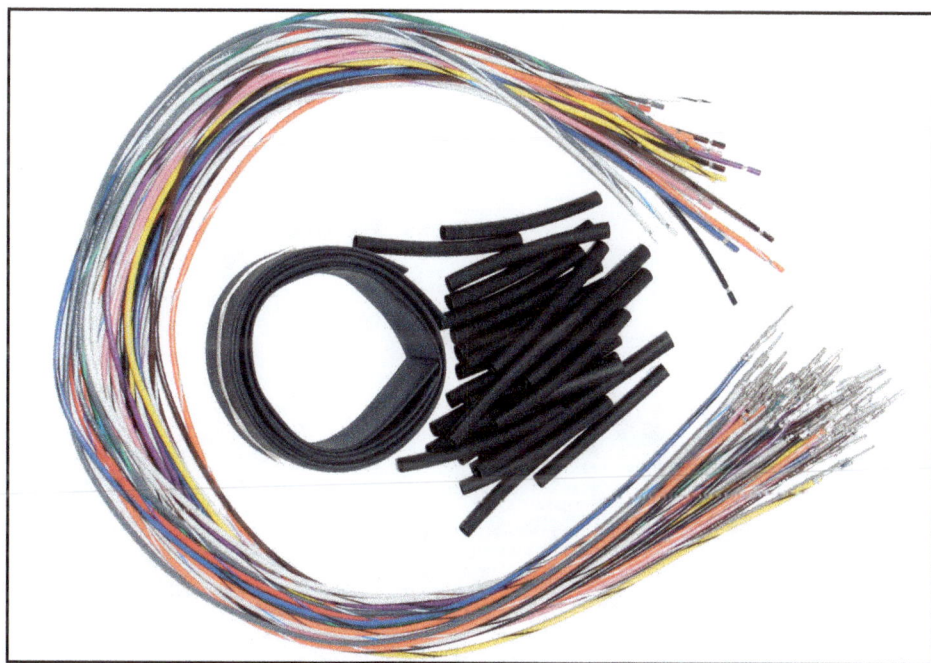

These NAMZ universal NON CAN-Bus handlebar switch extensions come terminated on one end for easy re-installation into the connector, and stripped on the other. Gives the installer the ability to stagger cut and solder the wiring as they see fit. Comes with heat shrink for a perfect installation.

127

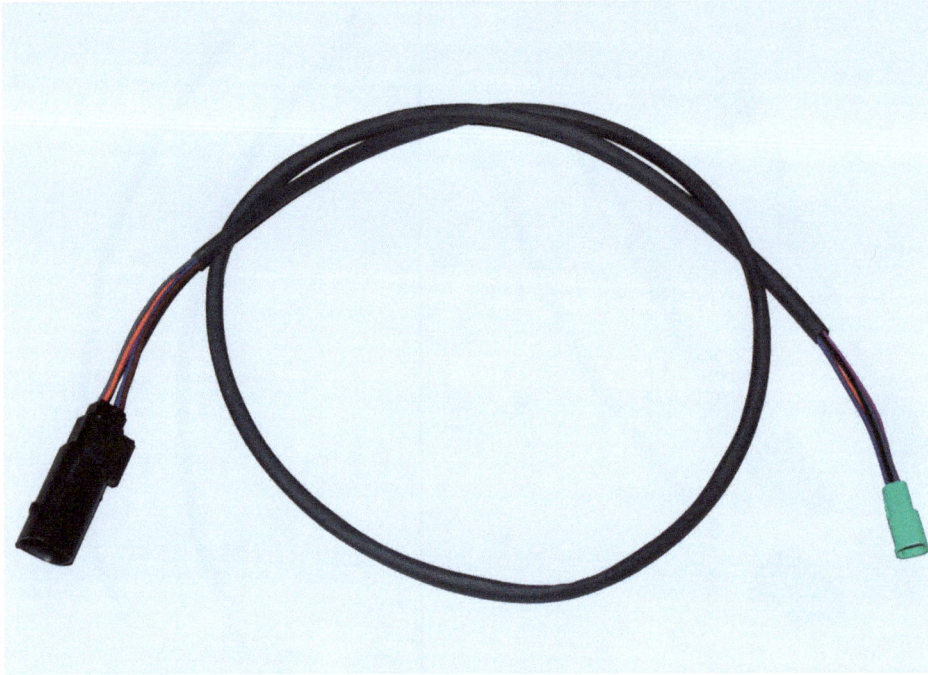

Our Throttle-by-Wire Extensions are an inexpensive yet safe method to get the job done right. The NTBW-4201 (shown) is much longer than stock and will fit up to 18" taller bars - a good choice for FL models. NAMZ

Two 02 sensors, the larger one used from 2006 to 2008, and the much smaller model installed beginning in 2009.

having risers and a clamp made for a very sleek front end. They were produced in 1 inch up to 1.25 inch OD but the larger outside diameter bars looked much better. Like most custom or aftermarket bars, the "t" bar was made for running wiring internally. The design was basic, very similar to a "drag" bar and the riser height was available from 2 inches up to 10 inches on some versions. Carlini was the first manufacturer to install a fishing string attached with rubber bands on every t bar they sold making running wires a snap. Still, like anything else, you needed to take your time as the slag or extra "weld-material" in the bar is usually very sharp and can really rip up a harness as the wires are fished through. If this is an option you decide on, be sure to de-bur the holes under the area where the switch housings would mount, and also run a tap through the threads in the risers to clean out chrome residue.

No matter what handlebar you choose, proper installation requires skill, the right tools, supplies and patience. Make sure you have all of the materials you need to get the job done right the first time.

O2 SENSORS

Talking about the introduction of oxygen sensors or O2 sensors could open a whole can of worms. They are installed for a reason although they're not always the best option when you are trying to gain performance. See, once you start talking about tuning or engine performance, EVERYONE has their own opinion, and the argument of who is right or wrong can go on forever. Some motor heads tell you to keep the O2 sensors and use an EFI tuner that works along with them. Others will say to take them out to get the most performance possible. Most importantly, mating correct EFI tuning along with the right engine modifications will allow you to get the best performance possible.

The factory started using O2 sensors when they rolled out the 96 cubic inch power plant on 2006 Dyna models. The new sensors created some challenges for the aftermarket exhaust manufacturers. Now they had to prepare for a new model year along with installing a female threaded bung up near the head to except O2 sensors. Nobody likes change and this was no exception. For 2006 Dyna or 2007 bagger models, finding a header pipe that was a direct fit with installed bungs was scarce. Some aftermarket companies were a little slow to react as you can expect so getting a new custom exhaust on your ride was not that easy. This was not a good thing as it gave shops and builders the idea to drill holes and install custom made O2 bung ports on pipes that were never intended to have them. A new technology that needed to be understood before it was customized. Unfortunately this didn't work out that way.

Harley's O2 sensors are used to measure exhaust gases exiting from the heads. In closed-loop mode, the narrow-band O2 sensors send data to the ECM, which uses the information to manage the fuel mixture – closed loop operation is defined as low and cruising speeds, before the system switches to open-loop mode. The addition of O2 sensors to a motorcycle

This is the computer that runs everything except the CAN-bus system on a late model Softail. Like all computers, these are getting smaller and smaller.

Make your rear blinker lights do more than blink with a quality run-brake-stop module from Badlands.

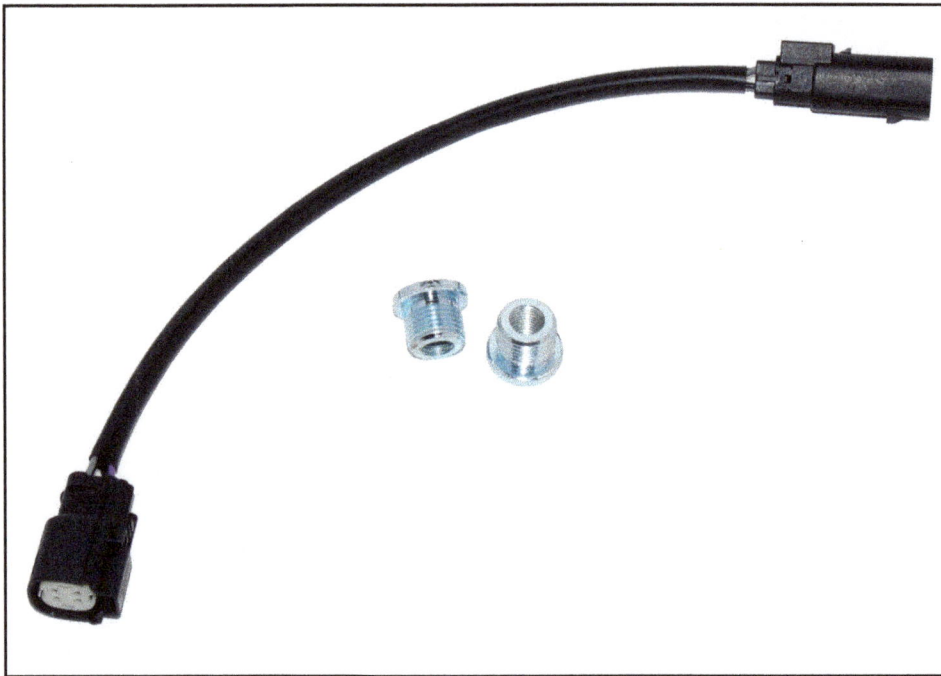

You want to install an early exhaust system on your new 2010 Glide model or a new 2012 FXST or Dyna? No problem. All '10 Glides & '12 FXST/Dyna's use a smaller 12mm O2 sensor unlike earlier models. So our kit allows you to extend the front O2 harness & install O2 bung reducers for any exhaust you choose! Plug and Play. NAMZ

The first bikes to come equipped with O2 sensors placed those sensors close to the exhaust port as shown.

equipped with EFI means the ECU knows almost instantly if the engine is a little rich or a little lean, and can adjust the mixture with more precision than is possible without the input from the exhaust sensors.

Ultimately, O2 sensors help to lower emissions, and also improves your fuel economy and overall ride ability – all good things.

So yea, in the beginning of 2007, not having a header pipe really put a dent in your plans for a custom exhaust, but waiting was not an option for most enthusiasts. Some manufactures of fuel injection tuners helped exhaust manufacturers as their tuners actually eliminated the O2 sensor altogether. This was similar to 2005-earlier models that relied on MAP (manifold absolute pressure) and TPS (throttle position sensor) to measure the load on the engine.

There is a lot to know about O2 sensors. From 2006 up through 2008, the 18mm sensor was heat treated to operate close to the head. It was also a two wire system using an AMP Superseal two position connector to attach to the wiring harness. In 2009, Harley changed the O2 sensor to a much smaller 12mm design that operated in lower temperatures and was located much further back on the header pipe. Unlike the earlier version, these sensors used a Molex MX-150 four-position connector where gray and black determined front and rear cylinders. The change only took place on bagger models, so again, trying to find a header pipe that fit properly can be a real challenge. NAMZ Custom Cycle Products came up with a fix to allow 2007-up header pipes to work on 2009-up glide models. The O2 sensor extension harness was just that, an extension to allow the wiring to reach the more forward location of the O2 sensor. The kit also comes with two bung reducing inserts that reduce the 18mm threads down to 12mm for new sensor fitment.

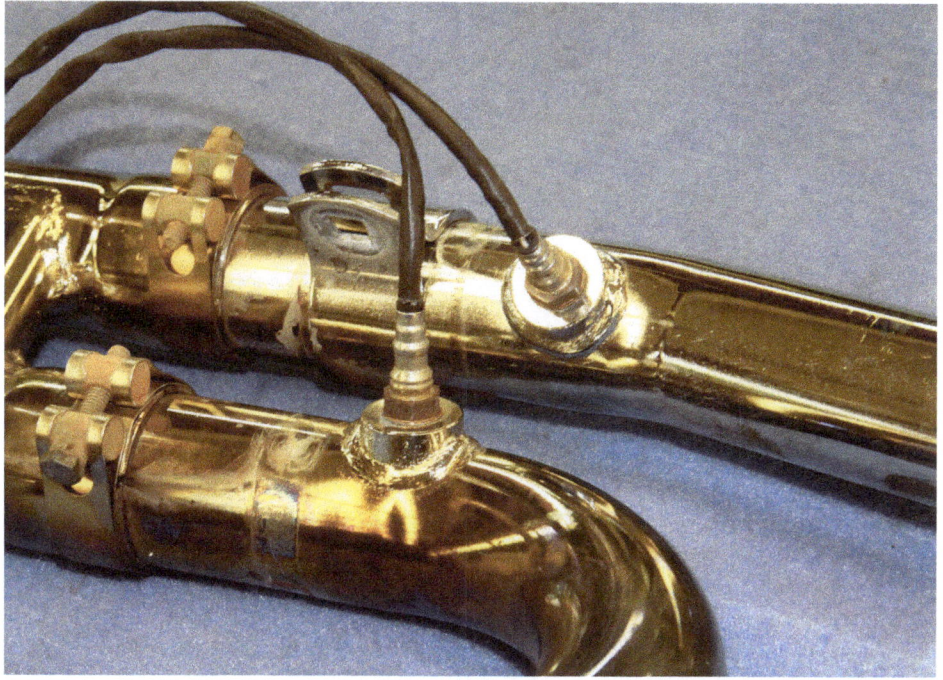

As opposed to the first models with O2 sensors, the current bikes position the sensors much farther back in the exhaust system.

Now that you have more information than you will ever need to know about O2 sensors, you should be able to make a better decision on which EFI tuner to purchase, which pipes fit what models, and why they were installed in the first place. Carburetor or fuel injection, a motorcycle runs the best when air and fuel are mixed just right and O2 sensors help get the mixture that much closer to perfect.

Yes, Victory has gotten into the "Bagger" market big time with a variety of models that sport hard bags, though finding aftermarket accessories is a little harder than with a typical Harley. Klock Werks

Chapter Twelve

Audio

Two-Wheeled Juke Box

For motorcycle riders, the audio boom, no pun intended, is upon us like it was in cars and trucks back in the late 80's and early 90's. So much so that even Harley Davidson has jumped on the audio bandwagon. Though the factory has had factory radios installed in touring models for years, they have taken motorcycle audio to a whole new level making audio products compatible for all models. Even the aftermarket has invested a lot of money in the audio segment. Big name manufacturers like Rockford Fosgate, Focal and Hertz are producing amps, speakers and switching devices for motorcycle specific applications. Harley models have amps, GPS modules, IPOD and

While a nice stereo was once a rarity on a Bagger, today there are very few fairing-equipped Harleys on the street that aren't equipped with a nice head unit, amplifier and at least two speakers mounted in the fairing. Klock Werks

IPhone docking stations to go along with the mainstay CB radios. The motorcycle aftermarket is thankful to have our own handful of highly talented and creative audio "professors" producing innovative products and accessories like Hawg Wired, J&M, Hogtunes and Biketronics just to name a few. Weather resistant speaker upgrades, amps the size of a business cards and installation hardware that makes us audio heads from the late 80's and early 90's wish we could have a mulligan!

HEAD UNIT RADIOS

Back in 2006, Harley Davidson partnered up with Harmon/Kardon to develop the Advanced Audio System for all touring models. A much better unit than what was available in previous years, these units boast AM, FM, single disc, WB and an auxiliary input for MP3 players. Watertight as you can make a radio, these units did the job rain or shine. One of the major drawbacks for any audio-minded enthusiast was the lack of power, and sufficient volume, when cruising down the highway at 80 miles an hour. Many people thought that changing the speakers would do the trick, but no, it wasn't that simple. Better speakers cleaned up the radio's sound, but the power was still not there. In the mid-2000's there simply were not any small amps available that could take the punishment

A perfect picture of an aftermarket radio installed in a batwing fairing, hard to even tell it's not factory installed.

A factory Harmon/Kardon head unit trying to find the right FM station.

Hawg Wired display system features over-size, 2-way front speakers with separate tweeters, driven by an aftermarket head unit and digital amp.

From this side you can see the adapters needed to attach the too-big speakers to the existing fairing opening. In addition to the speakers, the kit shown includes the cross-overs, head unit and amp, all designed to be plug and play.

of being installed in a motorcycle.

The story is different today. Once you've installed new speakers and still need more power, there are a variety of small amplifiers you can add and install in the fairing of your Glide model – that's really the only solution short of replacing the head unit with an aftermarket version.

Replacing the radio with an aftermarket unit will require the use of a marine grade unit with a waterproof cover for extra protection. Having too much extra protection is NEVER a bad thing. When manufacturers state that their radios are "marine grade" it does not mean that you can ride in a rainstorm and expect the radio to stay dry because that just doesn't happen, ever. Marine grade in my opinion, means "splash resistant" which is good for the occasional light mist every once in a while. More than that, the radio will more than likely fail. Corrosion is NOT covered under ANY electronics warranty under any circumstance. Some manufacturers even use litmus paper inside their products to detect water or liquid damage. Unless you purchased a police Road King that doesn't have a radio, it's best to stick with the factory Harmon-Kardon unit.

Adding an additional amplifier to the stock head unit is pretty easy. First, you need to choose an amplifier that has all of the options you want. If you are only going to keep the two front stock speaker locations, a simple two-channel amp will do the trick. Before going farther, we need to talk about the signal from the radio that you are going to amplify.

Low level output on a radio is unamplified - a pure, clean signal. High level out, or speaker output, is already amplified by the head unit, and therefore the signal is not as clean and likely includes some distortion and/or noise.

Since the factory head unit only has high-level output - or, speaker level/amplified, you need to purchase an amplifier that will covert high level to line level or signal-only. Most new amps have this feature or they have both high level and low level/RCA jack inputs. Only having high level outputs is the biggest drawback on the factory radio.

REAR SPEAKER OPTIONS

The other drawback of the factory radio is not having a fader to control output to the rear speakers. If you want to take your head unit to a Harley dealer, they can activate the rear channels of the radio enabling you to have the use of a fader. If you do not choose this option, the Harmon-Kardon radio will have front speaker outputs only, and you have to find another means of providing a signal to the rear speakers. The first step is to purchase a 4-channel amplifier. Next, you would want to split the sig-

Note the compact amp and the very neat wiring. No cutting or soldering required. Efficient digital amp makes good power without a lot of heat.

Here is a really big, aftermarket Arc Audio 4-channel amplifier that will provide PLENTY of power for any 4-speaker system.

nal to the front speakers to feed both front and rear channels on the amp. How do you do that? It's pretty simple, remove the wires attached to the front speakers and make short jumper wires for each wire which would give you four wires for the right and four wires for the left. Attach these wires to the high level input on the amplifier. Be sure to get the polarity correct!

What is polarity you ask? The term polarity is generally used to speak to a characteristic associated with electrical charges. These charges are given the terms positive and negative. For example, speaker wire has a mark or strip on one of the conductors to help identify polarity of the wire. When installing speakers to an amplifier you need to observe the proper polarity. If the polarity is not followed then your system will have a poor balance of sound and some frequencies will be cancelled out. The speaker should have an indication of plus (+) or minus (-) and some speakers even use a large .25 inch male terminal and smaller .125 inch male to help distinguish polarity. You can also revert back to the service manual of your model which will tell you positive and negative.

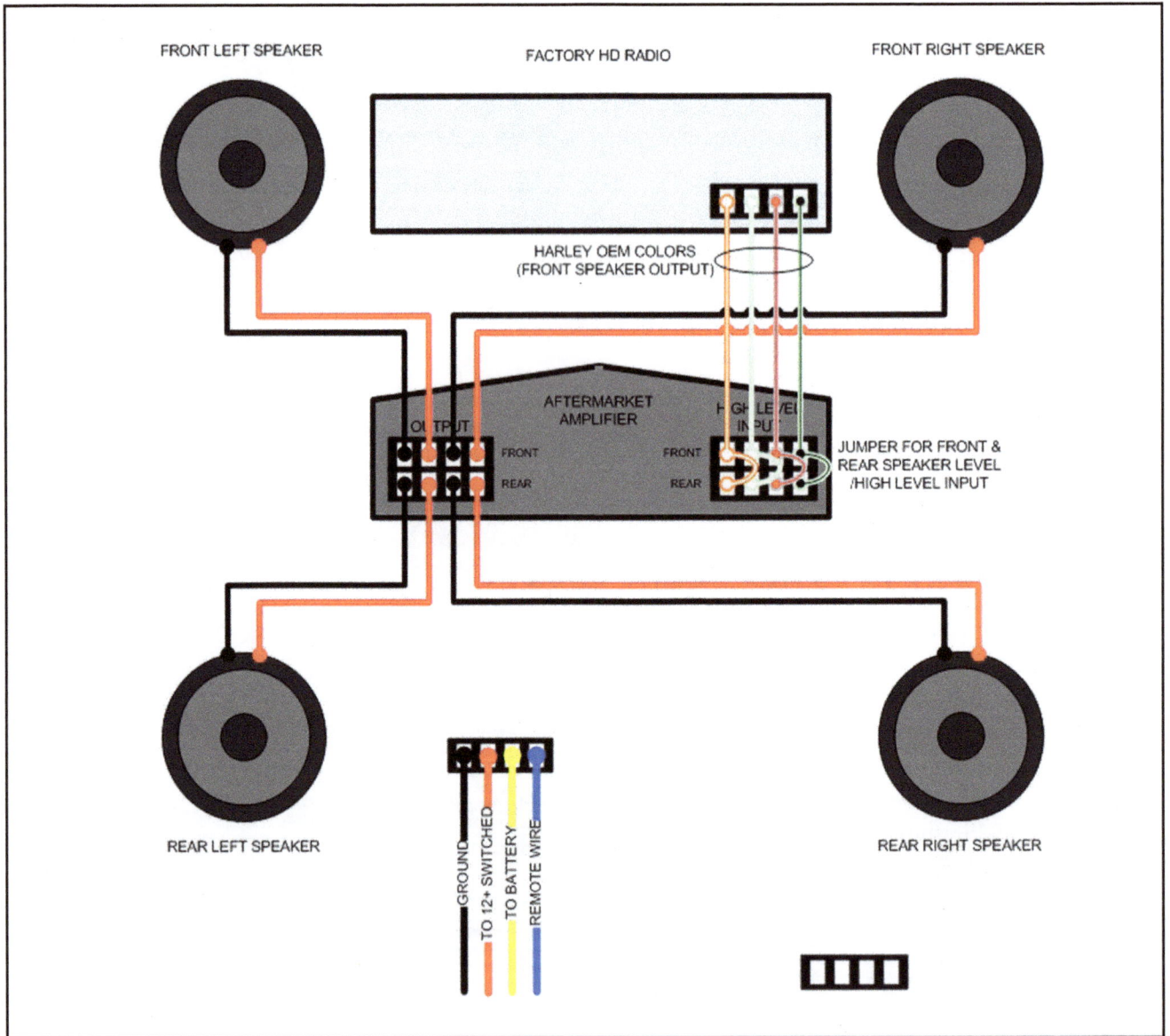

Here's a schematic for a typical situation where the factory head unit has only front-speaker outputs, and you want to use a 4 channel amp and feed power to both the front and rear speakers. Note the jumper wires mentioned in the text.

AFTERMARKET ANSWERS

Now if you choose to install an aftermarket radio, be sure to follow the instructions that come with the unit. On most head units, white and gray colors are used for front speaker outputs and violet and green are used for the rear. Note, there are actually two wires to each speaker, or a total of four wires for the front speakers: a white (positive) and white with black stripe (negative) to one side, and a grey (positive again) and grey with black stripe (negative) to the other side.

This also holds true for the RCA or low level output from the radio to the amplifier. In this case, be sure that you install white for left and red for right. Then, when installing speaker wires from the amp to the speakers, be sure that you keep track of polarity as mentioned in the preceeding paragraph. If you're in doubt about the end result of your installation, a true audio enthusiast can tell if an audio system is "out of phase" (polarity mis-match) just by listening to it. If there is ever a time when you want to sure that you have all of your connections correct, this is it. Having to take off the outer fairing again can be a real pain!

So now, with or without the added jumper wires mentioned above, you decide to use a 4-channel amplifier and you know the correct polarity for right and left. Why not replace the

A nice pair Hertz Audio 2-way, 6.5 inch front speakers. Notice the + and − on the back of the speaker, important for proper polarity.

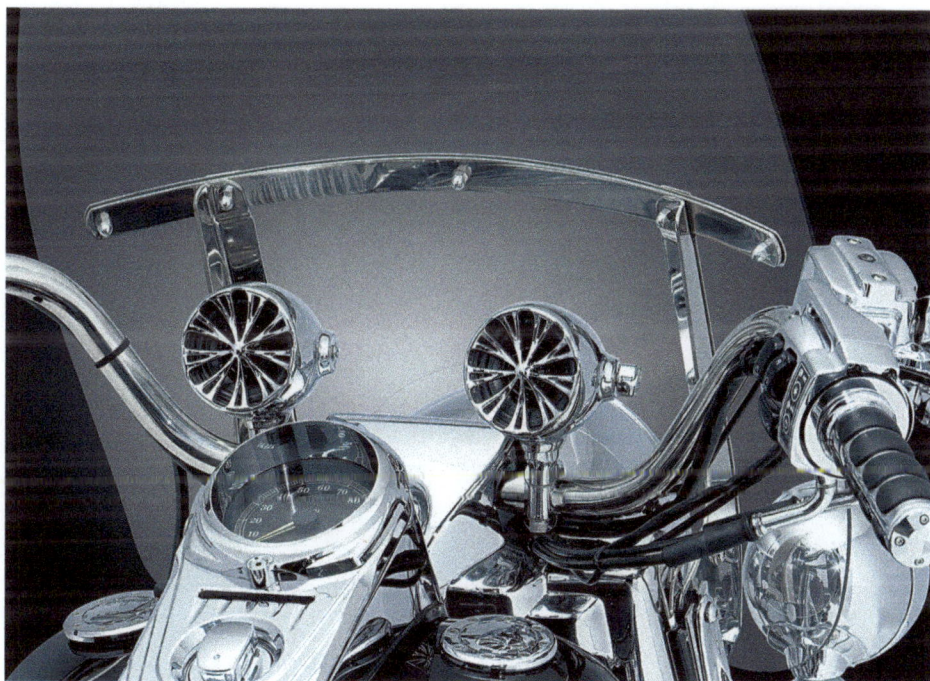

Just because you don't have a fairing doesn't mean you can't have nice speakers. These 3 inch speakers from Kicker mount to the handlebars and include an integral tweeter. Kuryakyn

137

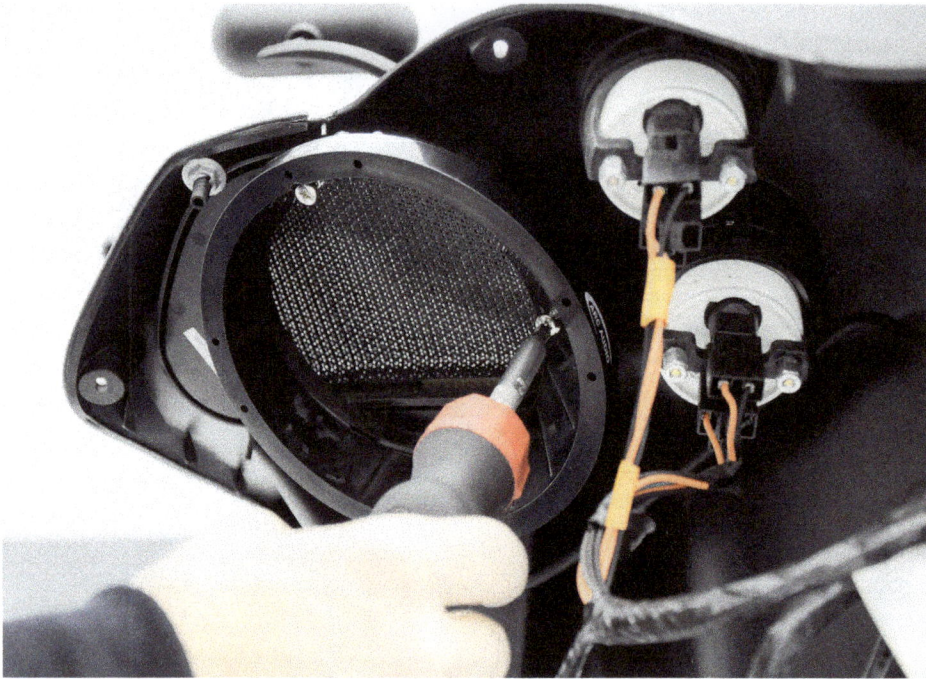

This 6.5 inch trim ring is a must for fitting a 6.5 inch speaker in place of the factory 5.5 inch version.

Make installation of rear speakers simple, just buy the lid covers from Kicker, complete with marine-grade 6X9 speakers, separate tweeter and high-pass crossover. Kuryakyn

stock front speakers with an oversized 6.5 inch two or three way speaker? Go for it, get it all done at once and you will be glad you did. When upgrading to larger speakers, make sure you also purchase speaker ring adaptors which allow for proper mounting at the stock location. First, install the adaptor rings as they get screwed into the inner fairing on Street Glides, Road Glides and Ultras. Then attach the speakers to the speaker ring and tighten accordingly. Now you need to find out where you want to install the rear speakers.

Nowadays, there are many options for rear speaker placement. You can buy a tour pack and the mating speakers that come with Ultra models. You can place the speakers in the bag lids, either by modifying the lids you already have or buying new ones designed to accommodate speakers.

The rear speakers can also be installed on the front side of your saddlebag or even inside the saddlebag facing the rear wheel. No matter which option you use, except for the factory tour pack style, installing speakers into your saddlebag or the lid can cause issues and take up a lot of needed room. Before you go too far, ask yourself what your final goal is: A custom show bike or an everyday rider with a nice stereo system? Let's stick with the everyday rider for now.

For our story, we will

go with speakers mounted on the top of our saddlebag lids. Yes, the speaker will make the lid pretty heavy and yes you need to watch out for wiring when you open and close the bag. You also need to take a bit more care when loading the bag with your goodies once the speaker is installed. Lastly, you also have to make sure that the speaker is mounted properly to prevent a leak when riding in the rain or cleaning your bike. Water can damage your speakers just like it does to radios and other electronics. Water can also ruin your Ipod, cell phone or other keepsakes when it gets into your saddlebag. Either way, for every step forward, you must be prepared for one step back, unless the job is done right from the start.

Now you need to wire those speakers in your saddlebags. The best thing to do is to make all of your connections at the speakers first. Be sure to keep the wiring away from the latch mechanism, and most importantly, away from the gasket that seals the lid to the saddlebag. If you run the wiring over the gasket (a common short-cut), you will prevent a proper seal and possibly damage the wire as well. Take the time to drill a hole in the bag, install a rubber grommet that will seal tightly to the bag and the wire to the grommet. Drill the hole for this behind the bag, close to the shock so that it's not visible when the job is done. If the wiring

Harley Davidson has jumped on board the motorcycle audio bandwagon with the introduction of their rear speaker bag lids.

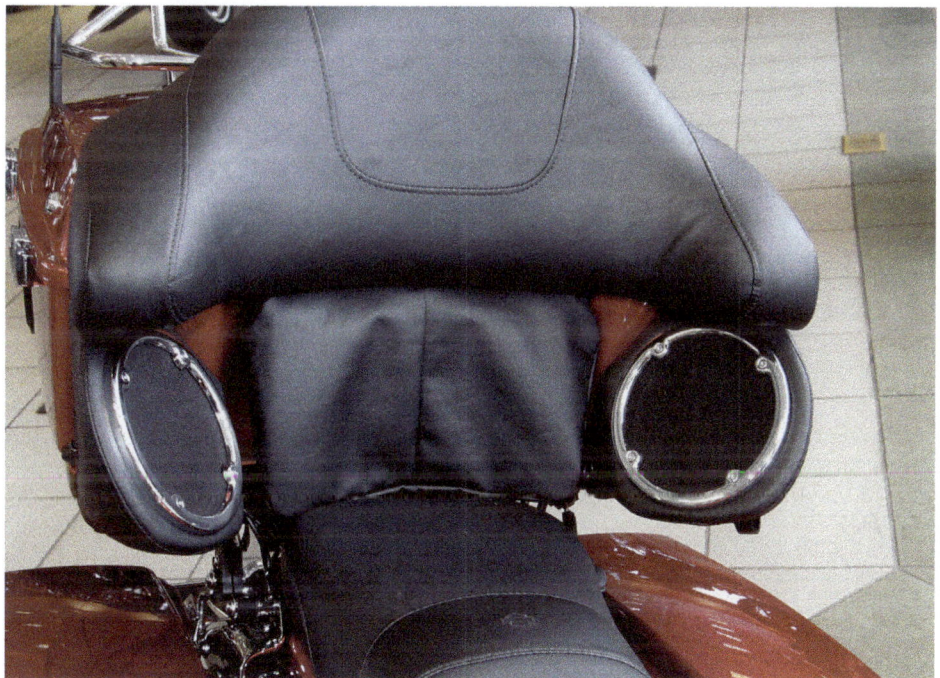

On their tour-pac equipped bikes, The Factory likes to mount the rear speakers as shown.

From Kicker comes this 5 channel amp - 4 channels of full range sound plus 100 amps of sub-woofer power. Digital signal processing makes for an efficient amplifier. More power and less heat inside your fairing. Kuryakyn

This compact Rockford Fosgate amplifier from Paul Yaffe is easy to install and fit in any fairing, and boasts plenty of 4-channel power for front and rear speakers.

harness to the speakers does not already have a mating connector for quick disconnect of the bags, now is the right time to install one. It's best to use a well-known and durable male and female connector for ease of servicing down the road. Try to keep the connection hidden behind the bag or close to the seat to keep it out of site. Now when you take your bags off for servicing or cleaning, simply separate the connection and remove the bag.

Now you can remove the seat and fuel tank to finish routing the speaker wires up to the amp in the fairing. Always keep the wiring covered in PVC extruded tubing or heat-shrink tubing and use cable ties in order to keep it all clean and neat. Once the speaker wires are in place, route the amp's red heavy-gauge power wire from inside the fairing back to the battery. It is best not to install the fuse until you are 100% done and ready to test the system. Connect the ring terminal to the (+) side of the battery and tighten with a 10mm wrench. Be sure to slide black heat shrink or extruded tubing over the red wire where it is visible between the fairing and the fuel tank. This will keep the wire from being an eye sore when the job is complete. Now attach the ground wire to a good, grounded bolt in the inner fairing, metal to metal. Actually, it is preferred to run the black ground wire back to the battery (-) as well since this is a best ground on the bike.

Now for the last step, finding a "remote" or trigger source. This is a 12+ powered wire that is only energized when the ignition switch is in the "ON" position. The best and quickest source is the backside of the cigarette lighter. There are two ways to connect both wires to the same source. First, you can install a female .25 inch quick disconnect with male piggy back. This is not the easiest part to find but it is the cleanest method. Second, you could cut off the OEM female quick disconnect and crimp on a 18 to 16 gauge remote wire along with the original power wire onto a new fully insulated female disconnect. Either way will work. This wire will be short and, along with the power, ground, speaker inputs and output wiring, can be attached to the amplifier according to the instructions.

Finally, remember about polarity, keep all the connections tight and secure and install the fuse at the battery last! Once you are ready to test, take the time to work through all of the audio settings on the radio, dial in the EQ and gains on the amplifier before your reinstall the outer fairing. A good rule of thumb is to never turn up the amp gains past 75% as the amp will clip quicker and tend to distort faster as well. Loud is one thing but loud and clear is a whole other thing.

When installing an external power amplifier on your ride you will need one of our wiring kits. The #8 gauge kit, shown, is for up to 900-watts (#10 gauge kit available for up-to 600 watts). Both kits come with EVERYTHING you need to install an amp properly the first time! #10 Wire, (2) RCA cables, fuse holder and terminals. NAMZ

When nothing but the best will do, you need a subwoofer powered by this small, but kick-ass mono amp from Kicker. 85% efficient, features 200 watts into a 1/2 ohm load. Kuryakyn

Books from Wolfgang Publications can be found at select book stores and numerous web sites.

Titles	ISBN	Price	# of pages
Advanced Airbrush Art	9781929133208	$27.95	144 pages
Advanced Custom Motorcycle Assembly & Fabrication	9781929133239	$27.95	144 pages
Advanced Custom Motorcycle Wiring - *Revised*	9781935828761	$27.95	144 pages
Advanced Pinstripe Art	9781929133321	$27.95	144 pages
Advanced Sheet Metal Fab	9781929133123	$27.95	144 pages
Advanced Tattoo Art - *Revised*	9781929133822	$27.95	144 pages
Airbrush How-To with Mickey Harris	9781929133505	$27.95	144 pages
Barris: Flames, Scallops and Striping	9781929133550	$24.95	144 pages
Bean're - Motorcycle Nomad	9781935828709	$18.95	256 pages
Body Painting	9781929133666	$27.95	144 pages
Building Hot Rods	9781929133437	$27.95	144 pages
Colorful World of Tattoo Models	9781935828716	$34.95	144 pages
Composite Materials 1	9781929133765	$27.95	144 pages
Composite Materials 2	9781929133932	$27.95	144 pages
Composite Materials 3	9781935828662	$27.95	144 pages
Composite Materials Step by Step Projects	9781929133369	$27.95	144 pages
Cultura Tattoo Sketchbook	9781935828839	$32.95	284 pages
Custom Bike Building Basics	9781935828624	$24.95	144 pages
Custom Motorcycle Fabrication	9781935828792	$27.95	144 pages
George the Painter	9781935828815	$18.95	256 pages
Harley-Davidson Sportster Hop-Up & Customizing Guide	9781935828952	$27.95	144 pages
Harley-Davidson Sportser Buell Engine Hop-Up Guide	9781929133093	$24.95	144 pages
How Airbrushes Work	9781929133710	$24.95	144 pages
Honda Enthusiast Guide Motorcycles 1959-1985	9781935828853	$27.95	144 pages
How-To Airbrush, Pinstripe & Goldleaf	9781935828693	$27.95	144 pages
How-To Airbrush Pin-ups	9781929133802	$27.95	144 pages
How-To Build Old Skool Bobber - 2nd Edition	9781935828785	$27.95	144 pages

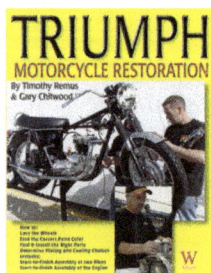

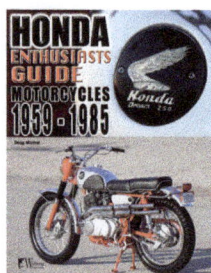

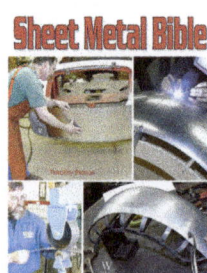

Books from Wolfgang Publications can be found at select book stores and numerous web sites.

Titles	ISBN	Price	# of pages
How-To Build a Cheap Chopper	9781929133178	$27.95	144 pages
How-To Build Cafe Racer	9781935828730	$27.95	144 pages
How-To Chop Tops	9781929133499	$24.95	144 pages
How-To Draw Monsters	9781935828914	$27.95	144 pages
How-To Fix American V-Twin	9781929133727	$27.95	144 pages
How-To Paint Tractors & Trucks	9781929133475	$27.95	144 pages
Hot Rod Wiring	9781929133987	$27.95	144 pages
Into the Skin	9781935828174	$34.95	144 pages
Kosmoski's *New* Kustom Paint Secrets	9781929133833	$27.95	144 pages
Learning the English Wheel	9781935828891	$27.95	144 pages
Mini Ebooks - Butterfly and Roses	9781935828167	Ebook Only	
Mini Ebooks - Skulls & Hearts	9781935828198	Ebook Only	
Mini Ebooks - Lettering & Banners	9781935828204	Ebook Only	
Mini Ebooks - Tribal Stars	9781935828211	Ebook Only	
Pin-Ups on Two Wheels	9781929133956	$29.95	144 pages
Pro Pinstripe	9781929133925	$27.95	144 pages
Sheet Metal Bible	9781929133901	$29.95	176 pages
Sheet Metal Fab Basics B&W	9781929133468	$24.95	144 pages
Sheet Metal Fab for Car Builders	9781929133383	$27.95	144 pages
SO-CAL Speed Shop, Hot Rod Chassis	9781935828860	$27.95	144 pages
Tattoo Bible #1	9781929133840	$27.95	144 pages
Tattoo Bible #2	9781929133857	$27.95	144 pages
Tattoo Bible #3	9781935828754	$27.95	144 pages
Tattoo Lettering Bible	9781935828921	$27.95	144 pages
Tattoo Sketchbook / Nate Power	9781935828884	$27.95	144 pages
Tattoo Sketchbook, Jim Watson	9781935828037	$32.95	112 pages
Triumph Restoration - Pre Unit	9781929133635	$29.95	144 pages
Triumph Restoration - Unit 650cc	9781929133420	$29.95	144 pages
Vintage Dirt Bikes - Enthusiast's Guide	9781929133314	$27.95	144 pages
Ult Sheet Metal Fab	9780964135895	$24.95	144 pages
Ultimate Triumph Collection	9781935828655	$49.95	144 pages

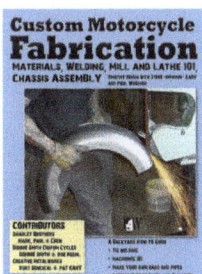

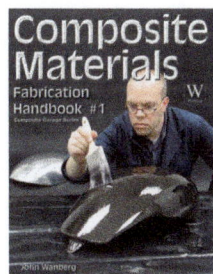

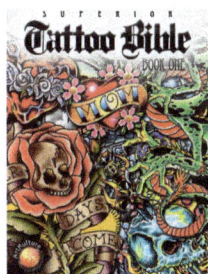

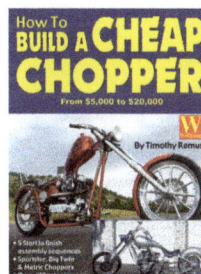

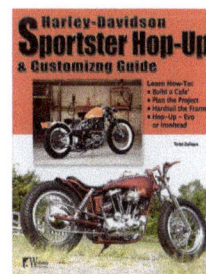

Sources

Accel
www.accel-motorcycle.com

Anderson Studio
2609 Grissom Dr.
Nashville, TN 37204
615.255.4807
www.andersonstudioinc.com

Cycle Visions
4263 Taylor St
San Diego, CA 92110
619.295.7800
www.cyclevisions.com

Cleveland Motorcycle Co.
clevelandmotorcyclemfgco.com

Custom Chrome
www.customchrome-online.com

Dakota Digital
1 800 593 4160
www.dakotadigital.com

Donnie Smith Custom Cycles, Inc.
10594 Radisson Road NE
Blaine, MN 55449
763.786.6002
Fax: 763.786.0600
www.donniesmith.com

Hotop Design products can be found in the
Drag Specialties catalog

Kuryakyn
www.kuryakyn.com

NAMZ Custom Cycle Products
169 Boro Line Road, Suite B
King of Prussia, PA 19406
610.265.7100
Outside Pennsylvania: 1-877-277-NAMZ
Fax: 610.265.7188
namzcustomcycleproducts.com

Perewitz Cycle Fabrication
910 Plymouth St.
Bridgewater, MA 02324
508.697.3595
www.perewitz.com

RWD
Russ Wernimont Designs
37100 Applegate Road
Murrieta, CA 92563
951.698.9495
www.russwernimont.com
Fax: 951-461-7066

Wimmer Custom Cycle
www.wimmermachine.com

www.ingramcontent.com/pod-product-compliance
Lightning Source LLC
Chambersburg PA
CBHW062008150426
42812CB00013BA/2573